SAPPHO WAS A
RIGHT-ON WOMAN

SAPPHO WAS A RIGHT-ON WOMAN

A Liberated View of Lesbianism

SIDNEY ABBOTT and BARBARA LOVE

STEIN AND DAY / *Publishers* / New York

Copyright © 1972 by Sidney Abbot and Barbara Love
Library of Congress Catalog Card No. 77–160348
All rights reserved
Published simultaneously in Canada by Saunders of Toronto, Ltd.
Designed by Bernard Schleifer
Printed in the United States of America
Stein and Day/*Publishers*/7 East 48 Street, New York, N.Y. 10017
ISBN 0–8128–1409–6

DEDICATION

To those who have suffered for their sexual preference, most especially to Sandy, who committed suicide, to Cam, who died of alcoholism, and to Lydia, who was murdered; and to all who are working to create a future for Lesbians.

ACKNOWLEDGMENTS

We would like to thank:
Sue Schneider, whose poem gave us the inspiration for the title of
this book:

> *Thinking Back Lesbian*
> Off the Asia Minor coast glided birds
>
> Of cultist hymns glide-song incantations
> Upon the sea brimmed beach,
> As the red-rimmed phoenix imprints
> into ashes of sand ribboned recollections:
>
> Of her gentle gaiety, of she-goats sacrificed
> Among sister blood only: Atthis, Dica,
> Gryinno, Hero, Timus, and clear-eyed Cleis.
> Those nippled buds of lilac breath
> She bore a noble nemesis.
>
> The love of the arts was worth more
> To her than the sharpness of Diana's darts.
> Lyrist of Lesbos left to remnant reincarnations.
> We weave our minds round your Grecian words
> Of the Mused collective consciousness:
> 'Lesbians Love Now'
>
> Sappho, you must have been a 'Right On' woman.

and:

Rita Mae Brown for starting it all; Jill Johnston for the gift of herself;
Kate Millett for her depth of feeling and incredible courage; Vivian

Acknowledgments

Gornick for publishing our first article on Gay Liberation in *Woman in Sexist Society;* Pamela Oline for reading parts of our manuscript and giving us the benefit of her perspective as an existential psychotherapist; Dr. Jean Mundy for seeing us when things got rough; Bici Forbes for her Celtic wisdom to inspire the world with the radiant force of spirituality, which touched our lives; George Caldwell, Barbara Towar, and Mary Solberg, our editors, who remain our friends; Ivy Bottini for her presence which gives strength; Father Robert O. Weeks, who has made religion meaningful to gays in general and us in particular; Sasha, our Alaskan Malamute, who obligingly ate our worst drafts; our parents for trying to understand; and finally our oppressors, for making us so angry that we finally decided to get moving.

CONTENTS

SAPPHO WAS A
RIGHT-ON WOMAN

INTRODUCTION

When people ask us why we are in Gay Liberation and why we wrote a book, when we could easily continue to hide, we reply that our ambition is to be most ordinary people. Our goal is to be able to go about our lives—as human beings, as women, as Lesbians—unselfconsciously, and to be able to spend all of our energy and time on work or fun, and none on the arts of concealment or on self-hatred. But we know that such a simple goal will be achieved only by sweeping adjustments in the way many people think.

The Lesbian is one of the least known members of our culture. Less is known about her—and less accurately—than about the Newfoundland dog. In the 1960's, two books on the Lesbian appeared. Both were written by men, and both were liberal attempts to deal with the worst stereotype about Lesbians—which says they are men trapped in women's bodies. Both failed to destroy the stereotype, since they only described behavior and since the authors were largely unable or unwilling to deal with the Lesbian's emotional life. Neither book was the product of any social scientific discipline. There may still not be a first-rate psychological or social-psychological study on Lesbians.

Today, for the first time in American history—perhaps for the first time in the history of Western civilization—hundreds of Lesbians are coming more or less into the open. They are functioning as Lesbians in Women's Liberation or Gay Liberation. Recently, too, experts have begun speculating that there may be more Lesbians than was previously thought—perhaps as many as or more than the number of homosexual males.

Who are these women? What are they like? What does their emergence mean? From the quick glances that newspaper, magazine, and television coverage have afforded the public so far, one thing is becoming clear—gay women are too varied and too individualistic to be lumped under any one stereotype.

As Lesbians and as authors, we are living through this historical transition period in two ways. As Lesbians, we share with gay sisters a new experience: we are laying aside fear, guilt, and self-hatred and are exhilarated by a new pride. As authors, we have tried to explore this process—and write about it. We have used our experiences as catalysts for thought, and as some of the implications of our experiences sink in, we have also asked serious questions of church and state.

Some strong emotions fueled the writing of this book. There was rage—at the energy and time wasted dealing with the terrible lies our society told us about ourselves, lies that we half-believed. There is soaring hope—that at the end of this cultural struggle no homosexual woman or man will have to suffer the ridicule and degradation that has been the lot of gay people. There is barely qualified excitement—at the advent of a new age of freedom.

Looking around, we see gay people finding confrontation with the culture preferable to invisibility, and a few good friends preferable to the conditional goodwill of nameless and faceless strangers called society. We see the Lesbian's life as still filled with complex conflicts which make terrible demands on her. One of those conflicts is a double-bind, a no-win situation, where she can either have external approval and no internal integrity by keeping silent, or can achieve integrity and lose approval by coming out publicly.

We see that it is not Lesbianism that makes some Lesbians prone to alcoholism, suicide, or drug abuse: it is the self-degradation our society went to such pains to teach us, and which is hammered into us not only by the overwhelming force of public opinion, but specifically by lost jobs, lost homes, and—if we are mothers—by lost children. Yet—and it is a wonder—most Lesbians find ways to deal with the crushing condemnation of society and build meaningful lives.

Today there is a new, positive sense of self in Lesbians exposed in person or by the media to the Liberation movements. Too bad it is too late for the dead, the habitually drunk, and the permanently psychologically disabled, our casualties of this insidious kind of war.

We heard about a gay bar called the Lost and Found, and thought the name reflected the problem of the Lesbian losing and then finding her identity. The idea of "lost" (and alone) is dealt with in the first half of the book, "What It Was Like." The idea of "found" and all the good things it connotes is dealt with in the second part of the book, "Living the Future."

The Lesbian in the first part is frightened, and lives fragmented and tranquilized by society's methods of discouraging her. She is manipulated to sell out her identity. The Lesbian in the second half has found the stimuli and support to reject the negative things she learned about herself—on the best authority—and fight the catastrophic impairment of her self-esteem. She somehow establishes an opinion of herself that is radically different from that the world holds about her. She endorses her feelings about other women and her lifestyle; she finds them valid.

To some, this separation of the book into two parts may appear simplistic. Part one may appear too grim; part two, too hopeful. But the separation reflects the Lesbian's existential struggle between the past and the future, between shame and pride. In most Lesbians these are mixed to one degree or another. Even the most militant and political activist is not one hundred per cent consistent. Who is? The past and the future exist in each Lesbian activist; the present is most often felt as a collision between the two.

In the first half we mean to say, perhaps especially to our younger sisters, in whom we see a new pride emerging, remember never to forget that Gay Liberation is the result of an historical process. In the second half we want to reflect the full pride Lesbians are striving for, although few have yet achieved it.

The Lesbian is not the first to make a dramatic break with commonly held values. Feminists, Black activists, and student activists go through a similar psychological process; all risk the familiarity of the present for an uncertain future. We know little about this process, but something basic is at work here that may reach epoch-making proportions.

At the time of this writing, the Lesbian's own liberation movement is highly introspective, more concerned with internal than with external changes. Together in consciousness-raising groups, Lesbians are trying to understand who they are, and who they want to be.

Introduction

Insights help free their minds of conditioning and permit new possibilities to surface. Life goals emerge that are conscious, meaningful, and socially oriented.

For more than two years, the authors have participated in consciousness-raising groups. We owe a great many of the new, good feelings we have about our lives and our new perspective to our sisters in these groups. The questions raised there have compelled us to learn something about politics, psychology, religion, economics. Not oriented to any one political ideology, we have tried to learn as much as possible about the structures and processes that create oppression.

The second part of the book begins with the story of the Lesbians' hard-won battle for recognition in the National Organization for Women. This is the first time this story has been told in its entirety. We were Feminists before we were Lesbian activists, and we know that both Feminists and Lesbian activists fight to become self-reliant; both find dependence on men unnatural. The common political goals of the two groups make sexual preference seem an unimportant difference. Then, too, Lesbianism is far more than a sexual preference: it is a political stance. At the present time, when women are struggling to shape their own destinies, Lesbianism seems to have far-ranging social significance.

It is by changing attitudes that we, and all Lesbians, can become most ordinary people. The attitudinal changes asked by women, Blacks, and homosexuals add up to a new set of values based on an appreciation of both the differences and the common humanity existing between individuals and groups. The new society we are looking to—and working for—is based on pluralism, as opposed to today's society, which tends to hold up one way of doing things as the right way, and measure everyone against that single standard.

Finally, it is true, as a little thought will verify, that heterosexual people will not be free of their sexual fears so long as the homosexual person is used as a pariah to create and perpetuate those fears. Granting us our full humanity means granting it to heterosexuals as well.

SIDNEY ABBOTT
BARBARA LOVE

New York City, May, 1972

16

part one
What It Was Like

I GUILT: THE PARENT WITHIN

In my marvelous new feelings for her I felt I had discovered myself. I went walking, celebrating sun, sky, and trees, and myself as somehow center of it all. Then I stopped as if I had come on the edge of a chasm there in the woods. A word came clawing up from the depths of my mind. I didn't want the knowledge that was coming, but my wish didn't stop it. The horror of the word burst upon me almost before the word itself—sick, perverted, unnatural, *Lesbian*. The trees that had seemed so close drew away. The sky looked remote. I was a shadow, a wraith hurrying across the landscape as I ran home.*

Guilt is at the core of the Lesbian's life experience. It is her heritage from the past; it controls her present and robs her of her future. The dynamics of guilt pervade and order her days, draining her energies. Once set in motion, guilt works almost as an autonomous mechanism, independent of the individual's will or of the original cause. Because guilt becomes a constant, internal force, actions of flight are of no avail: the Lesbian withers under its influence, or is forced to try to understand it—historically and personally—and vigorously to struggle free of it.

A Lesbian who consents to guilt for her sexual preference is her own worst oppressor. She accepts and internalizes prejudices and uses them against herself.

Before guilt there is innocence.

Innocence is a kind of sacred ignorance especially prized in matters of female sexuality. Germaine Greer, in *The Female Eunuch*, describes the destructive effects of this enforced innocence. She reminds us that

---

* Throughout this book the authors have drawn on their own experiences and those of other Lesbians. Unless a specific source is indicated in the text or in a footnote, quoted material paraphrases personal experiences.

19

until recently women in Western society were not supposed to have sexuality at all and that even now female sexuality is defined in terms of response to the male's sexuality.[1] Girls are not taught the location and nature of their sexual organs and may not experience an early exploration of their sexual responses through masturbation as boys do. They may remain unaware of their sex organs even after puberty.

A girl may in fact discover genital sexual feelings when she is first touched by a boy. His apparent knowledge of her body may make her feel helpless, at the mercy of feelings she does not understand and dares not yield to. Even when this early guilt is resolved by marriage, sexuality can be seen as the gift of the male and not as something a woman possesses in her own right.

It seems paradoxical that women, whose worth is counted in sexual terms, are denied an understanding of their own sexuality and are not taught or permitted to be at one with the physical means of expressing love. This can only be viewed as a control mechanism suppressing female sexuality.

Lesbianism is not only seen as biologically unnatural, but, given the male idea of women's sexuality as simply a response to an aggressive male, it is unthinkable. If there are Lesbians—women who fulfill one another sexually—then perhaps women are not the passive creatures men make them out to be. To recognize the existence of Lesbianism is to admit that women are sexual beings in and of themselves, and that they do not *need*, though they may want, men in this basic way. Such independence from men is a *de facto* challenge to the idea that women exist for men. This may be one reason that, although Lesbians have not suffered the police harassment male homosexuals have, Lesbianism sometimes seems basically more threatening to the patriarchy, so threatening that recognizing it, even to punish it, is avoided. Society prefers to remain ignorant of Lesbianism, and innocent of its implications for female sexuality.

A Lesbian's guilt may begin long before a sexual experience, with just the feeling of being different. Guilt comes from not fulfilling society's expectations, as instilled by parents. Multiple levels of expectations are tied to sex roles. Trying out or incorporating behavior or mental sets generally encouraged in the male and discouraged in the female carry the seeds of guilt, since so many aspects of behavior are sex related.

In our society a girl who is assertive and rebellious is sometimes granted a period of immunity before she must acquiesce to the endless restrictions and conditions of the female sex role. This is the tomboy phase, a period of grace, a free time before rules of femininity are enforced. The tomboy is tolerated and jollied along humorously. She may even be admired. Men may say, "For a girl, she's got guts."

One on-going study by psychologists at the Post Graduate Center for Mental Health in New York City shows that of 225 Lesbians, 78 percent reported being tomboys in childhood versus 42 percent of the control group of 233 heterosexual women.[2]

Girls going through a tomboy period are not imitating boys as much as they are experiencing a fuller range of activities that will be permitted until puberty brings an end to their freedom. Childhood is a time of exploration and innocence, until one day the mother looks with horror at her long-legged, mini-bosomed daughter in tee-shirt and jeans sliding down a tree trunk and sets out to make a lady of her.

Young boys are permitted no such leeway. Very early on they can be labeled "sissy" and goaded to develop manly traits and mannerisms. As one writer points out, a father may say of his young daughter, "Yes, she loves sports. She's our little tomboy," but no one would dare say of a small boy, "Yes, he's our little marygirl."[3] That people who are horrified at an effeminate boy can express approval of a tomboy indicates that high value is placed early on what is considered male. This message, although usually not articulated, is clear, and it is heeded by many girls.

The tomboy claims qualities usually believed to belong to men. She does not see why they cannot be hers also. She wants freedom and wants to be like those who appear to her free—men, who seem to have the opportunity for achievement and glory within their grasp.

> I always wanted to be the heroes in the movies. I certainly didn't envy the hero's girl, who had nothing to do except to just wait around.

Girls are thought to identify with their mothers. But how can a tomboy, who aspires to be President or play first base for the Yankees or find a cure for cancer admire her mother, a washer of dishes, a

21

maker of grocery lists, whose life is apparently taken up with trifles?

Learning the approved female role can create conflict in some girls. A few young women are literally torn between selecting qualities known as female, for which they are rewarded, and qualities or characteristics seen as male, for which they are at first gently teased, then ridiculed, and finally punished. To some women, then, the narrow boundaries of the female role have made heterosexuality unattractive, and the independence and self-determination of Lesbians appealing.

The fate of those who do not relinquish tomboyishness is seen in the conflicts of the female amateur athlete and the negative experiences of many female scholars.

Skiing, swimming, tennis, track, and other sports develop strength, courage, independence, endurance, and general physical hardiness, qualities seen by society as essentially male. In the subculture of sports, however, women are not criticized for possessing them. Inherent in athletics for women is a value system in which assertive traits are encouraged and respected. In this small universe, women are relieved of guilt for acting aggressive or competitive. They are even given medals for it.

At the same time the young female athlete is always surrounded by girls or young women in school or in the neighborhood who do not appear to want or value what she does. Even if she feels superior to these relatively passive creatures, she also feels herself the target of unspoken criticism. She senses that there is something alienating in her achievements. She feels tolerated rather than accepted. Away from coach and teammates, she may become ambivalent about what she has attained as she becomes more and more alienated from others learning their female role. She may be defensive and rebellious, in which case she may even learn to fail at sports.

The female athlete's training and commitment to her sport take her further and further from the women her own age who are learning to use their energies to watch, admire, and support men. The female athlete develops her own potential. To win, she must develop a strong personality and sense of self-sufficiency. She may not even be aware at the time that the physical and psychological strength and courage rewarded in athletics are in glaring conflict with the femininity that is rewarded socially. When she leaves the sports world, she learns that she is "not a woman" if she persists in being competitive or aggressive and independent. These qualities are no longer appreciated, and she may even be asked by those who love her to conceal them or "play them down."

Guilt can be felt for the simple desire for knowledge. Until recently, and today to some extent, scholarship has been considered a male province. Some men would disagree, but most men still feel threatened by a woman who knows more than they do. If a girl listens to her elders, she may be exposed to the lingering idea that men won't appreciate a smart woman. One woman said, "My aunt told me that if I used big words and read books all the time, I'd never be popular and no one would want to marry me." The academic world, which tolerates some female achievement, is, like amateur athletics, a haven for women who want to develop as individuals and not be simply supporters of men.

But the price for development as a person is insecurity in the female role and more or less guilt for not desiring wifehood and motherhood before all else. Moreover, women graduate students report that their motives are continually reduced and simplified by those who feel that women enter graduate school only to look for a husband and to work with men. Queries made by Columbia University Women's Liberation and other college Women's Liberation groups show that a serious woman scholar seeking advancement in the academic community will more than likely be disappointed. She must thread her way around and between suspicious men, and occasionally women too, for the too few academic places open to women.

What connections, if any, are there between ambition and Lesbianism? After all, heterosexual women, too, have felt guilty for trying to expand their roles; it is a Feminist complaint. No one knows what makes one woman a heterosexual and another a Lesbian. But some gay women, looking back, find a correlation between intellectual or athletic achievement and the subsequent breaking of the heterosexual rule. They realize that they have sought freedom and independence in many ways, and that most of these ways are considered masculine in our culture. The female role is so specialized and small, that if a woman moves very far in any direction, she finds she is trespassing on male territory.

The successful female can hardly avoid being called malelike, when success is almost always defined in male terms. Because men often see a woman who fulfills her potential as either threatening or foolish, the woman who seeks achievement may find support, understanding, and affection from a woman like her.

Adolescent girls commonly experience crushes on teachers, older girls, or female classmates. Friendship rings are sometimes exchanged. Girls may learn to dance by dancing together. They may compare notes on their sexual feelings and show their "best friend" their diaries. These bonds are seen as normal until the age for dating boys arrives—and now that age sometimes can be as early as eleven or twelve. A girl is expected to grow out of all this and learn to transfer her love and trust to men.

Sometimes a young woman who tries to substitute boy friends for girl friends is not satisfied. Although dating boys, she may maintain extremely close friendships with women well into college. She feels comfortable with women, and likes to spend time with them. Time spent with men, on the other hand, may bring feelings of constraint. As one Lesbian said, "I felt exhausted after a date; it took so much energy to contain my energy." She prefers to explore other women's minds and emotions. As soon as she perceives that the logical extension of her caring might be physical intimacy, she becomes frightened, especially if she does not have strong desires for intimacy with men. However, since information about Lesbianism is suppressed by society, she may not know what her emotions mean, what name is applied to them. She may even enter into a Lesbian affair without fear.

During the period of awakening to Lesbianism, a general uneasiness usually precedes awareness. Intimations of Lesbianism occur in dreams—sometimes explicit, more often symbolic. Such common dream situations as falling, getting lost, being out of control occur, stimulated by women rather than men. It may be some time before these dreams will be interpreted.

At some point, of course, she will begin to wonder if she is different from most of the women around her and what her difference means. She may go to the library, to a counselor, psychiatrist, or minister to find out about her feelings. What she reads on the pages of a psychology book, what she sees on the face of a family doctor or minister, may reverberate through the rest of her life.

The jokes and references heard on the playground, in the street or at home grow clearer. She still may not know the proper name for what she is, but she knows the slang for it; she knows she is "queer." The realization comes tumbling down on her that she is hated, despised, and ridiculed, or would be if her queerness were known. She had absorbed this information previously, hardly knowing she knew it, had learned it as naturally as she learned the color blue or the letter A. She is shocked to find out she is one of the hated people others whisper about.

Some Lesbians clearly verbalize the core experience of guilt:

After my first Lesbian experience, I thought I was being followed and stared at, although I knew nobody could have known what happened to me. I kept turning around; I felt haunted.

When I pass the women's jail, I imagine in every detail what it would be like to be in there, including sleeping with rats running over my blanket. I feel I will be caught, because there's some criminal in me I'm hiding. I feel I should walk in there and confess to something—I don't know what.

Political scientist Roger Smith calls guilt a "concept with blurred edges."[4] No one abstract statement can define it, although it can be seen at work in its subtle as well as obvious manifestations.

Smith describes guilt as beginning when a person crosses a socially accepted boundary. His analysis applies accurately to Lesbianism.

[First:] A boundary is transgressed, and the offender is separated from the rest of society (sometimes physically, sometimes through withdrawal of solidarity); various attempts are made (Nemesis, guilt feelings, punishment, etc.) to reassert the boundary, and finally the boundary is either restored or a new one takes its place (reconciliation), and society finds itself at one with the offender (atonement).[5]

What Smith is describing is an act or event, the crossing of the boundary, followed by acts or events that lead to reconciliation or atonement. But how can a gay woman pay for her crime when her crime is her identity? Refusal to fill her role as wife-mother puts her beyond social boundaries with far-reaching consequences. She may not know exactly when she overstepped the line, but she senses intuitively that she has gone too far. Lesbians, who step outside the female role, can never be reaccepted into society without renouncing their homosexuality—that is, without denying their sexual identities and sociosexual patterns of interaction.

The Lesbian oversteps the boundaries of "woman" simply by being. The system responds by isolating her and withdrawing support. Alone and panicked, she tries to find her way back within the old boundary or to redefine the boundary without renouncing her Lesbianism. She tries all logical avenues back to acceptability, and plays many tricks on herself and society in the process, but she cannot achieve atonement and remain herself.

Women and men both have contracts with society. The social contract for a female child, agreed upon long before her birth, specifies the role of wife-mother. Meeting these terms brings rewards of love and approval, of security and status commensurate with her husband's social and economic position. The social contract for a woman is more narrowly drawn than the man's and has fewer options.

Sexuality and reproduction are not the exclusive criteria of manhood. A male can be a scholar, scientist, or priest and still be called a man by virtue of his accomplishments. Genius and rationality are typically believed to be male, and may to some extent be substituted for potency and virility as marks of manhood. But a female, no matter how successful, is seen to achieve womanhood, that is, adulthood, only through her role as wife and mother; for full admission into society, she had better have those credentials in order. Her femaleness can only be proved by putting a man's interests before her own, permitting and encouraging impregnation by him, and using her body as a vehicle to bear a child.

A Lesbian may never marry, or if she marries or has affairs with men, she may never relate to them emotionally in all the societally prescribed ways. She may marry but choose not to have children. She may have children, and then find that only her love for her children ties her to her marriage. Even when the married Lesbian conscientiously fulfills her duties as wife and mother, she may feel guilty for not being happy in the female role.

At what moment does a woman step outside the boundary of

acceptable relations with women? When she feels emotion for another woman? If she has one sexual experience with a woman? If she becomes bisexual? Only if she sleeps for a time exclusively with one woman? Even if she has had a single sexual experience with a woman, she will be labeled a Lesbian if the experience becomes known. A psychiatrist with many homosexual patients, when asked to define a Lesbian, replied, "A Lesbian is a woman who says she is." That is, no one event or emotion makes a woman a Lesbian. Use or acceptance of the term Lesbian may precede or follow Lesbian sexual experiences.

Many women have homosexual experiences, but those with some heterosexual identity seem to enjoy relations with women with less guilt, evidently because their experiences are just that, experiences, and not their identity. A woman can spend equal time in bed with men and women, and still call herself a bisexual or heterosexual. And yet, women who have never dared to touch another woman sometimes call themselves Lesbians.

Once a woman is known as a Lesbian, both she and society often feel that no other fact about her can rival the sexual identification. As a woman speaker, a leader in her field, walked to the podium at a national convention, a man sitting in the audience remarked to a companion, "Do you know who that woman is? She's a Lesbian." No matter what a Lesbian achieves, her sexuality will remain her *primary* identity. The role others expect her to play distorts or negates the value of all her behavior. They may see her through a kind of filter: the same words, the same actions as before now appear to have special meanings. There is something strange about her that they did not see before her sexual preference was revealed. Others may be afraid to associate with a known Lesbian. That association with her invites negative social results, the Lesbian well knows.

Many women who fear Lesbianism in themselves plunge into marriage or try to drown their guilt in numerous relationships with men. Some may confine themselves to work or study to avoid confronting their Lesbianism. If a woman admits her homosexuality and tries to live it out, she may find that she makes society the target for antisocial attitudes. Often this means apathy or withdrawal, hurting only herself. Others build super-respectable lives, conservative in all aspects, including the political, and contain their Lesbianism in a small, dark closet. Through tactics like these, Lesbians try to anesthesize guilt.

That Lesbianism is considered deviant is apparently reason enough to cause Lesbians to behave in certain unsocial or guilty ways.

Where does the Lesbian's guilt come from? First of all, from the family. Guilt begins at that tender age when children learn what their parents consider right and wrong. The family is society writ small, laboring to implant in its children what it understands of morality and religion, law, and mental health practices—all of which staunchly advocate heterosexuality. The media reinforce parents in teaching the notion of heterosexual superiority. Radio, television, records, and magazines depict happy housewives, husbands as providers, and beautiful children.

Margaret Mead, in an essay applying Freud's original concept of the development of the superego to anthropology, names as the source of guilt an internalized parent, the psychological structure typical of Western society that is often called conscience. Dr. Mead stresses the development of conscience in a child through the rewarding and punishing parent. "Such an upbringing develops in the child the capacity to feel guilt, to award oneself either in anticipation of an act not yet performed or retrospectively in terms of a past act, the type of suffering or reward once given by the parent."[6]

Parental reward and punishment, as it is carried out in Western society, trains the child to take early responsibility for her actions, and to project punishment for herself. Thus, if a child steals and is caught by her mother or father, she is made to return the object and is spanked or otherwise punished. If she steals again, she knows exactly what punishment should follow and what the extent of her wrongdoing is.

The child knows that the parents will reward her for marriage (gifts, parties, expressions of affection and approval), and "knows" there must be a punishment for other sexual behavior, even if she is quite ignorant of Lesbianism *per se* and of any proscriptions against it.

While the police and the law largely ignore homosexual women, the parent within metes out punishment. The more Lesbians try to avoid punishment from external sources, the more the fantasized punishment grows.

Over time, the real parents can become more lenient than the parent within. Parents may begin to realize that their daughter is seeking happiness in the only and best way she can, or their initial outrage may be replaced by a sad kind of guilt. But to a Lesbian, the parent within does not age or mellow but remains the oversized, nearly omnipotent parent of childhood. Long after a parent is able to punish in fact, the parent within can remain strong and threatening. Lesbians say that they don't want to tell their parents about their homosexuality because of the physical and mental pain they may cause them. Sometimes, however, it seems the Lesbian is mollifying her real parents in order to propitiate the parents within.

C. G. Jung says of the mother:

> In the unconscious, the mother always remains a powerful primordial image, coloring and even determining throughout life our relationships to women, to society, to the world of feeling and fact, yet in so subtle a way that, as a rule, there is no conscious perception of the process.[7]

A mother's love is believed to be unconditional: the mother is the only person in society who is supposed to love, no matter what. But, knowing society's views on homosexuality, the Lesbian fears that no parental love, not even that of a mother, could stand before her Lesbianism.

She has heard stories of mothers and fathers who have ostracized their daughters, or rushed them to psychiatrists, or thrown fits of hysteria. She has learned vicariously, if not actually, that the home generally is not a protective, care-giving unit for Lesbians.

There is fear that a parent would say: "Why do you want to hurt us? We have been good parents and we love you." One Lesbian says bitterly: "Ever since I told my parents, they have blamed all their ills on my Lesbianism, from overweight to colds, varicose veins, and heart attacks." Some Lesbians carry around a terrible sense of power, which is their own guilt. One Lesbian imagined she could even electrocute her parents with the revelation of Lesbianism, or at least be a precipitating cause of their deaths. But guilt does not end with the death of the parents if "the parent within" lives on.

What It Was Like

The interior guilt and pain often lead the Lesbian to act against her own best interests, perhaps to punish herself, or perhaps because she has already identified as a failure. The Lesbian's guilt becomes, if she is not careful and exceptionally strong, a lifelong burden; her efforts to throw off the weight of it represent a struggle to return to innocence.

Guilt is not the only enemy. There is also shame. Parents, focusing on a cause-and-effect relationship in society, show the child how others will respond to her actions. Young girls are indoctrinated with a special sensitivity to a withdrawal of solidarity. Girls are taught to please. They learn that they should dress, act, and look in certain ways that meet social approval. Thus, the disapproval of friends, neighbors, and society as a whole weighs very heavily.

Margaret Mead points out that shame is disapproval by either positively or negatively valued groups.[8] Thus you can feel shame if anyone, no matter what their position in the social scale, knows something about you that should not be known. Unlike guilt, which is internalized, shame can be avoided simply by knowing what is shameful and concealing that part of yourself. Groups are not felt to be omnipotent and all-seeing like the parents within. Shame is easier to master.

To avoid shame, Lesbians may withdraw from heterosexual groups and live more or less completely in a gay subculture. While this ensures them some support, it does not necessarily lessen the fear of groups outside the subculture. Others remain in heterosexual groups and conceal their Lesbianism.

Parents also fear shame. This may be one reason why they generally dread a verbal confrontation with Lesbian daughters. Acceptance or tolerance, on their part, might lead to their daughter's being open about her sexual preference. The community might learn of it, and the parents would be shamed before their peers. Many parents, forced to choose between allegiance to their child and allegiance to society, betray the child and choose society. Guilt follows immediately upon shame. The inevitable first question is some form of "Where did we go wrong?"

The Lesbian's guilt demands self-punishment. But it is so pervasive, so basic, that the required punishments are too severe to be imposed directly. The self defies annihilation, and coping mechanisms come into play. These mechanisms, which transfer, channel, or otherwise divert the guilt and shame and make them manageable, can be termed denial, debt, and damnation.

If a woman cannot accept homosexual feelings for women, she may deny she is a Lesbian even, or especially, to herself. This is possible when Lesbians go through some traumatic experience that is intolerable to the memory. Every Lesbian's nightmare is to be caught in bed with another woman. If such a thing happens—and it has—a woman may repress all memory of it. The idea of loving other women may arouse too much fear.

There are other ways to avoid anxiety, but the most pitiful way is by absorbing society's hate into one's own thoughts and actions. How many Lesbians have destroyed other Lesbians to protect their own façades? "Where people cannot escape from threatening forces from without, they will often incorporate the hostile forces and identify with the aggressor, as in the case of some members of a minority group taking on the prejudice of the majority toward them."[9] As disturbing as this is to Lesbians who are trying to hold their heads above water, this kind of reaction to fear is nearly always unconscious and automatic.[10]

Freud's classical "defense mechanisms" seem to provide the only explanation for the perplexing and agonizing reality that a Lesbian can deny who she is and actively participate in ridiculing or degrading another Lesbian.

There are many degrees of denial. A woman may deny her feelings for other women. She may recognize the feelings but deny herself any physical expression of them. She may sleep with women but deny the label Lesbian and all it means. Finally, she may toy with the idea that she is a Lesbian but insist to the outside world that she is not.

There are some things you don't tell the world; others you don't tell your friends; one you don't dare tell yourself—this is love for a woman.

Society rewards denial by continuing to treat denying women as heterosexual. The extremely limited cultural stereotype of the Lesbian makes it easy for many women to persuade themselves that they are not really Lesbians, that they are somehow different:

> I was a woman who loved other women, not a Lesbian. Lesbians wore black leather jackets, trousers, and did things in toilets.

Women who fear they might love other women may get involved in heterosexual affairs or in marriage:

> For years I denied myself contact with women. I never mentioned my feelings to anybody so that there would be no opportunities. At thirty I married a man I didn't love because I believed that was the only way to happiness. At forty I began to worry—so many women I could have loved had passed by. At fifty I had my first Lesbian experience.

> I refused to recognize my love for women and went to bed only with men. I said I was heterosexual. Finally, I began sleeping with women as well as men. I still said I was heterosexual, but why miss a little extra fun? Slowly, I stopped seeing men, always intending to resume when a really attractive man came along. I felt I had high standards for men, and sleeping with women was not so serious. I called myself a heterosexual. One day I whispered to myself that I was a Lesbian. It was a long time after that I was able to accept it, and not until Gay Liberation did I feel good about it.

To say one is a Lesbian means not only coping with the freak stereotype, it means admitting to oneself the hostility of society. It means that one can be in danger. A parallel is a Jew who denies that he is Jewish. He not only does not attend synagogue and tries to pass for a Gentile with friends and co-workers, but denies any meaning in the entire history of Jewish oppression. Saying to oneself, "I am a Lesbian," is to stand outside traditions, laws, religious beliefs, and family ideals, and to begin to identify with the oppression of all homosexuals. Since this identity is too threatening, denial may also mean holding oneself back from one's lover, who is living proof that one is a Lesbian. The object of a gay woman's love is at the same time the cause of much anxiety. For this reason it can be as much a relief as a sorrow to end a Lesbian relationship.

One way of denying is to decide that the lover is the Lesbian:

> We had a relationship for two years; the first Lesbian experience for both of us. Near the end we fought more and more violently. One day, she screamed, "You're a Lesbian, I'm not!"

Denying Lesbians often have one-night stands or brief, chaotic relationships.

The Lesbian may try to forget who she is by focusing on her work. She denies herself any time to think about herself. Since attempts to ease off on her work only give her more time to dwell on her guilt, the situation worsens. Denial of her sexuality in this way involves a kind of self-desertion. The Lesbian tries to become a robot who just eats, sleeps, and works to avoid coping with her feelings.

While the denying Lesbian struggles with guilt, the debt-paying Lesbian acknowledges her homosexuality to herself, and feels somehow subservient for it. She is in society's debt if she is allowed to keep a good job and straight friends. She accepts her Lesbianism but only as a guilty secret. Her tactics are designed to prevent the addition of the burden of shame—that is, to prevent others from knowing.

The debt-paying Lesbian also still hides her Lesbianism from others and, at the same time, tries to make up for it. She may seek and value a responsible job in nearly any field. She sentences herself to hard labor for the "crime" of being a Lesbian.

Often she will work in a care-giving field, like social work or teaching, perhaps to compensate for the antisocial nature of her sexual preference. One study indicates that people who are considered deviants or whom society considers deviants are likely to be more sensitive to others' problems and assist them, as this gives them a feeling of "goodness" society generally denies them.[11]

Being successful on the job and being known as a good person with co-workers and friends are important for feelings of respectability and financial security. The debt-paying Lesbian's family may also have an important place in her life. She wants to maintain a good relationship with them, and may devote her holidays to them at the expense of her lover. If a lover cannot abide by this program, a new lover is found. Gay friends, who share these values and who are at all times discreet, are carefully selected. This Lesbian may present a rather simple, artless, and open self to straight friends and co-workers, but barriers for the protection of her secret are always present, particularly when she discusses her roommate, friends, or men.

A married Lesbian may work extra hard at her marriage in order to pay her debt to society. Often this kind of gay woman seems to be saying, "I may be bad in one way, but look at me, and my life. I am as good or better in other ways. I make up for my fault."

The debt-paying Lesbian makes an implicit attempt to create a new, enlarged boundary of societal acceptance that would include her. On a more conscious level, she undertakes this with the knowledge that society will probably not allow the boundary of acceptance to move even one inch. Sometimes, however, she may feel confident of her record and attempt to show herself.

Sometimes the debt-payer's hard work seems at least partially to pay off, but not always. One woman had a good position with the YWCA. She had worked to innovate and put into effect a series of programs that she felt were helping people significantly. She was respected in the community and liked on the job. Then, her landlord went to her superior and said he had reason to believe that she was a Lesbian. Confronted with this, she admitted it almost gladly. "I've wanted this out in the open with you," she said. "You know my work and what kind of person I am, and I'm sure that you see this doesn't mean anything." She was fired. The YWCA could not take the risk of the word spreading in the community. Never again did she make the mistake of thinking she had proved anything by her life-style, though she has maintained essentially the same life-style.

Another woman, conservative in all her values, including the political and religious, was called in when her employer was tipped off by phone that she was a Lesbian. He acknowledged her excellent performance on the job, but advised her that if she could not survive the investigation that company regulations called for, she had better resign. She cleared her desk and left the same day.

A third woman, who had become a Lesbian late in life and who was valued on the job as a hard worker, finally told a friend and co-worker about her Lesbianism. She felt it could not possibly make any difference to her friend since they had known each other for a long time and since her good character surely was evident by this time. Her friend was unable to cope and betrayed the confidence. Resulting office gossip cost this woman her government job.

Society's harsh treatment of the debt-paying Lesbian is manifestly unfair, for she is the "good nigger" of the homosexual world. She believes in society's values and does not challenge them in any way but one. Yet she is not accepted. She is always on a tenuous and necessarily hypocritical footing, yet her one longing is to be honest, and she stores up points toward the day when she may risk it. But as time passes, and perhaps after one or two experiences show her that she can neither make it back across the boundary nor enlarge the boundary, she can come to feel a good deal of bitterness at the unjust treatment she has received. Her self-respect erodes slowly as she realizes that she is trying to pay a debt that cannot be paid.

She may begin to feel unworthy or may fear taking risks. This may mean turning down new jobs or friendships that would entail unnecessary exposure. She may move to the suburbs or country to get away from gay life. When she is older, she may break completely with any homosexual life-style and live quite alone. She rarely analyzes the reasons her one difference is not tolerated. She cannot understand why straight men and women can commit adultery and not be as severely punished, for example, while she must suffer for being a Lesbian. She is always somewhat puzzled or hurt at being considered evil or degenerate, particularly since she tends to rather long, monogamous relationships.

A Lesbian who feels damned by her sexual preference may take full advantage of her outcast status. If society expects her to be irresponsible and amoral, she will be. Being beyond the pale of decent behavior seems to suit her just fine. She can enjoy riding the "golden chariot to hell."

Seductive, she haunts the gay bars looking for kicks. She may be out for a one-night stand or to betray a lover. Unlike the debt-paying Lesbian, she does not feel obligated in any way to be good. She knows that is useless. She tries to be as good a Lesbian as she can be, by society's definition of Lesbian—irresponsible, promiscuous, tough.

For the most part she lives from hand to mouth, supporting herself by little short-term jobs. She may be too fond of alcohol and late hours to keep a good job for long. And anyway she may refuse jobs that compromise her Lesbian image.

Such women give the air of being almost deliberately, willfully damned. In the bar, too, are the helpless damned. For a variety of reasons, these women prefer an appearance that is sufficiently masculine to prevent them from getting many kinds of employment and that acts to limit them to the gay subculture. Often of working-class background, where sex roles are taught strong and early, where all the human world seems divided up into masculine and feminine—dress, behavior and activities—Lesbian to them means tough, hands-in-pockets behavior. If everything is perceived as masculine and feminine, then what does not seem feminine must be masculine. They may have been labeled queer as children by their families, who unconsciously drove them to the stereotype. Like the effeminate male homosexual, they are on the fringes of even the gay world, and have an air of loneliness. Also among the helpless damned may be the older Lesbian who has not plotted her escape from the bar before time caught up with her.

Role playing is important to the Lesbian's damnation; in shouldering all the baggage of the stereotypical Lesbian image, she also subscribes to the division of gay women into two groups, male-identified women and female-identified women. She shows that she accepts the heterosexual idea that a woman who loves women is against nature. Much irony is generated in the gay world by people who are in conflict with themselves and the society, whose deliberate distance from, and perspective on, heterosexual life at times gives them biting insights. One gay woman calls their gestalt "gay soul."[12]

These Lesbians have severed relationships with their families. It is even more likely that they were thrown out by family, school, or husband. In some ways, they know more of the hard truth about being homosexual in this society than do their uptight, closety debt-paying sisters.

Heterosexuality is the only way; homosexuality is evil. The damned Lesbian fully acquiesces to this with as much style and verve as she can muster for as much of the time as she can muster it. Beneath her unending gaiety, the damned Lesbian has a profound insecurity and a sense of unworthiness, gifts society has made certain she has received.

The Lesbian who wants to stay in the system must conspire with society to fulfill its most important requirement: invisibility.

Invisibility has saved many Lesbians from economic discrimination, but it has geometrically increased the psychic agony of guilt. In contrast, Blacks, for instance, can rarely hide their blackness. People are careful to conceal their prejudices in the presence of Blacks. Gay people, who hide their gayness, are often exposed to cruel jokes and obscene remarks. Worse, they often feel they must appear to enjoy them to maintain their protective isolation. Lesbians, as personnel directors, media censors, admissions counselors, and in other positions, are even asked to enforce discrimination. Some attempt quietly to work for more lenient measures; other completely conform to the rules to keep their job.

Invisibility is a condition of getting a job and keeping it. If Lesbians were purple, none would be admitted to respected places. But if all Lesbians suddenly turned purple today, society would be surprised at the number of purple people in high places.

The need for invisibility, like other measures discussed in this book, is not limited to Lesbians. Any peripheral social group has a special social contract to remain invisible. The poor, for instance, who are poor due to some moral failure according to the puritan ethic, are to stay in their ghettos out of sight. Criminals are put away in prisons, and other groups are exiled in one way or another.

Nothing around the Lesbian offers her validation. Everything carries the message of heterosexuality. Lesbians are shown by society as a whole, by the media—especially television—that women love men. This is not only omnipresent, it seems fixed, final. A challenge to an entire culture would seem incredibly arrogant. The sheer weight of history, of multitudes of lives, makes the Lesbian's experiences in life seem insignificant, invalid. The few movies that deal with Lesbians are considered sensationalistic erotica by society, and do not in any case reflect Lesbianism as lived by most Lesbians (who do not go to French boarding schools). The novels are mostly a sad lot. Although occasionally well-written, they are almost purposely dreary and discouraging and filled with foreboding. The subject is not discussed in school, church, or home. Consider the loneliness and pain of participating in a culture that absolutely refuses to recognize your existence.

One of the most haunting cultural experiences of invisibility must belong to the homosexual Jewish children for whom their families have sat shiva. Sitting shiva for a person is equivalent to holding a funeral. After the ceremony, the family considers the person dead. They do

37

not speak to her, see her, hear her, or appear to feel her if she touches them. This is a salient expression of the ostracism that all Lesbians suffer in society.

Denial, debt-paying, and damnation lead to exile and imprisonment. The overwhelming social necessity for most Lesbians to remain invisible and alienated is a contributing factor to both exile and imprisonment.

Exile and self-exile take many forms. Lesbians are sometimes told to leave home or not to come home, an obvious form of exile. This is especially cruel to the young girl in her teens who may not have the education, survival skills, or emotional strength to take care of herself. Many gay women run away from home, a form of self-exile. The majority close off their real lives from their families, and conceal themselves, preferring to exile their identities.

Young boys, beaten up and tossed out of small towns across the country as village queers, often become street people in large cities, ripping off for survival like many of the oppressed young. Young girls often try to call for help. This is made more poignant by the fact that the only organization they are likely to know about, the Daughters of Bilitis, in the past has felt nearly powerless to help them if they are under age, for fear of arrest on the grounds of contributing to the delinquency of a minor or corrupting the morals of a minor.

One Lesbian, whose name had appeared in a large metropolitan newspaper in conjunction with Gay Liberation, for weeks received desperate phone calls from a fourteen-year-old girl. The girl was afraid to identify herself, or even to see a psychiatrist, for fear her family would find out. But the Lesbian, on the best counsel of friends and a lawyer, had to refuse to see her. The girl might be about to explode to her parents, who could then decide that the villain in the piece was not their daughter but the older Lesbian. The girl was jail bait. But her guilt and shame were probably increased when she understood that she might endanger the very person who tried to help her. Thus the girl learns that to be a Lesbian is almost always to be alone.

There is a kind of exile—a geographic cure—where one tries to leave oneself behind. Eastern Lesbians move West; Western Lesbians move East. The experience of being cut off from family and society, of rootlessness, can lead to a pattern of fleeing, as in this fantasy:

> The only way we could imagine living as Lesbians was to have a fast car and lots of money. To set up a temporary life somewhere for a few weeks before moving on, to live an interim existence between discovery and discovery.

Running away, mentally or physically, does not lead to a productive life. But this couple felt that whatever they achieved would be destroyed the instant their love became known to others.

If the desire to get away and the parents' desire to have the daughter away coincide, leaving occurs by mutual consent; but it is still exile. Parents still send troubled or restless daughters to Europe, or to live with relatives away from bad influences, or outright pay for them to stay away.

In the old classic story, some Catholic families have tried to exile their daughters to a convent to keep them away from bad influences and thereby solve homosexual problems. In this connection Dr. Clarence A. Tripp talks about the effectiveness of such a decision for males:

> It would be far quicker and cheaper to get the patient to join the Trappist Monks; that would "cure" a homosexual problem, any heterosexual problem, and since the monks don't speak it would fix stuttering too.[13]

Parents also send their Lesbian daughters to psychiatrists, which is exiling the Lesbian in their daughter if not the daughters themselves.

Once in a while parents, even of adult Lesbians, resort to an extreme but reliable means of convincing the Lesbian she is guilty: exile as commitment to a mental institution. This is not as rare as people may think and serves effectively to strip a Lesbian of civil rights, self-respect, and responsibilities, all of which she must have to prove her sanity. By reducing her from person to patient, those who would commit a Lesbian for her sexual preference ignore the possibility that a Lesbian who denies guilt for her sexual choice could be in her right mind.

They also exile the Lesbian in their daughter when they refuse to believe her if she tries to tell them, or label her sexuality a "phase." The daughter usually understands from this that they do not wish to hear about her Lesbianism, and so she shuts off much of her inner self.

The parents' feeling that their daughter could not possibly be homosexual is a function of what Jung calls "self-knowledge," most of which he says is dependent on social factors influencing the human psyche. Parents are likely to say that such-and-such does not happen "in our family" or "among our friends." At the same time, the parents hold illusory assumptions about the alleged presence of good qualities, which merely serve to obscure truth about the family.[14] Thus parents too are apt to say, "It must be the other girl. We are sure you didn't want this." They exile the identity of their daughter, whose emerging capacity to love may be expressing itself in a Lesbian relationship.

Psychic exile can also occur when parents subtly forewarn daughters not to let them know, not to tell them. Thus, the parents avoid having to make any decisions. But the girl gains the impression that what she is is too terrible to be discussed and that she is not fit to be part of the family.

Lesbians, like other alienated or oppressed peoples, find life more tolerable if they can make themselves semiconscious. This kind of "living" can be achieved by alcohol, tranquilizers, sleep, and by continuous denial. The alienation, the lack of a validated identity, becomes more tolerable when both mind and body are deadened and the troubled Lesbian settles for living a small fraction of her potential.

Gay role-playing is another way out of confronting oneself. If a Lesbian plays a male or female role in a relationship, she is living out roles written by the society. Whatever role is played, butch or femme, the Lesbian will eventually find it hard to be herself, to know who she is.

Another form of role-playing is a pretense of heterosexuality. This act may include dating men, having affairs, maybe even marriage.

The Lesbian—although literally a sexual criminal in all but a few states—is rarely imprisoned in body, but is often imprisoned in her own mind. One kind of mental prison is the "closet," in which one encloses and locks away one's Lesbianism by limiting it to certain times and types of interaction. The debt-paying Lesbian often literally imprisons her gayness.

This aspect of her guilt, and of society's demand for invisibility, means that she suffers emotional imprisonment. Spontaneity, freedom of expression, and the direct expression of personality are not hers. A woman who has been more or less alone for a year meets a marvelous woman at a party. She gets the woman's phone number, but hesitates to call. She sits at work, thinking about whether to dial the number; her phone rings. It is the woman she met. She is very happy, but she has no way of telling her co-workers about her happiness. She must hold it in, lock it up, or lie about it.

> If I am not with my lover or one or two good friends, I must hide the intensity of my emotions, especially at work. I might be in love and ready to climb mountains or shout with delight. I must act as if there is nothing more important in the world than a late subway. I move from ecstasy to pain while never showing any emotion at all, even to some who feel they know me very well. In the office, the young girls and the married women talk about every thought their husbands or boyfriends have, and about every time they take them out to dinner or a show. It is hard not to feel a barrier between us. They think I am out of it all, and tolerate any occasional lies. They must think I never feel anything deeply. No doubt they think I am so cold no one could ever love me, or I them.

A sense of imprisonment, shutting different parts of herself into different compartments, can stunt the Lesbian's growth emotionally, intellectually, professionally. To grow, a person must feel free and self-confident. She must be open to inspiration, and take advantage of the full range of her personality, creativity, talents, and skills. She must be together enough to try new paths or to double back and start over—to be adventurous. Above all, she must respond to her inner experience, "the real me." Only in this way can she be intensely alive. Anything short of this is a half-death.

Coping with guilt eventually takes its toll of personality, and at some point one's remaining self-respect and working relationships with the outside world may break down. It becomes clear to the Lesbian that her life isn't working. She hates the lies and the control tactics that she knows are necessary to survive. Yet the thought of withdrawing further from society may intensify her anxiety. Feeling the futility of the web of façades, lies, and delusions she has spun around her, a web that can be easily torn by the single stroke of a careless or malevolent hand, she may experience despair, try confession, accept insanity, or even let herself fall into violence.

A woman by upbringing—that is, socialized to be dependent on the opinions of others for a great deal of her opinion about herself—the Lesbian is often tied to her efforts to relate to the larger human community—to re-establish herself within the boundary or to enlarge the boundary. As a woman, she is often psychologically maladapted to operating from a strong inner sense of self. Trying to live in a society that does not want her, she is never entirely immune to the insults and rejection.

Abject confession is another last resort to regain the lost love of the external world. Confession is a plea for understanding and simultaneously a testing of the environment. Gaining the sympathy and continued friendship of a straight friend is powerful medicine. Although it changes little in the rest of a Lesbian's life, it does offer hope. Rejection is a bitter blow.

As Theodore Reik notes, secret knowledge clamors to be revealed. The Lesbian like many other "criminals," is obliged to confess her "crime," if not to a friend, then to a minister or psychiatrist, who can offer protection or comfort. If she bars confession, her unconscious urge for self-betrayal may find expression in ambiguous words that stimulate questions from her listeners. When the moral tension is unbearable, words that allow of only one interpretation finally break through. "Surely some emotional effort was required to repress certain ideas or impulses. The very term 'repression' implies that. Also, a certain amount of repression is required to keep them in that state. . . . The repressed thought and tendencies have, mind you, the strongest inclination to return by themselves, to be voiced and to be realized," writes Reik in his *Compulsion to Confess*.[15]

Despair, leading sometimes to insanity, is also a last resort. Frequent use of any of the altered states of consciousness, the half-deaths, indicate a buildup of despair. Some Lesbians say that they cannot believe they will live past thirty. While this reflects the emphasis on youth in our culture, to the Lesbian it can be a symbolic statement of the impossibility of solving her life and of a suspension of attempts to deal with its problems. It can mean that despair has already set in.

Some Lesbians panic and cry out, "I was wrong. Let me in. I will change." They resume relations with men and perhaps seek psychiatric help.

The greater number seem not to see that all of their ameliorating efforts must fail, since their evasive tactics and camouflage do not include renouncing Lesbianism. "I am doing everything in my power to be a good person" is not enough so long as the original cause of stepping outside the boundary exists. The Lesbian remains truly outside the perimeter as long as she remains a Lesbian; she realizes this on occasion, perhaps during personal crises when she has need of emotional or financial support, and when there is no one there to help. At those times, her isolation becomes a reality that no tactics will disguise.

Frustration with her situation in life can lead to sporadic outbursts of violence—usually psychic, occasionally physical. Violence is a form of temporarily giving up and giving in to the powerful forces society directs against her. The Lesbian is teeming with inner turmoil and fury. She may strike out at people or things around her, as if by striking out anywhere or everywhere she can hit the center of the omnipresent oppressor. There is the desire to punish as she is punished. This is irrational only because it does not gain the Lesbian anything except temporary relief. Violence, internally or externally directed, is a predictable human response to intolerable, unrelieved suffering. Lesbian violence has often been noted, but has not been understood in relation to the overwhelming forces in the Lesbian's life running contrary to any affirmation of self or possible self-respect.

Most human beings cannot live without love from a chosen individual or individuals, but human beings have a broader social nature as well and need a sense of community, even, or especially, in this day. The two needs are mutually exclusive in the Lesbian: she can have one but not the other. The gay subculture has not been enough. It has been a specialized social network designed to supplement the basic culture into which the person is superficially integrated. Until Gay Liberation, the gay world was made up largely of places to meet potential sex partners. Not satisfying for many Lesbians as a full-time commitment, it cannot substitute for all the rest of society.

The tension between a Lesbian's needs for love from individuals and from the community cause personal crises, internal confusion, and erratic behavior. Her love for her lover becomes murky with self-hate. She may come to hate her love partner, the tangible evidence of her break with the community. Fear and guilt temporarily dissolve the love. She strikes out at her lover and at herself too.

What It Was Like

Suicide is the ultimate violence to oneself. It is the most extreme reaction to guilt, a final solution. The machinations of guilt take over the personality and mete out a punishment more severe even than society would wish. Can heterosexual society comprehend the agony a Lesbian has gone through who conceives of death as the only solution?

Every Lesbian knows of women who have taken this final route out beyond their peripheral and despised position in society to nothingness. Gay women may attempt suicide as a desperate cry for help. Emotional and psychological pressures have become too much to bear alone. They may have tried to ask their parents to hear them and may have paid a professional listener (therapist), and still felt they were not heard. Instead of destroying unjust laws and attitudes, they destroy themselves. Alone they feel helpless and fear life more than death.

The suicide's anger turns upon herself; a Lesbian activist's turns outward. Both are saying: "I cannot and will not live any other way, and I cannot live my way the way things are now."

2 A STAKE IN THE SYSTEM

When a young woman begins to be aware of sexual feelings for other women, she realizes with a deepening sense of shock that if she becomes a Lesbian, she is identifying herself with a minority group that is hated and despised by all racial, religious, and ethnic groups, including her own. Her sexual preference places her at rock bottom in society's eyes, no matter how much or how little her stake in the system at birth.

Almost at once a Lesbian begins fighting to hold onto her place, to survive. She does not strive to gain so much as she attempts to prevent loss. She runs and runs to stay in one place—passing for straight is her survival skill. A good deal of energy is devoted to it. On the job, in the street, or at her parents' home, the Lesbian who can pass for straight is accorded the privileges attendant upon what activists have called "the heterosexual assumption."

The tendency of people to assume straightness (acceptability) until "unfeminine" mental or physical characteristics are revealed, or until circumstances occur to arouse suspicion, is just what the Lesbian counts on, just as a blond, Aryan-looking Jew in German-occupied Europe in World War II might have hoped to avoid notice.

Like members of other minority groups, Lesbians are liable to paranoia, bad self-image, defeatism, and low expectations. All of these fears act to inhibit fulfillment.

Many Lesbians share with members of other minority groups an attitude that results from unfair treatment: gratitude for whatever society seems to offer.

Until the various Liberation movements started in this country, minority people tended to say that they were getting along about as well as could be expected, that things could be, or had been, worse. There was a tendency to locate such security as they did enjoy in the same system that oppressed them, a tendency to reduce expectations to the minimum so that they could be fulfilled. They were grateful for marginal, low-paying jobs with no security, for inadequate housing, for third-rate schooling for their children. Members of minority groups, aware of the underlying hostility of society, fear attention, which can erupt into open hostility. They cling gratefully to what they have, afraid to ask for more, reluctant to rock the boat.

Similarly, a Lesbian, like many other working women, is too often too grateful for too little. She can be grateful for a low-paying job that offers virtually no chance for advancement. She can be grateful that her employer and co-workers like her. The Lesbian tries to forget that if they knew her story, some—if not most—would undoubtedly withdraw their friendship and support.

A homosexual woman's fears are often justified. One of these is that advancement may put her personal life under scrutiny from her employer.

The hassle involved in asserting herself on the job sufficiently to improve her salary and position significantly can be frightening to a Lesbian in hiding. Allowing herself to be content, however, means accepting the limitations in housing and recreation that come with lower pay. She knows that she will be in the job market for most of her adult life and must count on supporting herself entirely.

Lesbians may well be exempt from marriage and pregnancy, which are perceived as drawbacks by corporations and used as excuses to avoid hiring women for responsible positions or to avoid promoting them. But how can a Lesbian turn this into an asset? How can she explain that she differs from most women workers in that she will not marry or become pregnant? Far from being an asset in business, her sexuality may get her fired or, at the very least, bring forfeiture of promotion. Even the suspicion of Lesbianism can cause relations with co-workers to degenerate to the point where the Lesbian will get jumpy enough to look for another job.

If I see someone in a work situation that I met in a bar, I never say hello. I avoid talking to her at all. I have a horror that one day the phone will ring and it will be someone from the bar. If that ever happens, I will hang up. If I see someone in the street, I avoid her eyes and just walk past, especially if I'm with someone from the office or someone in my family.

Not only does a Lesbian have to be extremely careful around straight co-workers, she must keep information about her life and job to a minimum around gay acquaintances. Lesbians are rarely black-mailed, but revenge phone calls to employers are not unheard of. Many Lesbians are so fearful of discovery that they do not wish to get phone calls from gay friends on the job at all.

Personal contacts are important in advancing a career. Lesbians, as a rule, are reluctant to exploit the possibilities of business-related entertaining that gets new clients, strengthens alliances between executives, leaks information not shared during office hours, and offers entrée into otherwise closed circles. The Lesbian may shy away, too, from the opportunities presented by professional organizations. Problems, real or imagined, surrounding her sexual preferences may keep her from less formal professional meetings and gatherings.

There are in fact Lesbians in key jobs, particularly in the communications industry and in the service professions, who might offer each other support. But usually a Lesbian is afraid to take advantage of these acquaintances. Experience has taught her extreme caution about her own secrets, and she reasons, realistically, that she may be rebuffed as jeopardizing another gay woman's sexual identity.

Lesbians, on all levels, identify their interests with their jobs in a more concrete way than many women, since for them Prince Charming is not going to come galloping up and, if and when he does, he will be rejected. Lesbians seem frequently to take on extra work and responsibility; this fits in with their self-image, for capability and resourcefulness are necessarily desirable and attractive qualities in Lesbian life. But hiding may rob the Lesbian of a real feeling of accomplishment, since it is her façade that gets the accolades.

Any setback or failure is magnified. There is conflict between the demands for success, both internalized and from without, and the drains of a woman's Lesbianism on her energy. It is hard to feel good enough of the time to compete successfully if one is bearing in addition to the burden of being female, the burden of a hidden identity.

In the office the tension of creating a façade complete with men and dates, the need to account for vacations and weekends, can make the job a hated place—a place to get away from.

What It Was Like

A number of Lesbians devote their main energies to their personal lives and are satisfied with jobs that are not time-consuming beyond regular working hours. In this they resemble many other working women.

If the qualifications for a job are ability and responsibility, one wonders what Lesbianism has to do with it. Once the subject is out into the open, the Lesbian is in jeopardy. Knowledge of her sexual preference seems actually to change an employer's perception of her work, as if the architect who is now known to be a Lesbian can no longer make a good design, the executive can no longer make sound judgments, or the secretary be counted upon for accuracy.

Holidays are particular times of stress. Inquiries about personal life are stepped up. Straight people seem lucky; most of the holiday decisions—where to go and who to be with—have already been made by tradition. The Christmas holiday also brings the dreaded office party. Employees are encouraged to bring husbands or wives, and an unmarried Lesbian is expected to ask a man. A gay woman has three possibilities, each fraught with problems. She can make excuses and not appear at all, which may make bosses and co-workers question her interest in the job or her commitment to the company. She can bring a straight male friend, but complications can result from this deception, which is also apt to put her lover on edge. Finally, she can ask a gay male friend and hope that he is good at passing for straight. Thus an ordinary office party can be a blatant reminder that a Lesbian couple is not part of the system. In the holiday cheer around her, the Lesbian feels excluded and is reminded that she is an outlaw.

Minor daily stresses accumulate. Most usual of these is the phone call from a lover, who requires reassurance or a loving word. These can't be given over the phone. If the lover is also calling from work, the inability for both to communicate renders the call both ridiculous and frustrating. They have to try to talk in code, and serious confusions and misunderstandings result. These phone calls occasionally aggravate a situation to the extent that both may rush home after work to talk alone and straighten out the mess. Many Lesbians would like to forbid lovers to call them at work, but few have the heart to mention this.

Even something as basic as a lunch hour can become intolerable. If she is in a work situation where the same women eat lunch together day after day—like a secretarial or clerical pool—she is forced into a social situation in which the main topic of conversation is dating or husbands. If she has the social skill, she lies. If not, she sits in silence or goes off alone. One homosexual woman went to a psychotherapist because, though a trained bookkeeper, she could not hold a job, she said, because she had developed a horror of lunchtime pressures to contribute to discussions on personal and sexual topics. Women in managerial or executive positions often use lunch for business appointments and thus avoid this particular pressure.

Office clothing becomes a costume, helping the Lesbian to stay in character, to play the role, serving to remind her that she is among heterosexuals and that she must control her conversation and behavior accordingly. Work clothing, then, takes on a nearly magical function. It offers the comfort of protection, and adds to self-confidence and ability to deal with the situation. It tells her to keep her mouth shut. One woman often wore a long necklace to the office. "These are my straight beads," she would say. She said she wore them in situations where she feared she would relax and make a slip.

For the suppression she undergoes at work, the Lesbian compensates by priding herself on her skill at the game of deception. She may see herself as manipulating the office situation rather than being manipulated by it. Nevertheless, energies are given over to concealment at a cost to the more productive aspects of her job.

Hiding around straight people may lead a gay woman to invest more and more in her Lesbian relationships, where she has a sense of self, and perhaps plunge deeper into the gay subculture of bars and parties.

Is the Lesbian really fooling the straight people she sees regularly? The game of social expectations and requirements can become quite subtle. In the larger urban centers at least, it does not seem to be required that she actually deceive everyone, but simply that she make a respectable effort to do so. Most people can sense the bogus, and today, when sex and interpersonal relations often come up as topics of conversation, people are keener at detecting homosexuals.

The basic demand of a work group seems to be that members try

49

to conform to the standard of that group in order not to cause strain. Employers and employees often try to close their eyes to such questions as sexuality, accepting a Lesbian's efforts to conceal on a functional rather than deeper emotional level and trying not to believe what they suspect.

Increased openness and chatter about interpersonal relationships does not mean that anyone tells the whole truth. After all, status is at stake.

The lack of privacy in many work situations and the absence of real office friendships causes most people to present a somewhat superficial version of themselves and their alliances or marriages. This acts in the Lesbian's favor. Co-workers may hold barely formulated reservations about a Lesbian but never express them unless asked directly or unless some particular stress situation arises. Apparently they wish her to hide, since this enables them simply to accept her as a worker. Disclosure would mean that they would have to cope with a condition that they don't understand; it would mean, too, that they would have to take a stand, which most people will go to great lengths to avoid. The group may make some effort to "believe" the Lesbian, ignoring, for example, slips she may make. If they like and value her in a work context, they may actually suppress perceptions, since they also have a stake in things as they should be, and this stake does not accommodate co-workers who are homosexual.

The work situation is inherently degrading for a Lesbian. It means hiding and a denial of self that is very detrimental to self-respect. It means an inordinate fear of financial loss. Hannah Arendt tells how lack of financial security can become profoundly threatening, over a period of time, until any relief from financial fears and the humiliation of poverty will be sought:

> Each time society, through unemployment, frustrates the small man in his normal functioning and self-respect, it trains him for the last stage, when he will undertake any function. . . . A Jew released from Buchenwald once discovered among the SS men who gave him the certificates of release a former schoolmate, whom he did not address but stared at. Spontaneously, the man stared at remarked: "You must understand, I have five years of unemployment behind me. They can do anything they want with me."[1]

A search for freedom from pressures on personal life motivates the Lesbian who drives a taxi or who starts her own business. Starting a business is not uncommon for Lesbians, at least in the larger cities. It may be undertaken with a lover or gay friend, thus partially decompartmentalizing their lives. A number of Lesbians have done well with their own—usually small—companies, finding more autonomy and greater fulfillment in the process. The chances are, however, that the death rate for Lesbian businesses would be in proportion to the very high national death rate for small businesses, which are often undercapitalized or started without sufficient management or planning experience.

Not surprisingly, it is often the Lesbian who has created her own business, or who has stepped out of the mainstream, or who has dropped out to be on welfare, who is the happiest. These Lesbians are individualistic and find office conformity a waste of time when they have already chosen a nonconforming sexual life.

Lesbians in the artistic and academic fields suffer more from discrimination than other women in these fields. Women writers probably get the best breaks, whether heterosexual or homosexual, but some Lesbian sculptors and painters feel that the galleries and exhibitions are especially stacked against them, as they are the target for discrimination as a matter of course, not only from heterosexual male gallery owners, who might give a break to an attractive woman, but from homosexual men in these areas who are inclined to advance a young man's career.

Both gay and straight women seek careers. But it is interesting to speculate on a possible difference in the motivating dynamic .

Lesbian career women may have had encouragement from their fathers, but perhaps the key to their strivings, which may reach beyond those of most women, lies in their relationships to their mothers. Some Lesbians, in consciousness-raising sessions, have called this "living out the dreams of their mothers." No matter the degree of hate, resentment, or ambivalence expressed toward the mothers, there seems to be a deeper level of identification. At some level the mother communicates to her daughter what the daughter has to do to live out an active life in the larger society outside the home, to live out the life the mother did not or could not have. Lesbians seem to have been, or have been made to be, very alert to their mothers' subliminal discontent or sense of entrapment.

A Lesbian's mother, like any mother, will tell her to be pretty and winsome and catch a young man and will expect her to do so. But she may also reveal, perhaps nonverbally, her frustrations and deepest longings, perhaps never even articulated. The mother may long to write, travel, study, earn money, be a more complete person in her own right. Lesbians often become their mothers' psychic protectors and, in families where physical violence is expressed, their physical protectors as well. These ties, which run very deep, are far from understood, but in many ways some Lesbians seem to live so as to avenge their mothers' deprivations, to make their mothers' lives worthwhile in a way that the mothers themselves could not.

Conversations with heterosexual career women suggest that the fathers of heterosexual career women are more influential in their lives. These men seem to have marked their daughters out for accomplishment, sometimes because they did not have a son, sometimes because they had more rapport with their daughter than with their sons. In major piece for *Esquire* magazine in 1970, Sally Kempton, daughter of writer Murray Kempton and herself a successful writer, wrote movingly about this kind of relationship, in which the father treats the daughter as a close intellectual companion, although always with the assumption that she will never quite become an equal and hence never a worthy competitor.

Unless she marries and has children, the Lesbian's original family is likely to be the one permanent social unit in her life. Her family is her emotional stake in the system, another element that makes it hard for her to make a clean break and create a full gay life.

On the family's side there is continued concern about an unmarried, hence unprotected, daughter. Lesbians, as women, have been socialized to be dependent and although they may resent and fight it, vestiges of this dependence may last for the lifetimes of the parents. Whatever the quarrels with Mother and Dad, it is nice to have them there in time of crisis. Eventually the family may become the Lesbian's last link with the great heterosexual majority surrounding her, the last place she can go to fit into this majority for a few moments without question. She may be very ambivalent about her homosexuality and about her parents and yet, for some of these reasons, not want to break completely with her family, the protective unit she may need late into life.

If Christmas creates a bad situation in the office, it presents an impossible situation within the family. Christmas is the day on which most Lesbians confront the split in their lives. At this time of the year when people are expected to be with those closest to them, a gay woman is asked to divide herself in two. There is not time to serve fully two conflicting identities—gay lover and loyal family member.

Christmas means a choice between the family she loves and the woman she loves. A Lesbian feels like a puppet. It is just a question of who will pull the strings—lover or family. On this emotionally loaded day, she may feel she has to treat her lover as though she did not exist. Christmas Day can emerge as a focus of contention as early as spring or summer. A symbol in any case, it acquires great meaning in terms of priorities. A couple may split and each go to her own parents' home. Or one lover, who has broken with her family or whose family is geographically distant, may spend Christmas alone. If a Lesbian is able to go home but chooses not to, often she cannot explain her choice convincingly. The parents may try to second-guess the problem and say, "We understand; bring *him* home."

Lesbian couples sometimes spend Christmas together in the home of one lover's parents. There may be an expressed acceptance on the part of the parents, but more often than not, understanding is unconscious or unspoken.

One way some Lesbians remain in touch with the system is to continue seeing men. Dating may be an aspect of denial, or it may represent an unwillingness to break yet another symbolic tie with the larger world.

One way to live was to go out with men every night until 12 P.M., and then to put on slacks or pants and go to the women's bars. Another way, especially at college, was to be with women during the week and date men on weekends. Later, some women go out frequently with gay men, to dinner and to women's or mixed (men and women) gay bars.

Lesbians have been brought up as heterosexuals, and they take parts of the system with them into the gay life. The primary way they continue to subscribe to their heterosexual orientation is by forming, and trying to maintain, couple relationships. If living as part of a monogamous couple is the only way a woman can live respectably as a heterosexual, perhaps it is the only way a woman should live as a homosexual.

Becoming attracted to a third woman, and perhaps sleeping with her, is usually taken to mean that the couple relationship has failed. Often, then, though not always, it breaks up. Repeatedly trying and failing in monogamous relationships is the one element of her life most apt to break a Lesbian. To give up this ideal can mean too great a break with her upbringing to tolerate. It threatens what she has been raised to consider her identity as a woman, and her conditioned way of relating to the people she loves. It is a pattern to which she will cling, knowing the odds are against her. This element has to do with the expectations of permanence in relationships that she was brought up to have. Lesbian relationships last a year or two, and often longer, but there is no contractual guarantee for permanence even in one that has lasted ten years. To dissolve a relationship, you merely pack your bags. Typically, then, a Lesbian has a series of monogamous relationships. Serial relationships require a different mental set than that for marriage. Impermanent monogamous relationships are described in Alvin Toffler's *Future Shock*[2] as a life-style of the future. However, to a woman who has been brought up to value and honor only one love relationship in a lifetime, having several relationships can be very upsetting.

There is, of course, tremendous pressure, subtle and obvious, to break up the Lesbian relationship. Unknowing parents say: "Why have you been living with that girl for five years? Don't you want a place of your own so you can entertain men? When are you going to become interested in men?" At the same time they make the Lesbian constantly aware of the awards and approval incidentally accompanying a heterosexual contract: the showers, the big wedding for everyone in town, the newspaper announcement, the honeymoon.

Some of the evidences of permanence in Lesbian relationships are the same as those used as indicators by heterosexual couples. "When we both signed the three-year lease for the apartment, I cried. I felt I was holding a marriage certificate in my hands." Lesbian couples buy houses, cars, furniture, and pets together, and these possessions serve to stabilize the relationship.

A Lesbian with children feels that she must remain much closer to the system, that she has a stake in continuing to relate to as much of the system as possible, that stake being the happiness of her children.

Children are often a stabilizing element in a Lesbian relationship. Donald Webster Cory, in *The Lesbian in America,* written ten years ago, says that Lesbian couples with children in the home are rare.[3] A recent study by Daughters of Bilitis, however, shows that about one-third of their members are mothers, although not all choose to leave their husbands or to live with their lovers or felt they could live with lovers if they did leave their husbands.

The difficult part of having children in the home is apt to be borne by the adults rather than the children. Children in a Lesbian home imply the virtual elimination of psychic and physical space in which to be oneself. This is to some extent true for heterosexual parents as well, but for a Lesbian couple who feel it is in the best interest of the children to conceal the relationship from them, it is a greater hardship. Nevertheless, Lesbians and Lesbian couples undertake it.

Of course, hiding affection for each other from the children shows guilt, and the Lesbian's guilt goes very deep. Heterosexuals too conceal their sex lives from their children, but the Lesbian mother may hesitate to show her partner any affection around the children. She is particularly sensitive to charges—real or imagined—of influencing her children toward homosexuality.

The sum total of stresses involved in a monogamous, marriagelike relationship attempted outside any area of support such as the heterosexual couple receives from family, friends, indeed the whole social environment, sooner or later catch up with the Lesbian couple. The couple breaks up, and often both parties soon plunge into other similar relationships. Few stop to ask what life-style would actually suit their female homosexuality. Few ask if a Lesbian relationship should be like a heterosexual one or work to discover what it can be in itself.

Family, job, and love relationships do not make up the entire social system in which the Lesbian finds herself, of course. From time to time, she becomes involved with other major social institutions. Most social institutions have a social-control function, but this function is more explicit, less subliminal, in the institutions relating to the law, education, religion, and psychiatry.

Lesbians do not necessarily encounter the law in the course of their gay lives, but the law both sums up a cultural norm and verbalizes it so that it forms a base for the rules and regulations in such areas as education, civil service, industry, and the military.

The law in turn has been shaped by various religious beliefs and more recently by inputs from psychiatry.[4] What we have here then is what appears to be a closed system with the most ancient aspects of our culture embodied in religion, giving the chief input to laws governing homosexuality, re-evaluated but supported by psychiatry, which until recently has been so culture-bound as to have been unable to assess sexual minorities fairly. In turn, as mentioned above, other major social institutions build their attitudes and regulations on aspects of the outputs of religion, law, and psychiatry.

It is in an indirect manner that the law most often affects Lesbians. Most Lesbians go their ways scarcely thinking about the laws that make their way of life criminal. Sometimes they do not even know of the existence of the laws or do not believe that the laws apply to them, as for example in states where the catch-all sodomy laws obtain. After all, they do not commit sodomy except as sodomy is used in law to mean "unnatural acts." Behind the Lesbian's removed attitude is the psychic distance that most women maintain from the legal/governmental system. Women traditionally have been trained to confine their interest to areas that immediately concern them. They have rarely been aware of systems—whether legislative, judicial, or governmental —probably because they did not create them and rarely administer them. However, it is not true that there is no legal or police oppression of women. Women have been pulled out of gay bars and beaten by the police and by roving gangs of boys, with tacit police approval. Women in the military are under equal, if not greater, scrutiny for homosexuality than the men, with the same penalties and punishments.

Lesbianism has been ignored much more than it has been punished. This reflects the lower value placed on women in the society, Victorian attitudes about nonexistent female sexuality, and the threat Lesbianism poses for the male establishment. Men would rather not believe it exists and, in any case, how can sex between women be serious? Oddly enough, being ignored by the law is also a form of oppression.

The most acute legal problem facing many Lesbians is the one confronted by Lesbian mothers. In any child custody case, Lesbianism is in itself grounds for being declared an unfit mother. This "fit mother" clause in effect controls the personal lives of many mothers, when judges who disapprove of Lesbianism can apply this open-ended clause. Thus, many Lesbians, whether they remain with their husbands or divorce, live in fear. Husbands who suspect their wives of having Lesbian affairs, or who know of their Lesbianism, can and do threaten them with loss of the children if they do not stop, or if they try to get a divorce. Some Lesbians who love their children very much willingly give up their children in divorce because they have been *convinced* they are unfit mothers. One Lesbian mother asked that her children be given to her husband, and the judge exclaimed that he had never heard of such a thing before.

For many homosexual women the most cruel oppression—one that they perceive in an institutional sense—is in the area of religion. Rejection by the churches sums up the hurt and symbolizes a severing of relationships with the human community. For some, being cut off from the church means being cut off from God. Not to be able to attend church, to go honestly and participate as oneself before community and God, is a source of anguish. Even in this nonreligious age, it is hard for the individual ego to assert itself against centuries of ecclesiastical authority.

The college or university also appears to operate from long-sanctioned authority and from wise and moral precepts. A number of Lesbians say that they had trouble in college, perhaps flunking out and then returning, or perhaps leaving for good. College years are the time when a woman begins to define herself and to explore the possibilities of adult life. These are also the years when she may have her first Lesbian relationship.

The discovery that she is a Lesbian is both joyous and draining. Some women say that, at first, their grades went up with the presence of newly liberated energies. But they also say that as they recognized the implications of their choice, their grades plummeted. Until recently dormitory life has been carefully supervised for women, and off-campus living has often been prohibited or discouraged; under these conditions a natural attraction between two compatible human beings can often turn into fear. Fears are compounded by the furtiveness required to maintain a relationship at college. Sneaking into little-used buildings, hugging in the bushes, renting rooms in nearby towns, constantly justifying seeing a woman and not a man, soon make the relationship into a kind of hell.

Being young and having no one to talk with can be devastating for the Lesbian. Little suspecting the outcome, the young woman sometimes tries to talk with the college chaplain or the college psychiatrist. But these officials are not bound to confidentiality. In fact, Lesbianism is considered such a threat to the college community that officials are sometimes required to pass on the information to the dean of women. The Lesbian can find herself first under observation, and then out of school. Women's colleges, in particular, have periodic Lesbian purges.

In these purges a particular pattern emerges. Often only one of the two women involved is expelled. The administration attempts to determine who is the aggressor in the relationship, which *one* is the Lesbian. The woman who appears more masculine or who admits to prior Lesbian experience is the one expelled. Or the woman expelled may be the one who breaks, who talks to the psychologist or to her dorm mates. In the last case the reasoning is that this is the woman who will cause confusion and upset in the dormitory, and she is thrown out, even though she is probably the more ambivalent one about the relationship.

College, then, is a training ground, a place to learn the necessity for playing it straight to maintain one's stake in the system. The psychic damage caused by college policies is enormous. The economic damage done to women who may have to earn their own livings for the rest of their lives is not even considered. The assumption is that Lesbianism will spread like wildfire, being a kind of disease or evil. This attitude is due partly to ignorance about Lesbianism and partly to a prevalent view of college women as children, unable to think for themselves or to take care of themselves.

Consulting a psychotherapist has traditionally been a dangerous business for the Lesbian who wants to preserve her way of life.

Even in private practice, let alone in the military, university, or industry, the psychotherapist is a cultural policeman on the side of the heterosexual majority. He works on the assumption that what the majority is doing is correct.

Some Lesbians are caught in a seemingly unending dependence upon a therapist. The patient relationship is essentially that of a child to a parent and, in the case of the Lesbian, this is compounded by the attitude that women are somehow childlike and that Lesbians are immature women who have not made it to the final, heterosexual level of development. In short, the view of the patient as childlike, immature, undeveloped, may influence the therapist into relating to the patient as though these things were true.

In a New York *Times* story on male homosexuality, the psychiatrists interviewed said they have noted that few Lesbians enter treatment, and even fewer do so to change their Lesbianism, in comparison with male homosexuals.[5] This may mean that homosexuality has a different meaning for a woman than for a man.[6] But for those women in treatment, unless they have been lucky enough to find an unusual therapist, the implicit goal of therapy is to examine her life with a view to changing her sexual preference. As a last recourse, adjustment to her homosexuality is undertaken. But this also means adjusting to some kind of third-class citizenship and to the misery caused by the societal oppression of homosexuals.

The majority of Lesbians who do not enter treatment, or who do so only briefly in times of crisis, sense that their psychic task is somehow to maintain equilibrium despite all the social pressures. The wonder of it all is the resilience and control of most Lesbians. Few Lesbians are in mental wards, as well they might be; few are out of contact with reality. Most Lesbians struggle to live as well and as fully as possible.

Oppressed not only by numbers of people, but by the institutions those people endorse and the power they delegate, the Lesbian is aware that her feelings cannot find spontaneous expression. She is painfully aware of her helplessness and insignificance as an individual in an authoritarian sexual system. She is fighting the traditions of millions over the centuries who take for granted that she is flawed.

The popular misconception that Lesbians wish to be men is so pervasive that a Lesbian herself may believe it. A Lesbian who has newly come out sexually may think that she must imitate a man, act butch, in order to be a good Lesbian. Later she discovers that a woman who wants a woman usually wants a woman.

The truth is that most homosexual men and women want to be their own sex; many, in fact, are chauvinistic about their own sex.

What does happen to most homosexuals as they explore their sexuality is that they become acutely aware of societal sex role constructs that serve to express and reinforce heterosexuality. For homosexual men and women, the sex role stereotypes are literally straightjackets, binding and limiting their choices and development. A Lesbian does not want to be confined to the poor half of human characteristics apportioned to her sex; she has, by virtue of being an outlaw, the chance to become a whole human being.

Having two sets of complementary characteristics for human beings seems absurd to homosexuals, for they know they contain a wide range of human qualities within themselves. They see no reason not to express a quality they value just because someone long ago assigned it, arbitrarily it would seem, to another sex. The enormity of their social crime is that they reject sex-role stereotypes:

> The sex typing of behavior and privileges is not only rigid and lasting but covers an expansive range. In most societies, the male is typed and trained for the superordinate role, but with social allowances for certain devious aggression against or sabotage of the male role. . . . It is then one of the essentials in the social development of the child that the social personality of each one shall match his sex in the biologic sense. . . . The system of rewards for sex-appropriate behavior, and punishments for sex-inappropriate behavior constitutes a large part of the social code in any society. . . . It operates with relative severity, begins early in the family's treatment of the child and is reinforced later by the controls of the school, the gang, the social clique, and the adult world.[7]

Kate Millett describes sex-role stereotyping in terms of "sexual politics." She points out that the division of human characteristics is not just functional or useful but hierarchical:

> . . . The formation of human personality along stereotyped lines of sex category ("masculine" and "feminine") is based on the needs and values of the dominant group and dictated by what its members cherish and value in themselves and find convenient in subordinates: aggression, in-

telligence, force and efficiency in the male; passivity, ignorance, docility, "virtue" and ineffectuality in the female.[8]

. . . The function of norm is unthinkingly delegated to the male—were it not, one might as plausibly speak of "feminine" behavior as active, and "masculine" behavior as hyper-aggressive.[9]

Studies of hermaphrodites and of children whose true biologic sex does not emerge until they are several years old, show that the children become the sex role they are taught, whether or not it conforms to biologic reality.[10] While there are undoubtedly implications of hormonal activity in the two sexes, it would seem that society, in search of an organizing principle, has overextended and oversimplified what male and female differences really exist. People have erroneously assumed that the choice of a partner of the same sex means a confusion of basic sexual identity.

Perhaps the earliest social distinction a child learns is his sex role. Before children are aware of genital differences in our society, they associate sex differences in terms of characteristics like power, aggression, and status. Children as old as four years may believe that sex can be changed by changing the style of hair or clothing.[11] Adult heterosexuals' fear of the homosexual may be based on just this primitive error.

When the Lesbian passes for straight, she is not hiding a biologically based masculine component, but a different way of life, a different self-concept and value structure—one that is profoundly threatening to a sexist society. She sees "feminine" as confining in physical as well as mental terms, and to the extent that she is aware of the controls governing her in her assigned sex role, she tries to free herself from them. Her unauthorized freedom is sometimes mislabeled masculinity.

She is not being "masculine" when she chooses to move, to laugh, to talk—to think and act—in a relaxed, expansive, and free manner. This freedom and exercise of choice, however costly, is valuable, and perhaps essential to the Lesbian's well-being. Women learn early to direct their minds down acceptable paths and to control the movements of their bodies: to sit up straight, to hold their arms in, to arrange their posture and their expressions. What the Lesbian feels she must monitor, both in terms of what she must not say as well as

61

what she must not do, says more about the role of women in our culture than it does about any masculine components in Lesbians.

A beautiful woman, a brilliant woman, or a Lesbian should be called deviant under the definition "differing from the social norm," or all three could be called individualistic. "The border between individuality and deviance is often arbitrary," says one psychologist.[12]

Yet we know that the word deviant is reserved for the negatively valued—freaks, criminals, and homosexuals. The word carries with it stigma and persecution.

Through controlled laboratory manipulation of a random population of 1,000 students,[13] experimenters Jonathan Freedman and Anthony Doob *convinced* a group of normal individuals that they were either deviant or normal. They found that the "deviant" subjects, worried about the kind of treatment they would receive from the "normal" people, attempted to minimize mistreatment by avoiding contact with them. They tried to please the normal group to compensate for prejudice, attempted to conceal their own deviance, and said they would prefer to be normal.

It is not surprising that Lesbians try to minimize mistreatment by hiding. Outside their home or apartment, women who care for each other do not feel free to show affection; they do not like to cheapen their love by exposing it to ridicule. The privacy of the home offers freedom, but in time the home can become a prison.

In the beginning, when they are totally engrossed in each other, they believe, like all lovers, that they have locked out the world, but Lesbians are apt to discover that the world has locked them in. Lesbians who have just found each other are reluctant to leave the safety of their shelter. Stepping out into the sunlight together can be an awkward and bitter experience. After going through that door there can be no more reassurances of love. They both know "Now we have to pretend we don't care for each other. But we know we are just pretending. I will try to hide my doubts if your pretending seems too real."

It is as difficult and painful for two Lesbians to pass for straight as it would be for two lovers forced to appear uninterested in each other. Lesbians try to conceal their love, but it is often bursting to be revealed. Guilt too is constantly demanding release. With these two formidable forces acting against her secrecy, the Lesbian must be supercautious.

Mere conversation is dangerous. It takes skill to cover up. Others may perceive gaps in the conversation about personal life or slight inconsistencies in simulated information.

Monitoring conversation is not enough. Expressions and gestures must be monitored, too. It is very easy to reveal deception with non-verbal clues. Actions may speak Lesbianism quicker than words. A touch, a look that lasts too long, a smile that is too warm, or any number of other actions may appear inappropriate or suspicious, especially to an interested man who is tracking a woman's interests.

Rather than smile or frown at the wrong time, it is often easier to adopt a masklike expression. Such inflexibility often appears cold or distant.

What is going on inside the Lesbian may be in flagrant contradiction to the blank façade. The Lesbian may be teeming with emotions, privy to all kinds of private information on the cost of hiding her love: a lump in her throat, nerves tingling, muscles tensing, stomach knotting, or heart pounding. The physiological changes are imperceptible to others, but they take their toll over time. And there are sometimes clues that she cannot hide, such as a sudden flush of feeling. She can betray herself in so many ways, even when she is careful.

For safety some Lesbians find it easier to ignore each other around people who would not understand; other Lesbians decide it just isn't worth the energy.

Congeniality with others can only be accepted up to a certain point—the point where others begin to penetrate the camouflage or the point where the lie extracts too much in self-respect.

A Lesbian's expectations of what life *should* have been, had she not been gay, constitute her stake in the system. This stake is what keeps Lesbians playing the straight role, to keep jobs and the love of their families, to protect their children. Like all women, they sometimes play the role of women as society writes it. But now, many heterosexual women also feel that at least some aspects of the feminine role —those that inhibit their drives, desires and development—are too costly.

All women sometimes play at being feminine.

However, for the Lesbian the situation is more serious. Her need for survival and acceptance guides her choices and can make her more conservative than a heterosexual woman, especially in this time when women are reaching out and exploring. To maintain her stake in the system, she too often sacrifices her self-respect. She becomes a hypocrite. If she somehow escapes guilt for being a Lesbian, then she is certain to feel guilty for being a liar.

"I'm not just a Lesbian in bed, I'm a Lesbian twenty-four hours a day," one woman has said. This conveys a feeling not only of Lesbianism as an identity, an integral part of the total being, but as a life-style related to and determining the nature and scope of the woman's interactions with society. This consciousness runs counter to the expressions of many liberal, urban people who maintain that Lesbianism is a private matter—"What you do in the bedroom is your business."

As long as the Lesbian is vulnerable to the written and unwritten laws of a society that has legally restricted sex to reproduction, as long as she can be fired from jobs, denied an education, kept out of government service, made unwelcome in churches and synagogues, and banished from her home, Lesbianism is very much a public matter. Unfortunately, what some people do in bed affects their involvement with the human community.

Liberals who say Lesbianism is strictly a bedroom issue condemn the Lesbian to eternal denial of her identity and what it means. If they understood what they were asking, they would not ask it. Passing for straight is a torture chamber, a daily task of lying and concealing. Since the Lesbian must conceal the many details that bear tangentially on her sexual identity, she must sacrifice more and more of herself to this effort.

Hiding, in turn, breeds self-contempt and self-hatred. Lesbianism can either be dismissed as unnatural masculinity on the part of women, or treated as though it were separate from the rest of the person and confined to the bedroom. Both views are wrong. Lesbianism is a way of living; with assumptions on the value and meaning of the self; it constitutes a kind of a statement of belief in independence and freedom for all females. Society denies itself an opportunity to learn more about women and how they can function by making the Lesbian seal off her Lesbianism in all her interactions with society.

Passing for straight can be thought of as a sort of *sane schizo-*

phrenia. Psychiatrist-writer R. D. Laing deals with schizophrenia not so much as an escape from reality as a technique for dealing with a threatening environment. As Laing describes it, schizophrenia involves the creation of a false self that acts as a barrier between the threatened personality and the threatening environment. The false self is quite consciously designed to buy off others, to satisfy what the schizophrenics think they want. Laing shows schizophrenia to be a rational, even successful action from the schizophrenic's point of view.[14] Using the term schizophrenic loosely, it sometimes seems as if the Lesbian, with her two identities, lives as a kind of sane schizophrenic. Common understanding of the term schizophrenic has it that one of the identities is fantasy. Sometimes it seems that one or both of the Lesbian's two selves—the real and the façade—is fantasy. She feels her life is strange—because it is. She is forced to live in two conflicting realities.

Like the schizophrenic, the Lesbian creates a false self, a façade or front, which she interposes between herself and the world. Only her lover and a few close friends may ever see her as an integrated being. If she has a good attitude toward her Lesbianism, the façade is a difficult but necessary tactic that allows her to retain social and economic status. If she is more at odds with her homosexuality, she may more closely approach having a split personality, identifying alternately with her straight behavior, and then with gay behavior.

A young Lesbian spoke of her sexuality in these dualistic terms:

> I had a good friend. I was very close to her. She became a Lesbian. I couldn't understand her at all. It was very hard because that Lesbian was me.

Sane schizophrenia uses psychic energies that should find more positive and creative expression. It diverts energy into building and rebuilding defenses against the threat of discovery, a threat that will never cease to exist. The outer self acts as a filter, a censor that examines all incoming and outgoing messages for threats. It is like thinking in one language and talking in another. For example, the Lesbian has to substitute "I" for "we" in describing life with her lover. The censor translates the word on the spot, so as not to bring up the question "We?" Threats to her façade spring up everywhere, from inside as well as outside, always having the advantage of surprise.

65

What It Was Like

The most unfortunate aspect of sane schizophrenia is that it reinforces, even creates, a kind of self-hatred that becomes almost palpable over time. The Lesbian daily experiences herself as so awful that she must be hidden away. Even for the middle-class Lesbian, who especially prizes the rewards and privileges the system has to give, this is a great price to pay for security. The Lesbian comes to have an investment in her straight façade and, justifiably, to be grateful for her ability to hide, but her life is literally in pieces, leading to psychic stress and damage.

Many straight women may work at satisfying all the demands of "femininity," laughing at male jokes, asking for help when they may not really need it, appearing more shy than they are to attract a man. For the heterosexual woman, this role is apt to be so habitual that she forgets she is playing it. Because the Lesbian plays this role only intermittently, she must work hard at it and often achieves an uncomfortable result. She may concoct a generalized female stereotype for herself much like the one society seems to value and then try to impersonate it. She may feel as though she is overacting her femininity as though she is in drag. Nothing she does seems spontaneous, and she may seem to others not so much masculine as lacking in spontaneity, or, since anything related to sex is very heavily censored, as not sexy:

> I felt as if I were a character playing a role, but could rarely come off stage. It was exhausting. I was careful about my language, always changing she's to he's, and her's to him's, substituting men's names for women's; making sure I smiled at men and not at women. All that I did, it was not me. I acted like the person I imagined I should be.

The Lesbian's sane schizophrenia is a practical and necessary response to real discrimination. Carl Jung has written:

> ... [a] human being can only meet the demands of outer necessity in an ideal way if he is also adapted to his own inner world, that is to say if he is in harmony with himself. Conversely, he can only adapt to his inner world and achieve unity with himself when he is adapted to the environmental conditions.[15]

Can the Lesbian have harmony with the system if she does not have harmony within herself, or can she have harmony with herself if she is not in harmony with the system? It is precisely the necessity for the unity of inner and outer realities that the Lesbian seeks to achieve in today's society. This has led the psychiatrists to try to change the Lesbian to heterosexuality and the Lesbian activist to try to change society.

Weakened by her personal struggle against pervasive and almost relentless oppression, the Lesbian craves a psychic space of her own to restore her ego and her identity. Where can she go to be free?

3 SANCTUARY

Living in an environment that is hostile or indifferent, Lesbians find themselves floundering for validation. They feel alien, uprooted—no longer able to count on acceptance from anyone or in any place. They feel that they don't count, don't exist, in a system whose social institutions and resources do not include them.

Not knowing what to do or where to go, not knowing even what it is that she wants, a Lesbian may escape the tensions of feeling different by daydreaming, taking long walks, or seeing endless double features. In another mood she may seek release in driving fast or a reckless run down a ski slope.

But it is almost impossible for human beings to live without community, the sense of belonging to something. Sooner or later, the Lesbian begins to see her carefully constructed and valued seclusion as forced upon her. Isolation drains her will, her conviction of the rightness of her love, even her passion and feeling. Her ingenuous feelings of love for another woman now present a new problematic face. For relief from the sustained concentration of exacting pretense, she seeks a sanctuary, a place where she will be protected enough to feel free.

Sanctuary has customarily been offered by the church, but for the Lesbian sanctuary is often found in the anonymity of the urban night, the amorality of the Mafia, who runs the bars for women, or the secretive sociability of the Daughters of Bilitis.

For heterosexuals, finding a partner has elements of a twenty-four-hour-a-day game of chance. A lover or a potential spouse can appear at work, at church, on the bus, or in a supermarket, or be a friend of your brother. But there is no everyday way to meet other Lesbians.

69

What It Was Like

One cannot—yet—look in the yellow pages for a gay computer dating service, or even buy a guide to gay bars, without first knowing where it is sold.

Night becomes a longed-for sanctuary. There is a sense of relief at the end of the day. With dusk, lines between conventional morality and immorality, rejection and acceptance, begin to blur, much as the hard edges of the buildings and streets lose their definition. Whatever destination she has in mind, the Lesbian is able to disappear into the hiding place of the night.

Perhaps dressed in dark tones or in black, in the fashion of old gay custom, the Lesbian blends into the environment, camouflaged like other life forms that develop protective coloration in hostile environments. By day she must contain her feelings in a dark closet; but protected by the night she feels she can allow her lightest moods to emerge. Day and night reflect the split in her identity that divides who she pretends to be and who she is.

One woman said that she began her hunt for others like herself by following women who looked gay down the street. Another said it took all the courage she had to ask a cab driver; and even then she was not sure of the right words: "I want to go to a place where only women go." "What do you mean, lady . . . the YWCA?" Frantically, "No." Pause. "Oh."

In many American cities there is at least one such place—inevitably a bar—and the Lesbian knows she must find it: this is where she belongs.

The bars are usually hidden away in warehouse districts, in lofts and cellars. Spooky at best, the deserted streets, with papers and bottles blowing in the dark, heighten the excitement of the forbidden. Often a bar is not marked; the entrance is unlighted, signless. Looking through the windows or through a peephole in the door, one can see very little. The door is frequently locked; if there is a bouncer at the door, he looks over each customer before admitting her. If the bar is called a private club, he asks for her card, which is usually signed with a pseudonym.

When the Lesbian enters a bar, she feels as though she is being let in on a secret.

I felt when I entered that I should give a secret handshake or a special code word. I did not know these women, but they were my sisters. I felt something like I was visiting another chapter of my sorority.

Inside the bar, the decor is often barren and seedy: red lights, wallpaper imitating brocade, a jukebox. The bartender on the scene, often a woman, has heard it all, seen it all, done it all. It seems a worn-out, grimy place.

Prices for watered-down drinks are high: You pay for protection. Order right away and pay before you're served. The need to keep drinking in order to be allowed to stay in the bar means that patrons drink slowly or hold a warm beer in their hands for hours.

Just how much security or protection does a bar offer?

In New York, bar after bar opens or opens under a new name with the same management. Bars exist today, in 1972, but they still serve as reminders of an underground life.

A well-known Lesbian bar that flourished in New York in the late 1960's featured a back room for dancing, open only to regular patrons. Although nothing went on there but dancing and talking at tables, this room was protected by a bodyguard, as was the street entrance. Police visits were signaled to back-room clients by sudden bright lights and the silencing of music. Women would stop dancing and return to their seats. The police would look around for the owner, presumably to collect a pay-off. Pay-offs seemed to be a part of bar life. When politicians are running for office and threaten to "clean up" the city, there are sometimes raids.

Fear of arrest keeps people away for a while, and then they come back or turn to another, safer bar, perhaps with still higher prices. The money from the patrons goes to the management and to the police, who function in the gay underground as oppressors and exploiters.

There is always the rumor, if not the probability, that in a raid the names of those arrested might be published in the newspaper. This is a threat that plagues the patrons who are always sensitive to police cars out front, or to the presence of policemen in the neighborhood. A kind of puritanical terror hangs over the clients of a gay bar, the clandestine, guarded nature of the bars heightens the fear of consequences. The feeling prevails that, should her excursion be known, a woman could be branded for life. The atmosphere of an illegal den of iniquity is promoted deliberately and with mastery by the management. It gives them power through fear, born of guilt and isolation.

The bar exaggerates the sense of the forbidden, and at the same time makes the protectiveness of the bar seem all the more necessary. The sanctuary is in many ways a trap.

Men sometimes wander in. They are permitted if they pay a cover charge. Gay men can make friends with the women because they are not afraid of being ridiculed or becoming sex objects. Straight men are both curious and threatening. Some are voyeurs who are titillated by the idea of women loving other women. Some want to win over a Lesbian: They consider it a supreme challenge. Making it with a Lesbian—to make the unmakable—would be a real trophy, positive proof of masculinity. Others just want to hassle Lesbians: "Take down your pants and prove you're a man."

The first visit to a gay bar is usually a shock to a Lesbian. Some of the young Lesbians in the bars look as though they would be more at home in an ice-cream parlor. Others would nevertheless look out of place in any bar. For many, the Lesbian bar is the first bar experience of any kind.

The first time one Lesbian went to a bar, she was greeted by an older woman who had been around the bars for years. The young girl was excited about being with other women like herself. She had driven a long way to come to this bar she had heard about in the city. The older woman's first words to her were, "Get out now and don't come in again. You'll be sorry. This is no way of life for you." This girl continued to go to the bars.

Lesbians have strong reactions to their first visits. Many say they were "freaked out." Some found it "repulsive, but exciting." One woman said it seemed "sophisticated, hip, exotic." Another said, "It was revolting. I started to cry and ran out." But they soon learn that if you are a Lesbian, this is the most you can hope for. And so they arrive from the suburbs, from other states, from miles away. The bars attract all ages, all socioeconomic groups, all races, colors, and creeds.

There is something in the bar in addition to the mystique of sexual vibrations. There is the need for identity; it is affirming, comforting, just to talk with others who feel the same way about their lives. There is a need to discuss, although the noise and the flirting leave little opportunity for discussion. There is a need to strengthen self-image, although the pressures of the atmosphere and the games of conquest often act to diminish one's dignity.

Sometimes a Lesbian finds in the bar a solitary kind of renewal. She comes simply to be alone among other Lesbians. She will sit by herself or stand leaning against a wall just watching. Or she may not even look around but stare at the jukebox or at her drink, with no intention of meeting anyone.

> The bar is the only relief I have from pretending. I can dress the way I want and think the way I want. I can truly relax for a few hours. I need this to carry on during the day, which has become increasingly exhausting.

After a while she may have enough verification, or whatever tonic it was she needed. She is satisfied that it is still there, a hard-to-define part of her she sometimes hides so well she loses the sense of its reality. It is still there because they are still there—other Lesbians. The minimal level of need has apparently been filled, and she leaves alone, perhaps without having spoken a word to anyone.

At first the bar, like a drug, can give a high: a moment of reassurance, a sense of security, a surge of confidence. But the security is false, the confidence dissipates, and the reassurance is groundless. The beneficial effects wear off quickly, leaving the hard facts of the Lesbian's isolation unchanged.

After their initial experiences in the bars, few Lesbians really expect to find anything positive there. Although they come for renewal, most of them learn to accept despair; at least it is a despair they do not suffer alone. They do not really escape society's hatred in the bars; they bring it in with them.

Because there are drinks and loud music, the bar is a way to reach a state of semiconsciousness. Here the Lesbian can let herself slip down to the bottom, where she can rest or give up. Just let her mind drift with the music, watch the smoke patterns, the motions of bodies swaying, and listen to the music, the voices and the glasses clinking. Perhaps for a moment the scene may even appear exotic; the lonely women may seem energized and happy.

For many the bar is an attempt to find a community. There is a desire to feel a part of the "in group," the bar clique. Some Lesbians make a point of getting to know the bartenders, bouncers, and waitresses by first names, and talking to the bar elite.

The support in the bar is superficial and so are bar friendships. Both vanish as quickly as the mood of a movie when you're out on the street again.

Bar life is centered around cruising, or looking for a sex partner, as the neophyte soon discovers. Traditional values don't count: the bar has its own set of values. Because there has been no other place to meet Lesbians, their homosexuality is the only common denominator.

One newcomer relates:

> For the longest time I just couldn't understand why I kept losing out in the bars. Whether I was an interesting person or wanted to meet another interesting person didn't seem to make any difference. My education and background didn't seem to impress anyone. Then it dawned on me that the only thing that mattered was whether someone thought you looked good. It was that simple. Those around me seemed so confident in their roles, so sure of the rules of the game. No one in the bar was interested in meeting someone she could take home to meet Mother. Mother wouldn't approve, anyway.

A bar is essentially a competitive place. It is not chummy or homey as described by Donald Webster Cory in his book *The Lesbian in America.*[1] The casual chatter is designed principally to increase bar status, to promote sexual conquests. The Lesbian who goes to the bar to find community, freedom, love, and ego support, finds instead competition, exploitation, degradation, and frequently loveless sex.

Couples who go to the bars often are taking a risk. But many must take that risk, or live in isolation. The number of friendships as well as opportunities for sexual relationships open to Lesbians are limited, and the bar is one of the few places to meet or dance.

Two women who want to remain together don't go to bars if they can help it. It is dangerous for one member of a couple to go there alone. Very often, women prohibit their lovers from going to the bars alone. Lacking wedding rings, common property, or any societal sanctions, a Lesbian relationship is treated as tenuous, even if both partners intend a commitment.

Nobody would deny that the most common reason for going to a bar is to find a love partner. Some are looking for love and "marriage" —a carbon copy of the heterosexual relationship—but a number of the women are contemptuous of the idea of finding a suitable long-term partner in such a place. They seek a lover for the night. An atmosphere of sexual urgency prevails.

For some there is pairing off at the end of the evening. Fear of rejection is acute, however, particularly since many feel totally rejected by society. Proving one's desirability by displaying or landing a lover is the critical aspect of bar life: it is important to make conquests, if only to restore one's ego. The final blow is to be rejected by the rejected and cast out by the outcast:

> I never expected a woman to dance with me, so I always carried a beer can with me when I asked. It was my security. If she said no, I could always say to myself that I didn't really want to dance anyway. Later I might boast that three women had asked me to go home with them.

Between two women, both socialized as passive, it may be difficult to get a conversation going or for one of them to get up enough courage and poise to be aggressive. Making the first move can be a long, involved process. Asking a woman to dance is often accompanied by trepidation or embarrassment.

Before even making a friendly gesture to another woman in a bar, it is necessary to stake out the situation by watching her for some time. Is she with a lover or is the woman with her only a friend? Is the lover possessive? Is there a potential confrontation? For the actual approach, one asks simple, ritualized opening questions: "What's a nice girl like you doing in here?" or, "Do you come here often?" or "Would you like a drink?" or "Would you like to dance?"

The lines are rigidly prescribed and deviation from them may be misunderstood and penalized. Here, too, Lesbians are bound by convention and restraint at the expense of spontaneity.

In this totally sexual atmosphere of dim lights, warm music, perhaps with pictures of nude women on the walls, it is inevitable that older women feel uncomfortable. The bar is for the young. The older Lesbians in the bar give off a sense of hopelessness. "Because I am a Lesbian, I have to live this way. I don't want it." Viewed from a barstool, life seems dismal; one cannot afford to become trapped for long in the dungeons left for Lesbians.

What It Was Like

The self-denigration that is a part of so many Lesbians' lives is only made worse by the bars.

Natural and unselfconscious ways of meeting other Lesbians are seldom available. Outside the bar, the façades that Lesbians put on to throw heterosexuals off the track often make them invisible to one another. Even in settings where everyone is assumed to be a Lesbian, contact is inhibited.

The bar fixes a pattern in gay women's minds. Whenever a Lesbian simply attempts to make friends, when she asks for a phone number or extends any invitation, it is apt to be interpreted as a sexual overture. This, of course, makes Lesbians shy about asking and cautious about accepting. This confusion, which runs deep in Lesbian life, indicates how thoroughly the Lesbian sees herself in society's mirror as a creature so exclusively sexual that friendship is unthinkable.

Many women come to the bar with an attitude of superiority—"I'm really not a part of all this. I'm above it." They are out slumming or just observing. They don't want to be in that place but they have to be. The truth is that nobody belongs there and everybody deserves better. The bar is the awful place you have to go to if you are gay.

Words like "dyke" and "Lesbian" are used in the bar with neutrality, except when a fight occurs and the bitter, hurting, hostile use of the words shatters any illusion of peace or security.

Lesbians who first met their lovers in the bar usually avoid acknowledging that fact. If they admit it, it's with embarrassment or apologies; but sometimes they make up a story of how they met. The bar scene puts a sordid tinge on relationships, for others as well as themselves. Even for the Lesbian the bar has a taste of the bizarre that is hard to identify but that is there.

Because the bar is the only place to go, there is a need to believe it is desirable, and yet reality cannot be avoided. Lesbians always say the bars *used to be* better, the women *used to be* prettier, everything was more glamorous. This kind of talk goes on year after year. There is talk of the elegant, sophisticated Lesbians who used to come around, the posh parties that used to be held.

Sometimes there is speculation on movie stars. "Is she or isn't she?" There is need for some status, to know that there are famous and successful Lesbians approved of in the greater world.

Perhaps bars seem disproportionately dreadful to the Lesbians who frequent them. Lesbians looking through the eyes of self-denigration may undervalue not only themselves but all that is attached to their gay life. One heterosexual woman said recently that she thought the women in the Lesbian bar she visited were beautiful. This may be true, but does not negate the fact that Lesbians, however beautiful, often look upon themselves with less self-esteem than other women, who already have a great deal less self-esteem than men.

When Lesbians from the bar meet accidentally in a professional or social environment, as complete people with jobs, families, houses, dogs, they are almost surprised. Only then is it obvious that they also are "too good for the bars," that there are warm, talented, successful Lesbians who covered up these qualities to be able to play the bar game.

Because Lesbians need the psychological space provided by the gay bar, they come frequently and often more frequently than they intend to. Women who are in the bars several nights a week will say that they don't go to the bars. They say things like:

"That's Judy. She comes to the bar every night of the week, poor thing."

"How do you know?"

"I saw her here."

Everyone denies they go to the bars, yet the bars are always jammed. It is an easy and understandable situation for a Lesbian to overlook her dependence. The pressure is great to forget the gay life when she leaves a bar, and she must pretend to friends, family, and co-workers that she was not there.

Some women use the word obsession.

I couldn't stop going. I went one Sunday and then another Sunday. I said to myself that it was for the buffet supper. Then I started going on Saturdays to see who was there. I soon went on Wednesdays because Wednesday was a big night. Then I felt I had to go Fridays to start the weekend. I found myself there every night. I was addicted. Hours, days, weeks and years passed in the bars.

Another gay woman:

I was itchy for the bar all the time. I couldn't wait for it to open and was sometimes still there at 4 A.M. I didn't want anything to happen that I didn't know about—although nothing ever really happened. I

77

wanted to keep in touch. If I was out to the movies or away for the weekend, I would always feel I was missing something, and would sometimes make excuses to get out of events just to go to the bar.

One woman explains how she discovered the importance of the bar in her life:

I used to watch Lesbians being thrown out for improper behavior, which could mean simply that they had refused to buy another beer. They were really treated badly. I couldn't understand why they came back. It seemed so humiliating and degrading. They sometimes begged to return. I wanted to say to them, "Why do you take it? You don't have to degrade yourself that way." Then one day I had an argument with the owner. Somebody had played a trick on me, and I was angry. I almost got into a fist fight right there. The woman who ran the place stepped over without even asking about the situation and told me to leave. I was a trouble-maker. I said, "Hot dog, I'm happy to leave this joint. I won't take this kind of treatment. I'm leaving forever. Goodbye." I was happy to stay home and read for a few nights, but I was not going with anyone and had no gay friends. I began getting restless. After a week I started taking long walks and sometimes passed by the door of the bar. I recalled all those pathetic scenes I had witnessed and knew I'd never do that. I could live in isolation. Another week went by and I was really lonely, I mean really lonely. My other friends could not give me any real support. Finally, a weak and silly fool, I led myself by the nose back to the bar.
"What are you doing here?"
"I want to come back. I'm sorry. I won't do it again. Please let me in."
"You're a troublemaker and we don't want your kind around. I'll let you have a drink, but watch your behavior."
That's how I learned that the bar was essential to my existence. There was no place else to go.

Around the country there is a need for these bars. In some strange way the bars have gained more than money from Lesbians fearful of discovery; they have secured a monopoly on the Lesbian's social life.

Where there are lakes or coastline, there may be gay beaches, where male and female homosexuals are the rule rather than the exception. Difficult to get to, not cleaned or guarded because they are not approved, the beaches offer some measure of freedom. Perhaps more important, there is some relief from the constant heterosexual beach scenes—from families, from muscle men carrying screaming girls into the water, from necking couples and bands of boys ogling and teasing girls. A pair of girls may hold hands walking along the water's edge, though this does not happen often since there are usually some wandering heterosexuals present.

The Lesbian couple may be ensconced in homes in the suburbs, the country, and summer places in spots like the Hamptons on Long Island near New York City. There are vacation places where the emphasis is not so much on couples. One is Fire Island, now nearly a legend, where female couples may go together, but both have summer romances or weekend romances while there in the luxury of sunshine. Another is Provincetown, on Cape Cod. There are Lesbian couples there of course, but there are masses of younger women who may not be in couples. They surge through the town, fewer in numbers than the gay men, but sufficient to open two or three new Lesbian bars at the peak of the season. Dancing, picnicking, going to the beach, parties in houses, sailing, constitute the fun. The atmosphere is relaxed; there is excitement in meeting and talking to people you will never see again. Lovers can walk down the street holding hands, and openly acknowledge each other in many ways. Even though homosexual visitors are the largest source of income for the pretty town, they are still confined to a gay ghetto, separated from the townspeople. Being free to be gay stops at a certain block of Main Street.

Lesbians with adequate incomes find the country a fresh-air sanctuary where people—and therefore prejudices—can be escaped. In the city or suburbs, Lesbians must always be conscious of what the neighbors will think—and do—but in the country, with the seclusion of a farm or a house off the road, a Lesbian couple can be spontaneous. They can invite friends up from the city or entertain other gay women from the area. There is often enough distance from the public to entertain out of doors, with barbecues, or play volley-ball, or swim, or just socialize in the sunshine. Warm sunshine and soft grass make Lesbian life seem more positive, simply because the necessity for hiding is reduced.

Sanctuary is also a circle of friends who share the same standards of discretion. The Lesbian subculture is fragmented into thousands of groups of friends. A careful Lesbian with a stake in the system will choose her friends as much for their ability to pass for straight as for more positive qualities. The pickings are apt to be slim, for cultivating new friends means dropping your cover and exposing yourself and friends to danger.

The hiding Lesbian, though she may know some Lesbians with masculine habits from the bars or the beaches, rarely encourages their friendship. She will usually shrink from any contact with them outside exclusively gay precincts. They represent a terrible threat to her, and the prospect of being publicly associated with a tough, unmistakable dyke is the stuff of nightmares. Even when she is quite obviously homosexual herself, she may think of her deception as more successful than it is and, ludicrously, avoid contact with Lesbians who are scarcely more detectable than she.

The cell-like structure of Lesbian society leaves intact the self-hatred which a woman usually brings with her into a gay subculture. As she has been contemptuous of the Lesbian in herself, she learns from other Lesbians to be contemptuous of the Lesbian in others.

Lesbian society is notoriously inbred. The line between friends and lovers is a wavering one, so that Lesbian friends may represent a real threat to an established relationship. This varies, to some extent, and, of course, with the individual, with the group. Some women are naturally more monogamous than others, and some groups have strong taboos on "home-breaking." It is not unusual, though, for a Lesbian to have had love relationships with several members of her group. It is a characteristic of Lesbians that their relationships with one another are not well diversified or delineated: Every friend tends to become a lover. With a small field of choice, and acting on society's vision of them as primarily sexual creatures, Lesbians often go to bed together when they really want to be friends, come on sexually when they mean to be sympathetic, take on a sexual partnership when it is a working relationship that interests them most.

There are destructive forces always at work to drive Lesbian lovers apart. There do exist in Lesbian life those dark creatures of the stereotype who feast on intrigue and who seem interested only in women who are already involved in love relationships. And even the best-intentioned Lesbian may find that without being aware of it, she has drifted too close to her best friend's lover.

In Lesbian society, where there is no marriage, no social or legal sanctions to help sustain relationships beyond the initial period of romantic love, insecurity and jealousy have a field day. On the other hand, those relationships that do last are usually very strong and deep, and very loving in the fullest sense of the word.

Some Lesbians find that the safest friends are former lovers. After the wounds of parting have healed, whatever originally drew the lovers together, and the good experiences they shared, may survive, along with the tenderness that lingers after sexual intimacy, as a friendship of remarkable closeness and warmth for which there is scarcely any counterpart in the heterosexual world.

Even with gay women's bars and organizations growing in numbers, you could not count the Lesbians by going to these places—you could only estimate their numbers. It may be that the majority never approach a gay meeting place.

Passive by education, the woman who is a Lesbian is often too insecure to take her life into her own hands and experience even the periphery of the gay subculture. Some women say it took them ten years to get up the courage to walk through the door of DOB. The risk is too great. A Lesbian might be seen there by a teacher or a student, a client or an employer, a friend or a colleague. And so the same is true of the bars, the beaches, the restaurants, the bookstores. "What if someone were to see me?"

Many Lesbians frown on organized gay life and refuse to enter a community of gays. They live in isolation and somehow solve—or don't solve—their loneliness in the straight world. For example, suburban married women are finally forced to write notices in underground newspapers with box numbers and pseudonyms. Others take the risk of approaching a desired woman in the "straight" world. Entering the gay community with body, face, and name, seems to be too risky.

Neither sanctuary, nor straight culture, can give the Lesbian all that she needs. She cannot live in a gay bar, on a gay beach, or even in the DOB Center. Recreation spots do not make a life. For most of the Lesbian's life, she has to walk the same streets, go to the same schools, work in the same companies, and shop in the same stores as heterosexuals. She is always in the midst of others who may hassle her if her Lesbianism is not tucked in.

The conflict between society and sanctuary is agonizing when one needs both. For necessities and opportunities in *life,* the Lesbian clearly needs to participate in the system; for nourishment in belonging and opportunities for *love,* she needs sanctuary. Often it seems decisions involve the difficult questions of integration or segregation, adaptation or individuality, compromise or integrity, hurting others or hurting oneself, social respect or self-respect, pretense or peace of mind.

Most Lesbians are intensely aware of the limitations of their gay resources. Sanctuaries—inadequate, temporary, often sordid—act as reminders of their dilemma and dramatize the need to make it in the larger world, or to create a larger world.

4 THE NECESSITY FOR
THE BIZARRE

The essential conflict in the Lesbian's life comes from society's conception of her as a bizarre creature and from the Lesbian's own feelings that some of the things she does to survive are bizarre.

In a day-to-day sense the idea of a Lesbian as grotesque bothers her more than her status as a criminal. Since the gay world to date has been largely made up of fantasies and fears cast off from the straight world, the Lesbian may find herself forced into strange feelings and behavior that frighten and bewilder her. Whether her actions reflect the stereotyped homosexual image or she emulates heterosexuals, she is considered bizarre.

Mary Jane is, let's say, a fairly average girl from a middle-class family that lives in the suburbs of Chicago. She was a beautiful baby to her parents and relatives, quite ordinary to everyone else. She lived with her mother and her father on a street lined with oak trees that led into the woods. The men in the neighborhood commuted to jobs in the city; the women were generally housewives. It was considered a good neighborhood by its own standards—no Jews, Italians, or Blacks. The people living there considered themselves moral and clean living.

Mary Jane was never a problem child. In fact, she was a nice girl who always aimed to please. She drank her milk without a fuss, learned to count earlier than some other children, learned to tie her own shoes a bit later than other children. She liked the garden around the house and was frequently seen in bare feet with a book in her hand. She had a puppy, Jo-Jo, which she cared for herself.

No doubt, Mary Jane had her faults. She didn't like to eat squash and she didn't particularly like to help her mother with the dishes, but reluctantly she ate the squash and helped with the dishes.

What It Was Like

She had long blond hair and blue eyes; she looked clean and fresh, in particular on Sundays when she was dressed for church and to go to her grandmother's. The neighbors described her as cheerful, helpful, and energetic.

Boys became interested in Mary Jane when she became a teen-ager, and she started dating. She went out with a basketball player in high school and became engaged while she was in college. She broke the engagement, and nobody asked any questions. She had other boy-friends.

Mary Jane was twenty-one when she started dating Keith. She wore his ring, but did not talk of marriage. Her parents never saw Keith. She would meet him away from home.

Mary Jane loved her parents and never wanted to do anything to hurt them. She listened to everything they said. Things like: "Our children are so wonderful. We are so proud. The poor Joneses have a daughter who is always in trouble. We are so lucky that Mary Jane is a good girl. It proves what children need is a happy, healthy family situation."

And she would hear: "We love you so much, Mary Jane. We will always be here for you. You can count on us, no matter what." Un-consciously Mary Jane put together the messages and came up with: "We will always love you unless you are different."

Over the next year Mary Jane changed somewhat, but nobody noticed. She started sleeping on the couch with her clothes on and seemed more quiet and contemplative. Jo-Jo sensed a change and no longer begged for his biscuit or came around for fun. The parents assumed that Mary Jane was deep in her studies and that Jo-Jo was just getting old. Mary Jane's grades went up, then took a sharp turn for the worse.

One day a friend of Mary Jane's mother called and said, "Your daughter needs to talk with you. She's hysterical."

Mary Jane confessed with tears that she also used the name Nancy Sue, and sometimes Michael, to protect her family from scandal; that her lover was not Keith but a woman named Marlene who used the name Keith; that the ring was from Marlene; that the Saturday nights at the movies were actually spent at a Lesbian bar because she could not bring Marlene home; that she was being blackmailed by a young hoodlum who had seen her go into the bar; that she had lied about all this when she had never lied before—because she loved her parents. Furthermore, this happy girl, who had been given everything, had attempted suicide.

The situation was beyond comprehension for Mary Jane's mother. Was her daughter still nice? Could a nice girl from a nice family have sexual feelings for another woman? Was her Lesbianism proof that she had never been nice?

Mary Jane did a great deal of thinking, too: "How did I get so deeply into this? All I wanted to do was love."

Soon the neighbors began to talk, and Mary Jane was asked not to associate with her friends. Rumors spread through college, and she was expelled.

The parents confronted her: "You're not the weird one. That Marlene is. She must come from a bad home."

Mary Jane tried to think of what to answer. Anger battled with a glimmer of hope that her parents might be right.

Sadly, the parents asked her to leave home. She was no longer welcome, and neither were any of her friends. They retracted their vows of support but said they would be there—if she changed.

In a very real sense they asked Mary Jane to continue the furtive life she had been leading: to continue using another name so as not to disgrace the family, to live in a ghetto and bars, and to lie to people about her identity—to live a life that she herself had found incompatible with her goals, values, and upbringing. And if she couldn't do this, which she had already indicated she couldn't, she was still not allowed to come home. No one saw any alternatives.

Mary Jane pondered over the event for many years: "Was parental love a myth?" The conflict of the parents was great, but was it not extraordinary that they would sacrifice their own child for their social status?

Mary Jane's is an unusually pure example of discovery and banishment, with little hope of reconciliation. However, there are thousands of gay women who know or guess that they cannot go home again because they are not welcome. They want to apologize and ask forgiveness, but for what? Their parents, who have given them as much as they can materially, have nevertheless withheld understanding and acceptance.

The story of one Lesbian's banishment from home, or school, or job reverberates through the bars. One bad incident breeds fear in the other Lesbians who hear it. The vicarious experience teaches the same lesson as the real one: be evasive, be hypocritical, be dishonest. This is how to survive.

Although a most ordinary American girl can be homosexual, the instant she accepts the label Lesbian, she is subject to new expectations in every area of her existence: dress, behavior, attitudes, values —especially at the point of entry into gay life, the Lesbian bar. It takes maturity to really define oneself as an individual, and a Lesbian spends many years floundering among straight and gay definitions of herself before she finds her own identity. That the straight world considers her bizarre is bad enough, but that she often must behave in ways she considers bizarre in order to fit into the gay subculture is worse. Both worlds reflect distorted images of herself like those in funhouse mirrors, and the more she runs and turns in the maze of other people's expectations, the more lost she gets and the more weirdly she sees herself.

The word Lesbian may conjure up extraordinary contrasts (a man in a woman's body!) and incongruities (what do two women do in bed?). The Lesbian is expected to be a depraved woman, given to orgies, drugs, promiscuity; or an imitation man, given to wearing men's clothing, beating up men, and seducing helpless maidens. At best, she is thought eccentric.

It is society's ideas of the Lesbian as one kind of freak or another that make the realization of an ordinary Lesbian impossible. When a young woman discovers she loves other women, she must cope with straight *and* gay popular fantasy, in which she is the subject of intrigue and scandal and suffers the pain and agony of her difference.

Given the stereotypes, the Lesbian is effectively denied the possibility of normal behavior. The stereotypes, which are all a young Lesbian initially knows about homosexual women, serve to separate her from the rest of society, to put her in two or three clearly labeled compartments, over there, away from the heterosexual world.

But even more than this, a paradox is involved: What is bizarre behavior for anyone else is what society considers normal for the Lesbian; what is ordinary behavior for anyone else is actually what society considers bizarre for the Lesbian. People are able to be complacent about drugs or promiscuity in Lesbian life, but the closer Lesbian life approaches straight life in form or content, the more negative the reactions from some homosexuals and heterosexuals.

Lesbians are brought up to be heterosexuals. Since in some key ways their actions and opinions overlap heterosexual expectations, many Lesbians are confused as to what a gay identity or life-style is. For example, the question of secrecy and pseudonyms. A "normal" Lesbian is expected to act furtively, to deny her Lesbianism, and to exhibit evidence of guilt and shame or low self-esteem. A Lesbian who is happy, "together," outgoing, relaxed, and open about her sexuality is considered really perverted by "straights." Honesty in this case is bizarre. Psychiatrist Edmund Bergler in *Homosexuality: Disease or Way of Life?* remarked that some male homosexuals seemed amoral to him, apparently because they said they were happy with their way of life.

And other Lesbians also consider a happy, outgoing Lesbian as unusual and perhaps threatening. If she uses her own name and talks openly in a mixed group of heterosexuals and gays about her home life and her lover, she is considered suspect. She is breaking the gay code of secrecy. Recently closet Lesbians have accused some Lesbian activists of being heterosexual, apparently because their straightforward manner is totally incongruous to their sisters, who cannot understand it. No authentic Lesbian would act with such candor.

So in both the straight and gay worlds, the Lesbian who simply wants to live her life as most people live theirs is frustrated by a net of social expectations. She herself comes to feel that she cannot have an ordinary life, and that normalcy is stolen from her more by these expectations than directly by her sexual preference. She feels pushed more and more toward a bizarre identity as she internalizes society's concept of herself.

One Lesbian said: "I told my sister-in-law that I was a Lesbian and then said, 'I hope you don't worry about my baby-sitting now.' She said, 'Why should I?' What had I thought she would think: that I would proselytize my niece, teach her to hate men, molest her? That's exactly what I thought she'd think. That's what I had been taught to think."

What It Was Like

Although an outlaw, the young girl who first walks into a gay bar or a Lesbian party is not entering a free and unregulated society. She is entering a highly structured subculture, with its own rules and regulations, its own kind of recognition and success. She finds people who are striving for a kind of normalcy within the framework of being gay, whose deepest desires may be for an ordinary life complete with a good job and a house in the country. She finds couples desperately trying to protect themselves from irresponsible sexual marauders. She finds codes of dress and behavior that she must adopt or be left out and alone. After a period of initiation that may last weeks, months, or years, she finds that she has a choice between what Evelyn Hooker has called the open sexual marketplace of the bar[1] and the structure of a friendship group of couples and a few trusted singles.

Oddly enough, the world of the bar—the gay world most heterosexuals are increasingly aware of—is generally considered the normal environment for a Lesbian, and the unobtrusive social life outside the bar is relatively unknown.

At a recent filming of a national TV show, the audience listened with equanimity as gay men told of bars and cruising and one-night stands. But when one of the men described taking his lover of nine years home to meet his parents, a woman in the audience turned to her male friend and exploded, "How disgusting!"

As gay women mature, the life of the bars can seem shallow and destructive, much as it does to young straights who frequent urban "singles" bars. Most Lesbians seek stability and meaning in their lives, but somehow they are not supposed to want or have these things. If they achieve them, then how can society still consider them sick and arrested in development? Increasingly, heterosexuals seem to be expressing frustration and irritation as homosexuals elude their definitions and fail to conform to their ideas and specifications.

Unself-conscious behavior coupled with a healthy ego is associated with heterosexuality; self-conscious, studied behavior coupled with self-hate is considered characteristic of the homosexual. Both heterosexuals and Lesbians who have bought society's definition of themselves find honesty and openness and ordinary life goals unacceptable in gay women. A woman can be healthy or a Lesbian, not both.

One example of the rejection of an honest approach by a gay group: The Gay Activists Alliance of New York City applied to the

State of New York for a charter. Their application openly stated that the purpose of the organization was to act as a civil rights group for homosexuals seeking legal status for their lives. In the spring of 1971, the application was turned down on the grounds that homosexuals were practicing criminal acts, and could thus be considered criminal. The state could not issue a charter to such an organization.* But of course, without the tax-exempt status that comes with incorporation as a nonprofit organization, the struggle to throw off criminal status was hindered, and forced into semiclandestine operations. When the state declares you illegal, your fight to become legal is presumably not legal and cannot be endorsed or supported. Perfect circular reasoning! Other homosexual or Lesbian civil rights groups have gained legal incorporated status by promising the education and *adjustment* of homosexuals—that is, by accepting or pretending to accept society's negative definition of themselves.

Another example of circular reasoning is the Lesbian's typical dilemma with her church. Her participation in the rites and activities in most denominations is conditional upon her acceptance of homosexuality as a sin in and of itself. If she does not repent of her sexuality, she is acting under false pretenses, and she is a sinner in the eyes of the church. If she feigns repentance, she is untrue to herself, and it may be that she is a sinner in the eyes of God. A gay woman who is trying to be a devout Roman Catholic is presumably trapped into a weekly round of sin, confession, and repentance and can receive the sacrament of communion only on this basis. And all the time she is lying, unless she truly intends to forgo her homosexual life.

Lesbian marriages, Lesbian homes with children, butch and femme role-playing, and acceptance by parents of their daughters' homosexuality—in other words, those areas where Lesbian life most nearly approaches the heterosexual pattern—are aspects of Lesbian life that disturb heterosexuals most.

What is the accepted way for a man and woman to symbolize and express their love and commitment? Before a minister they announce their love and ask to be joined together before God. They may decide

* The Gay Activists finally won their case on appeal in the spring of 1972. But the state may appeal to a still higher court.

on a ceremony with friends, relatives, colleagues, followed by a large celebration with food, dancing, gifts, and toasts. They arrange for time off together for a honeymoon, and an announcement of the whole occasion appears in the society column of the newspaper.

The instant it is known that two women participated in such a ceremony, even in the daytime in a church with an ordained minister, a feeling of queasiness develops. In a Lesbian context, the common-place event, the goal of life for any female in our society, seems strange and unnatural. Some Lesbians who have relationships that are years old desire nothing more than such recognition and celebration of their love, as do older heterosexuals. Why? Although the institution of marriage is under attack from heterosexuals these days, in principle and by action, as indicated by swingers, group marriages, and perhaps by the rising number of divorces, the past exclusion of gay women and men from marriage has created a cultural lag.

Their reasons are classic. Marriage means recognition by the human community. In a down-on-sex culture, it legitimizes sex. It is supposed to express a mature commitment to another human being. Lesbians who want to be "married" are showing their socialization as women and, like a heterosexual couple, are seeking many things: to show honor for the love partner; to achieve respect for the relationship; to have pride in the relationship in the only way a society allows; to gain the sociosexual space to build and deepen the relationship into a permanent bond; to promise fidelity and trust; to heighten the relationship beyond the physical to the spiritual. They do not want to live together "in sin" any more than heterosexuals do.

Of course, Lesbian "marriages," even those performed in a church by a minister, are not legal. Homosexual men and women cannot get licenses or tax deductions. Recently, in New York City, the city marriage license office threatened to take action against Father Robert Clement for performing illegal marriages. Men and women of the Gay Activists Alliance zapped the New York city clerk's office, bringing a wedding party complete with champagne and a many-tiered wedding cake. What they were saying is, "Look, we are like other people, and we demand the right of all other people to bring order to our sexual lives and to celebrate our love before the community."

In June of 1971, an Episcopalian minister, Father Robert O.

Weeks of the Church of the Holy Apostles in New York City, long a crusader for homosexual rights, who had privately blessed a few homosexual unions in the past, asked for a couple willing to have their union blessed in front of a gathering of some fifty Episcopal clergymen. Two Lesbians, reacting with mixed feelings to an idea that seemed at once logical and bizarre, declined. A male couple responded, and the ceremony took place. No doubt the public found it bizarre that an ordained minister would do such a thing, and that other ministers would participate as spectators. Evidence of the decadence and dissolution of society! A gay ceremony recognizes an existing relationship, and usually does not entail vows of faithfulness or permanency unless the couple wishes them to be included. It is, in short, a new ceremony or form more suited to the realities of homosexuality—and perhaps heterosexuality, too—and not primarily imitative of the traditional "till death do us part" marriage vows.

On Sunday Father Weeks' church is used for two services: the regular Episcopal morning service, and a special afternoon service for homosexuals conducted by Father Robert Clement of the gay American Orthodox Church. Opening the church to homosexuals has thinned out Father Weeks' Sunday morning congregation to a few dozen people from the community. Neighborhood residents are reluctant to go to church with homosexuals. On Sunday afternoons, however, the church is crowded as hundreds of homosexuals attend Father Clement's service, joined by a few heterosexuals.

This situation is a statement of where urban America is at with homosexuals. "Do your own thing over there, but don't come into my territory. I'll come and watch your campy service and take in the groovy lavender vestments and lovely altar boys and marvel at the kiss of peace, but don't come in the morning and sit in the same pews at my service, or I'll just not be there."

A number of gay women feel that a "marriage" ceremony in whatever form between two women is bizarre. These women may also shun the more prevalent custom of exchanging rings. But, just as in heterosexual society, there are social reasons for these customs. The simplest and most basic reason for the ring or the "marriage" is to say "hands off," to gain some protection under which the relationship has a chance to grow. Thus the Lesbian may resort to the very extremes she has questioned.

When my lover asked me for a ring, I said she was crazy. I would never do a ridiculous thing like buying another woman a ring. Absolutely insane! But she was a beautiful woman. She was continually approached by other women at bars and parties. Everyone assumed she was free, even if we arrived and left together. If I didn't hold her hand constantly, our future seemed threatened. One woman danced with her and said, "You've been with her six months, now it's time to come with me." When my lover asked for a ring again to show others we were truly devoted to each other, I yielded. It began to make sense.

Some Lesbians use terminology like "marriage," "husband," or "wife," but there is a profound reason for this. These are the only words in our culture that convey love, trust, permanence, and responsibility in a relationship. The vocabulary of homosexual relationships comes from heterosexuals and is seldom appropriate to homosexual love. There are no equivalent words for homosexual relationships. "Lover" sounds furtive and focuses on sex. "Roommate," "friend," and "partner" seem to exclude love. All existing vocabulary is inappropriate, incomplete, even countercommunicative. Lesbians are simply unable to express their relationship in serious terms without sounding imitative or bizarre.

Older Lesbians are more apt to exchange rings and think in terms of homosexual marriages than young Lesbians are. There is a real generation gap. Two of the most prominent issues raised by the younger women are monogamy, which many younger Lesbians feel women desire chiefly because they are programed to want it, and the concept of the Lesbian couple as made up of one masculine and one feminine woman—one butch and one femme.

Apparently simple in its heterosexual origin, Lesbian role-playing is very complex in its manifestations. Presumably role-playing among Lesbians exists because Lesbians are raised in a role-playing society. Most human beings seem more secure and content if the content and obligations of their relationships are clearly spelled out. Butch-and-femme "marriages" have offered this kind of security to some older Lesbians, who have absorbed that a man wants a woman and a woman wants a man. They compromise their identity to be accepted in the traditional gay culture. Roles were sometimes learned by living them or cultivated consciously through the acquisition of techniques. To many women, however, they seemed so unnatural as to end by provoking a new self-consciousness and a new kind of contradiction with self. The role demands differed too sharply from life outside the gay scene. The transition was sharp and not all Lesbians could master the art of quick role changes as they stepped in and out of gay sanctuaries.

But younger women ask: if the choices are free, why label them butch and femme, which are by definition limiting to growth or change? The fact is that society can only see two women relating as man and woman; some Lesbians even believe this. The most common street-corner question hurled at two women showing affection for each other is: "Which one's the man?" This, of course, is to call the Lesbian "queer" in the sense of fake or counterfeit. The idea that two women can gain real sexual and emotional satisfaction from each other and live as two equal human beings is too bizarre to be part of popular thought.

That roles, duties, and attitudes are arbitrarily divided into categories labeled masculine or feminine demands that a woman who is independent and can perform a wide spectrum of skills be called masculine or butch. But only a Lesbian woman doing lawnmowing, carpentry, or painting would be labeled "butch." If the woman were just single, widowed, or divorced, this term would not be used. But even if both women in a Lesbian relationship appear feminine (or masculine), the "old bar culture" (before Gay Liberation or not) might try to separate them into butch and femme, depending on which one performs more duties usually reserved for one sex or the other.

Society sees most Lesbians as being in such relationships, when in fact only a small percentage observe defined roles. Many women don't label tasks "masculine" or "feminine" even if society does.

In the Lesbian bar particularly, butch and femme roles function as expectations that the young woman tries to live up to. Often she chooses arbitrarily whether to appear butch or femme. If she hesitates or refuses to make a choice, she is seen as "ki-ki," which means pejoratively that she plays both roles. In the old bar culture few women are interested in a woman with a "confused identity." Lesbians confronted with a ki-ki feel the same difficulty as heterosexual men and women who may not be sure if they are talking to a male or a female. The attitude in the bar is that any woman who is ki-ki is almost impossible to relate to; one doesn't know how to behave toward her. The ki-ki then, who relates to either butch or femme, has been treated as some sort of a freak by many Lesbians, just as society has treated Lesbians as freaks. As the heterosexual culture has had a need for opposites, so gay women have felt they needed opposites. Their needs were a carbon copy of the heterosexuals'.

> I would ask people, what do you think? Am I butch or am I femme? Some would say I looked femme and acted butch; others would say I looked butch and acted femme. Because I couldn't be typed, I was always looked on with suspicion and sometimes believed to be a police-woman.

Some say that role-playing is more prevalent among lower-class Lesbians, who have witnessed more role-playing in their families. In any case the role-playing learned in childhood is reinforced in the gay bars.

Since the bar is usually the point of entry into the gay subculture, the Lesbian is often unsure of her identity and is susceptible to new images. She knows nothing about who she is or who she's supposed to be as a Lesbian and is ripe for socialization by the subculture.

She has probably led a solitary life and, in any case, does not know how to behave as a Lesbian. Because she has been alone, she is probably insecure and unlikely to exert her own real personality. Besides, it is safer to hide behind a stereotype and not let other Lesbians, who appear threatening as well as attractive, get too close to her. So she tries to become a good Lesbian, emulating the practiced Lesbians she meets. After much contemplation, confusion, and questioning, she sees there is a proper behavior even in the Lesbian bar, so she relates to what Lesbians consider other Lesbians to be. She cannot afford to be excluded here; it is her last chance. She puts on the right costume, develops certain attitudes and gestures and the right language. She wants to look like what she now feels like—a Lesbian: "So this is what a Lesbian is like, and I am one of them." This false understanding that a Lesbian is these superficial things frightens some women who come into the bar filled with excitement and who leave in disgust. But many still feel trapped by this picture of themselves. If a Lesbian equals certain dress and mannerisms, and if I am a Lesbian, then I must dress and act accordingly. Thus the Lesbian has two identity crises: the first is over being heterosexual or homosexual; the second, over the old but still existent choice of butch or femme.

The new exterior adopted by the Lesbian is the way the Lesbian identifies herself. The exterior self is decorated to match the perceived interior self. In her honest search for continuity and sense of self, she must be able to see herself and her new image clearly in the reflection of the subculture. In her efforts to become her interior self, she takes on a new stereotype—that of the Lesbian. Whereas she has been impersonating a heterosexual woman, now she is impersonating a Lesbian. She gives herself over to a new image, also defined by central casting. The stereotype of the Lesbian becomes self-fulfilling.

The need to play a role can obscure the individual identity completely. The whole concept of "playing at being oneself" is discussed in terms of schizophrenia by R. D. Laing.[2] Laing's perceptions of schizophrenics seem to parallel those of Lesbians who have suffered a crisis in identity.

The gay woman who plays a heterosexual role feels that everything she does while playing that role is unnatural, and so to be a Lesbian, she does just the opposite and assumes that this is natural. The Lesbian does this when she switches from straight to gay at the end of the workday. She takes off one mask and puts on another. She sees her real self—Lesbian—in complete opposition to her false self—straight. She moves from masquerading to exaggerating without moderation or understanding.

The two roles never add up to a whole person. The Lesbian's true identity is never revealed, and her essential nature remains a mystery. She is at bottom a bit uncomfortable, studied, and unnatural in both roles. There is an overall loss of spontaneity, a difficulty in finding her own way. Literally the Lesbian is not able to pull her selves together.

The Lesbian seems to want to cry out "I'm me," and try to seek some individualistic ground, to take what seems natural from her straight and gay roles, which, however, are fixed and labeled and not susceptible to integration. In fact, there are bizarre results from the superimposition of the gay and straight roles.

> I was freaked out because I went to a Lesbian bar to get away from men, whom I found oppressive, and then discovered that the women in the bar practiced being just as aggressive as the men. I found myself relating to women just as I was relating to men.

95

What It Was Like

I was hit by my social inadequacy. I felt I couldn't be attractive as butch or femme. I had never been very feminine, but I certainly was not a bull dyke. I felt a kind of social inadequacy in the bars. I felt like a teenager again.

The Lesbian bar seemed to compound the worst in role-playing. I was self-conscious about my weight and inability to dance, and I didn't think I was attractive enough.

I could never walk with a wiggle, so I decided I must be the other kind: I was a boy. I wore a tie and jacket, and then people found me attractive.

A Lesbian switches roles if she finds the chosen role uncomfortable. If a Lesbian is not self-confident enough to be a butch, she may decide to let her hair grow, wear more feminine clothes, and act as a femme. That almost any Lesbian can switch makes it clear that the roles are just that—roles that almost anyone can play.

It takes some soul-searching and experiencing of the roles to realize that roles are simply aspects of social reality as we know it; many roles can and should be experienced simultaneously.

When a woman falls in love with another woman, must she then be made to feel that her own womanliness is in question? It seems extraordinary, but predictable in light of society's attitudes, that to love another woman, some women feel they must change their entire self-image. Because only a man is supposed to love a woman, some women new to Lesbian life imagine all sorts of strange things: "Am I a man in a woman's body?" "Do I really want to be a man?" "Do I not want to be a woman?" "If I want to attract women, do I have to pretend I'm a man?" Sometimes the new Lesbian forgets that for every butch there is a femme, or that many Lesbians feel no need to change how they dress or act. Acting masculine is clearly not a basic component of being Lesbian, but it is one that society has merchandised for its own reason—to keep Lesbians over there, bizarre and identifiable.

There is a strong possibility that heavy butch and femme role-playing serves the function of burying guilt. If only men can love women, then a woman who lives existentially as a man will not consciously feel guilty for loving another woman. In her own reality she will be seeing someone of the opposite sex, as will the femme. People can remind the butch she is a woman, but if she refuses to think she is a woman, she may be able to avoid much of the guilt that comes with Lesbianism.

The whole game fills many Lesbians with ambivalence: If she accepts the Lesbian butch stereotype, she fears she is part male, driven to imitating the male, which makes her a failure as a woman. Oddly enough, the butch may consider herself the Lesbian and her femme a "real woman." If she accepts the femme role, she is trapped into continuing hetero-female behavior and may not explore her sexual freedom any more than most women do. So the Lesbian is necessarily self-conscious about her social presence. She must come to the point of thinking out her own life, searching and analyzing to get to her own true personality as a whole without getting caught up in the pressures and roles of the heterosexual/homosexual culture that fragments her personality. In both worlds she finds it difficult to gain acceptance without playing the game.

The simple reason why Lesbians often base their behavior on the so-called natural behavior of heterosexuals is that the male-female paradigm for a love relationship is omnipresent in the culture. Lesbians, like everyone else, have learned this form of loving in more ways, through more media and over more time, than they have learned anything else. Literature, movies, records, advertising, and their own parents have taught them this. They know no other way. Lesbians have spent all their time in a culture that forcefully sells a way of life based on male and female dominance and submissiveness, independence and dependence, aggressiveness and passivity.

Actually attempts to emulate the so-called natural behavior of heterosexuals are necessarily rather tenuous since it has not been proven that heterosexuals are behaving oddly by assuming roles. Few situations are more absurd than a powerful woman acting out her role as a helpless female when she is completely in control and knows it.

Even homosexual styles that first seem grotesque and rare, irrelevant to most people's lives, turn out to mirror the needs and beliefs of us all. As sophisticated socio-psychiatric studies of all the homosexuals proceed, they will continue to force on us a clear view of the socio-sexual forest that straights live in and usually fail to see.[3]

Heavy role-playing seems like an exaggerated tragicomedy to many, but it is actually a kind of serious critique of superficial distinctions between the sexes.

Older gay women who today are examining roles sometimes say that they would not have gotten into the butch-femme syndrome if they had felt they had an option. Younger women are more aware of the ludicrousness of the roles, both between men and women and between women and women, and they refuse to play. Most young Lesbians today—those who have recognized themselves as Lesbian within the last five years—have rejected heterosexual role-playing and do not accept or even know about homosexual role-playing.

One woman who used to play a heavy drag butch role gives the following reason for adopting that role:

> I was told I looked like a man, dressed like a man, acted like a man, thought like a man, and threw a baseball like a man. I knew I was a woman, but even I began to doubt this after a while. I got so tired of all this that I finally found it was more comfortable to make a small effort and pass for a man so I would not have to apologize for not being what everyone else defined as woman.

A final statement on role-playing: If Lesbians do *sometimes* play roles, they cannot be criticized when heterosexuals are *almost always* into roles, and Lesbians merely imitate them.

As an outlaw, the Lesbian is also bizarre. She has defied society through her sexual preference; in many states she is technically a criminal. She must break some laws, yet she adheres to others. Rarely does she take full advantage of her outlaw status. As a lawbreaker, she might be expected to disregard all laws. Even in this she does not fulfill society's expectations.

Most heterosexuals are upset by the thought of children in a Lesbian's home. This is not only bizarre, it is sick, they say. The propaganda about motherhood describes a woman who could not possibly be a Lesbian, though of course many Lesbians are indistinguishable from heterosexual women. Interestingly, in what heterosexuals would consider a paradox, when the Women's Strike Coalition chose a Feminist who would also present the image of a mother on television, they unknowingly selected a Lesbian mother.

The Necessity for the Bizarre

Heterosexual society's prurient expectations of homosexuals are so pervasive that Lesbian mothers sometimes see themselves as unfit solely on the basis of social attitudes. Lesbians can internalize society's view and come to consider their motherhood bizarre simply because society does. Few human situations are more tragic than that of a mother who has been led to believe she is harmful to her own children when in fact she is not.

One common myth about homosexuals is that they are incapable of heterosexual intercourse, and hence of producing children, for children are regarded in our culture as proof of sexual normalcy. There are many homosexual parents. When there have been Gay Liberation events in New York City, Lesbians and male homosexuals have frequently set up child-care centers for gay parents who needed a place to leave their children.

Lesbian mothers often want to tell their children who they are. The secrecy is a barrier to the closeness they would like to share. Honesty and understanding are important values to them, just as they are to any mothers. But can a Lesbian do this? Society seems to say no. David Susskind, when he interviewed Lesbians on his TV show, made a point of saying that honesty was a value in his family and his children would tell him the truth, as he would tell them the truth. When a Lesbian mother on the show said she had told her four children, he indicated this was a very strange way of dealing with things. And yet if she hadn't, as many Lesbian mothers know, the children would feel distant and confused and suffer in silence the ridicule of those who use street language to describe their mother's love. Closeness and understanding are ideals in a family, except in the Lesbian family, where it is thought to be strange.

It is strange to expect a woman to use a pseudonym as identification in gay circles. She is expected to be so fearful and ashamed that she will put up with the complexities that result from the part-time lying that use of a pseudonym presents. Thus the Lesbian is deprived of her name. She is asked to be anonymous. Some women have found the need for a pseudonym imperative to protect government jobs, university professorships, parents, licenses in the psycho-therapeutic fields. Blackmail is not unheard of.

Daughters of Bilitis has a long-standing policy to protect people's real names. It is what some people call the "gay code." The pseudonym is the necessary protection from blackmail in all its forms. One Lesbian remembers her first meeting at DOB when she was greeted at the door. The greeter said, "I'm——. Who are you? You don't have to give me your real name (even your real first name)."

The Lesbian who has one name with her family, straight friends, and colleagues, and another name for Lesbian circles is likely to end up in some tricky situations. If she should run into a Lesbian friend in business, she may have some explaining to do when the friend says, "Hello Jane," and everyone in business knows her as Nancy Sue.

While such an encounter may never occur, it may haunt the Lesbian's imagination. What is important is that the Lesbian living with a pseudonym constantly lives with this possibility. Usually only close friends know both names, and the confusion resulting from mailing addresses, phone numbers, etc., makes an already complicated life even more difficult.

A less common phenomenon, but one which also has its legitimate reasons, is the male pseudonym for the love partner. When a Lesbian is talking to a friend at the office, it is very difficult for her to say she is going out with another woman on Saturday night. It is easier to say "Ken and I are going to the movies," or, "Ken and I are going away for the weekend"; "Ken gave me that gift," or, "I don't know if we can come for dinner; I'll check with Ken." A man's name sometimes comes in handy for lunch-table conversation, to maintain the façade.

It is actually the use of her own name in gay society that has been considered odd for the Lesbian. Homosexuals often cannot afford to use the same name in both gay and straight circles; it is risky to give the same name at the Lesbian bar as one gives in the office or in the community—to let sexual and social identities merge. For some Lesbians the need to be themselves and whole outweighs the risks. This shameless rejection of secrecy may be thought bizarre. Because of the very realistic reasons to use a pseudonym for protection, it is actually the Lesbian who uses her real name who is bizarre.

One Lesbian worked for ten years on Madison Avenue under her real name. She has also been a Lesbian activist under her own name. She received a letter from an older homophile leader in which the woman stated that she was "jolted" to discover the identities existed in the same person. Why? Perhaps because the lady herself uses a pseudonym for Lesbian business and perhaps found it bizarre that the younger woman *did not* use a pseudonym.

Society always focuses on the sexual aspect of Lesbianism. The Lesbian is rumored to be an explicitly sexual creature, although there is no comparable exclusive focus on sex in heterosexual life. Perhaps because her sexuality constitutes her difference, people identify her in solely sexual terms.

Contrary to public opinion, Lesbians do not react like men; they tend to have the same sexual values as liberated straight women; they are seldom attracted to women solely on physical merits as men often are. They are hardly likely to follow a sexy woman down the street or ogle a woman's legs or breasts. Lesbians, like women generally, respond primarily to a combination of physical and psychic attributes, to a manner, a personality.

It is necessary, too, that a woman indicate some response to a Lesbian's attention. In real life there is no such thing as Lesbian rape. Nor is there the conniving and trickery that characterize the baser forms of heterosexual seduction. The passive, reluctant partner who will serve a male to some purpose has no value in Lesbian sexual relationships.

Some Lesbians in the straight world strive to appear to be asexual, nondescript, even neuter. They do not want to look too feminine, which would put psychological restrictions on behavior and attract sexual attention from men, and they do not want to look masculine, which seems equally unnatural. The point is, a Lesbian is not an excessively sexual creature, as she is expected to be. But if she is indeed a total person, with sex an integrated part of her life, some may find this bizarre.

The most commonly accepted idea about Lesbian life, believed by gays and straight alike, is that it is a pain and agony trip, perhaps with poignancy the emotional high moment. The most common purveyor of this view is the Lesbian novel.

The idea that the Lesbian can have a good and a happy life in spite of the tremendous obstacles is almost unheard of. Happiness, which is the key message in heterosexual advertising, is not permitted in the Lesbian mystique. Happiness for Lesbians is considered bizarre.

Publishing houses have always been interested in novels about Lesbians that end in suicide, despair, and separation, preferably brought about by the introduction of the "right man" into the life of one woman who really wasn't a Lesbian at all. He, of course, takes her away to a better life. Beyond the fact that publishers don't want stories with happy endings about Lesbians because they might encourage Lesbianism, there is also the suspicion that they just don't believe happy endings are possible or realistic.

Isabel Miller, author of *Patience and Sarah*[4], a positive book about two Lesbians who lived in the nineteenth century, said that for years she found publishers unwilling to accept the plot, even though they gave her otherwise favorable comments. Having published two straight books with a major publishing house under another name, she had established her ability as an author. She says publishers wouldn't touch her novel because there was not enough tension, not enough conflict. In her own words: "What they really wanted to know was when does the horrible stuff start?" They wanted misery. So she first published the book herself, and in spite of the book's merits as literature, the book is commonly known as the Lesbian novel "with the happy ending."

Written by a man: "Sappho's love for her girl friends was so intense that there are those who, not knowing how passionate the love of woman can be for woman, still fail, despite the evidence, to recognize a love more sublime even than that for man."[5]

Why does the choice of a different love partner seem to imply a totally different life-style? If we take away the presuppositions that usually accompany the charged word "Lesbian," the belief that this one difference requires totally separatist behavior seems as illogical as the assumption that a person's preference for a green or red toothbrush would require different attitudes, interests, and general behavior. After all, Lesbianism is only a bedroom issue, isn't it?

The model for the straight-gay discussion of much of what is brought out in this chapter occurs in Radclyffe Hall's novel *The Well of Loneliness*:[6]

The mother confronts her daughter Stephen:

"In that letter you say things that may only be said between a man and a woman, and coming from you they are vile and filthy words of corruption —against nature, against God who created nature. . . . You have presumed to use the word love in connection with this. . . . I have loved your father, and your father loved me. That was *love*."

Then, suddenly, Stephen knew . . . there was one thing she dared not let pass unchallenged, and that was this terrible slur upon her love.

"As my father loved you, I loved. As a man loves a woman, that was how I loved—protectively, like my father. I wanted to give all I had in me to give. It made me feel terribly strong . . . and gentle. It was good, good, *good*—I'd have laid down my life a thousand times for Angela Crossby. If I could have I'd have married her and brought her home. . . . I will never forgive your daring to try and make me ashamed of it, there's no shame in me."

Then follows the classic: "The same roof mustn't shelter both of us". . . . "I understand. I'll leave". . . . And then: for the sake of her "father's honorable name," Stephen had to leave home on the pretext that she wished to study.

Disregarding whether one considers homosexuality sick or healthy, the day-to-day life-styles and goals of heterosexuals and homosexuals are similar in so many respects that the two must be considered either both healthy or both sick. If heterosexual life style is natural, it is difficult to label homosexuals bizarre, who are carefully taught as children to live this way. Actually, heterosexual and homosexual life-styles are mirrors of each other. Hard questions need to be asked about both.

Needs and desires and reactions to those needs and desires are basically the same for all human beings. The Lesbian is not an isolated individual but is one thread in the complex tapestry in society.

Over and over again, through many different examples, the Lesbian's so-called bizarre behavior seems much more socially intelligible than people like to think. Her attitudes about health are inextricably linked with those of the dominant culture. Her life-style, when analyzed, is totally in keeping with the reality around her. The essential difference is that the Lesbian loves and wishes to build her life with another woman.

What It Was Like

In summary: those things considered most conventional and valued in this society—honesty, commitment, straightforwardness, motherhood, and happiness—are just those things which society finds unacceptable for Lesbians.

part two
Living the Future

5 MIRAGE

The reader has turned the page and arrived in the future.

For Lesbian activists who confront society through the Gay and Women's Liberation movements, the possibilities of living openly and honestly multiply. But for the majority of gay women, who have reconciled themselves to a closed society, the out-front, assertive tactics of these Lesbians seem unreal, impossible, the actions of those living in the future.

Acceptance within the movements has not been as real or as ready to happen as it seemed at first. For the most part activist Lesbians have had to put much of their energy into fighting a Gay Liberation battle in Women's Liberation and a Women's Liberation battle in Gay Liberation. Lesbians have had to struggle to make a place for themselves. For a long time acceptance seemed a mirage.

Lesbians assumed they were included in the Feminist cause. After all, hadn't the first Feminists, fifty years earlier, recognized the right of women to control their own lives and bodies? The egalitarian rhetoric of today's Women's Liberation promised much for Lesbians, but in the early days there were few deliveries on the promises. Over the centuries women have often been divided and polarized —married against unmarried, young against old, rich against poor, black against white, daughter-in-law against mother-in-law. But nothing has been defined in such hard terms as Lesbianism, which has been driven like a wedge between women. Many women will not even say the word Lesbian. Ordinarily the two groups—heterosexual women and homosexual women—go their own ways. Straight women are drawn into dating and then marriage while Lesbians are involved in their own love relationships and usually jobs or careers as well. Different interests and different experiences even make conversation difficult. What happens when these two groups work closely together for a common cause?

Coming together has caused intense intragroup conflict over Lesbianism. Women's Liberation has struggled fiercely to maintain solidarity in the face of events that have threatened to divide the movement.

When Women's Liberation got under way in the mid-1960's, attitudes about Lesbians were virtually the same inside and outside the movement. Some Feminists who had come to the movement for relatively noncontroversial issues such as "equal pay for equal work" were frightened away by talk of Lesbianism. Many simply avoided the subject at all costs. A few had the insight to understand that the issues went much further, that all women had to be free, and that would ultimately mean acceptance of Lesbianism.

Today, the second women's movement provides the first open channel in history for communication between numbers of straight and gay women. The story of this dramatic change lies in events that took place in or around the National Organization for Women. From 1968 to 1971 some members of N.O.W., the most influential Women's Liberation group, moved the Lesbian issue from one engendering fear and silence within the ranks to one that has N.O.W.'s public support. Why is it that this group took a giant step in just three years, when the rest of Western society has not noticeably altered its attitudes and beliefs in thousands of years?

N.O.W. is large enough and has sufficient geographic reach to be of major interest to social psychologists and others oriented toward studying attitudinal change. Unlike most Women's Liberation groups, which operate on a loose and informal basis, N.O.W. is highly structured—along the lines of any large organization—one reason it has been able to grow into a broadly based national organization with some 200 chapters. All kinds of women make up its membership. Although most of its members have been relatively conservative—and its founders have always preferred to call it an equal-rights organization rather than a Women's Liberation organization—they could not be said to be totally Establishment-oriented. In fact, they have already taken the considerable step of questioning convention: they are Feminists. For these reasons, N.O.W. assumes importance as a gateway to change, and an examination of what happened in it may be useful to the gay movement.

Questions beg to be answered: Why was there initial panic? Could panic have been prevented? Was what happened—the destruction of reputations and the withdrawal of responsibility—inevitable, given the history of prejudice against Lesbians? When should principles come before image and image before principles? What was the turning point toward acceptance?

Lesbians have been able to become members of N.O.W. on the liberal grounds that all women were accepted and that what one does in bed is one's own business. In fact, in 1968 Inka O'Hanrahan, then national treasurer, accepted two Lesbians as members at the reduced "couple rate," which was of course intended for male-female relationships. But, for the most part, Lesbians joined N.O.W. in their straight disguises. At first they listened and watched quietly as heterosexual women wrestled with the same problems they had faced alone as independent women. They felt welcomed as they worked on the women's-rights issues that occupied much of N.O.W.'s energies—beginning with equal opportunities in education and employment.

Lesbians were permitted to work behind the scenes and even found their way to top offices if they could pass for straight and if they kept silent.

Young radical women were already making themselves felt in 1968, and the women's movement was not long to remain an equal-rights movement or a one-organization movement. Some women in and out of N.O.W. were getting restless. N.O.W. was too limited in its goals, they felt. These young women were questioning the entire role of women in society and were challenging society itself, which created and endorsed that role for women. They wanted liberation from roles and, some said angrily, liberation from men.

On October 17, 1968, Ti-Grace Atkinson, then president of New York N.O.W., and a dozen or so other radical women left the organization after a plan for a more egalitarian structure was voted down. There were heated words. Some women burned their N.O.W. cards. The women who left formed an important theoretical group which was later to be called The Feminists. The Feminists were the first group to promote the concept of equality in group activity and, later, the first militants to have an ideology favorable to Lesbians, although, in fact, it was more anti-male than pro-Lesbian.

Various of the radical groups then springing into existence came out for important new goals that focused on problems in the daily lives of women—child care and abortion on demand—influencing N.O.W. to take a stand on these issues. These new goals were also supported and worked on by Lesbians. Increasingly, though, Lesbians within N.O.W. were alternately exhilarated and frightened by the more personal direction discussions were taking.

Although N.O.W. had not endorsed consciousness-raising, the personal was becoming political. Women were talking about their personal lives and intimate feelings as a step toward their own analysis of society. Very active gay women who remained officially hidden had to work still harder to conceal their sexual preference as women began to discuss experiences with male lovers and husbands.

The fears of the hidden Lesbians caused a few of them to take reactionary stands when the subject of sexual preference was first brought up. Other Lesbians quietly left N.O.W. when they sensed there would be opposition to their presence. It was bad enough to have to hide from colleagues in the office, but to hide from other women in the movement was too much. Once more, when the inner life was up for sharing, it was difficult and embittering to maintain a façade.

Meanwhile, the press, friends, and husbands began Lesbian-baiting and using the assumed presence of Lesbians as a reason to discredit the movement. Feminists became increasingly anxious. Many Feminists and some Lesbian Feminists were telling outsiders that there were no Lesbians in Women's Liberation. Privately, they referred to Lesbians as "The Achilles Heel" of the movement. No less a person than Betty Friedan, founder and then-president of N.O.W., expressed fears by calling Lesbians a "lavender menace" and later referring to the issue as a "lavender herring."

Lesbians began to react angrily, but it did little good. Lesbianism was not an issue, they were told. Or worse, Lesbianism was death to the movement.

No matter how dim the situation looked at first, a few Lesbians realized that there was a crucial battle to be fought.

The Lesbian issue would never have been forced out into the open without the initial persistence of an attractive and fiery young woman named Rita Mae Brown.

The then-president of New York N.O.W. tells the story: "In mid-1969 Rita Mae joined N.O.W. She immediately announced she was a Lesbian. As she became more active on issues, I appointed her Newsletter Editor, which gave her a chapter board position. She became more outspoken about her Lesbianism and people were antagonized. The flak hit me, but I decided to give Rita Mae leeway. It seemed important at the time, though I didn't know why. I thought she should be heard even if she did antagonize other members. I was beginning to discover there were conservatives in N.O.W., and it was a rude shock.

"A panel discussion in August, 1969, on women discriminating against other women further raised the temperature. Rita Mae Brown pointed out how discriminated against a Lesbian feels and the psychic damage she faces when she cannot speak openly with her sisters."

"Members listened sympathetically and tensions seemed eased until the Women's Congress."

Some N.O.W. officers wanted N.O.W. chapters to meet with other women's groups and form coalitions to work on issues. In November, 1969, in California a Congress to Unite Women was held and the Lesbian organization Daughters of Bilitis was invited but was not asked to speak. Simultaneously in New York a similar congress was held. The first group to contribute money toward the congress was DOB, even though N.O.W. initiated the event. The single press release sent out after the congress omitted DOB as a participating group, though interestingly enough, New York N.O.W. was also left off the list.[11]

Says the then-president: "Rita, who had felt for some weeks that there were efforts to silence her, was incensed. And during this period, when the issue was emerging, Betty Friedan was saying, 'You can't talk about this. It will hurt the organization politically.' Her arguments were practical ones."

Pressure was building in N.O.W. In January, 1970, Rita resigned from N.O.W., along with two other women. They wrote an angry statement accusing N.O.W. members of being middle-class club women not ready to think about issues of race, sexual preference, or their own class privileges. In another section they mentioned Lesbianism. "Lesbianism," they said "is the one word which gives the New York N.O.W. Executive Committee a collective heart attack."

Trouble was also brewing at the national level. That same winter, unknown to most of the National or New York Chapter membership, an attempt was made to use Lesbianism against the National Executive Director who had spoken out on the Lesbian issue. At the National Executive Board meeting held in New Orleans near the end of 1969, Ms. Friedan spoke out strongly against the Lesbian issue and against the Executive Director in such a way that the two issues were linked in the minds of those present. At the same time, Ms. Friedan reportedly accused the New York chapter of being run by Lesbians. According to a national officer at the time, the explosive issue served as a means of shifting the national balance of power away from New York, where some disagreed with Mrs. Friedan on which issues were most important.

The then-president: "Incredible pressures were on the National Director as a result of the linkage. She couldn't discuss it with her friends. That would legitimize the question. She became physically ill. When a man she was dating said he heard a national officer say she was a Lesbian, the New York president asked the National Board to help. Press conferences and counter-press conferences were threatened over the Lesbian issue.

The next National Board meeting was in Chicago. Just before the meeting, Del Martin, a N.O.W. member and one of the founders of Daughters of Bilitis, had written a letter from San Francisco asking Ms. Friedan for N.O.W.'s stand on the issue. Ms. Friedan did not answer. However, at the Board meeting the New York chapter president and other women presented a proposed amendment to the N.O.W. Bill of Rights that would have guaranteed the right to "sexual privacy." They were forced to withdraw the motion. The Board did not want to be on record as voting against it. In another action the National Director was fired.

"The Director was fired softly," says the then-president. "The grounds were not made clear. Was it because in their view she did not do enough? Was it because it was evident that lately she and Betty could not work together? Was it because of the implications that she was a Lesbian?

"At that time a number of us realized this had to be important if you could have such total destruction over it. We had to deal with it, or it would be used again. We came home upset, but at least we thought we could move ahead on this issue, clear it up and get on with the business of the movement. However, this was not to be the case."

N.O.W. events triggered the creation of new groups of gay Feminists, whose activities would disrupt N.O.W. again. Rita Mae Brown called a meeting of gay and straight women to discuss sexism within the women's movement. One straight woman and thirty gay women attended. Not disconcerted by the absence of straight women, the Lesbians, who included several Gay Liberation Front women, proceeded to form three consciousness-raising groups, based on the experiences with consciousness-raising of several Lesbians who were in a Feminist group called the Redstockings. The meeting was historic in that it was the first meeting of radical young Lesbians without gay men, the first time Gay Liberation Front women had met with Lesbians from the women's movement, and the first time Lesbians from the women's movement had met each other as Lesbians. One woman remarked later, with tears in her eyes, that it was the first time she had met other Lesbians "in the light" outside a Mafia bar.

The Gay Liberation Front women there, who included Martha Shelley, took in the situation as described by the Women's Liberation women and N.O.W. women and proposed a position paper to be written by a collective, explaining the relationship of Lesbians to the women's movement. It would be circulated to straight groups.

Before the paper was even complete, it was decided that the one perfect way to introduce it would be at the second Congress to Unite Women in 1970. The Lesbians would return to the scene of earlier oppressive action against them with their paper entitled *The Woman-Identified Woman,* which today remains the best statement on the Lesbian in a sexist culture. The Lesbians, angered after pervasive and persistent oppression from other women, would not just take a literature table; they would take over the congress, and force the issue into open discussion.

Plans were carefully made.

On Friday night, as soon as the last drumbeat from Burning City theater's presentation ceased, the lights went out. When they went on again, there were twenty Lesbians at the front of the auditorium who wore T-shirts proclaiming them the Lavender Menace. They demanded the microphone, which was handed down from the stage, and a gay woman spoke, charging the women's movement with sexism, with discrimination against Lesbian sisters. Some of the 400 women in the audience had worked with the gay women on Women's Liberation actions but had not known until this minute that they were Lesbians. One or two Menaces talked effectively about their oppression, making it real, helping the sisters to see what they were doing. A call was made for women who agreed or sympathized to join them at the front of the room. At least thirty more women arose from their seats and went to the front. Most Lesbians in the audience were really torn. Some came slowly forward. Others never budged. The microphone was declared "open," and women lined up to use it.

One of the last women who talked had been a scheduled speaker for the program that never took place. She was a professor at Columbia, a founding member of Columbia Women's Liberation, and Chairman of the Education Committee of New York N.O.W. She was shy but she struggled to speak. "I know what these women are talking about. I was there. In some ways I still am there." The tension, the pain, were in her voice. Those women who had not yet risen to leave leaned forward to hear her words over the commotion. They could not know that this woman's personal life would become the focus of a nationwide movement hassle. This was the first time that Professor Kate Millett—a few months later to become a celebrated author and international Women's Liberation theorist—had spoken about her sexuality.

The next day spontaneous workshops held by gay women on the subject of Lesbianism were packed. Later the gay women invited the straight women to an all-women's dance at the church community center, which was the sanctuary for the two largest gay militant organizations—the Gay Liberation Front and the Gay Activists Alliance. After the refreshments were set up, there was an awful moment when the women thought no one would come. But then the Feminists began to arrive. The final turnout was good, and nobody seemed overly concerned about who was gay and who straight.

Although N.O.W. was not officially involved in the second women's congress, and in fact scheduled a meeting in Washington that same weekend, a few New York N.O.W. officers and members drifted in and out of the Sunday sessions. Attempts to block the Lesbian issue, which had dominated the second congress, were made at the closing session when the Lesbians wanted to report on their workshops; opponents argued that the Lesbian workshops were not on the agenda. But the Lesbians gathered enough support to read their resolutions to the assembly:

1. Be it resolved that Women's Liberation is a Lesbian plot.
2. Resolved that whenever the label "Lesbian" is used against the movement collectively, or against women individually, it is to be affirmed, not denied.
3. In all discussions on birth control, homosexuality must be included as a legitimate method of contraception.
4. All sex education curricula must include Lesbianism as a valid, legitimate form of sexual expression and love.[1]

There were many gay women at the congress who probably were not members of any gay organization. They had come to the conference from cities in the Northeast because of their involvement with Feminism. Some report being surprised, and embarrassed, at the Lavender Menace action. Nothing in their lives had prepared them for a group of radical gay women openly, warmly, and with humor affirming their Lesbianism and demanding the recognition of Lesbianism as a valid life-style in front of hundreds of heterosexual women.

The action frightened Lesbians who were hiding. The basic reason for their fear remains today. Each time a Lesbian speaks up, it decreases the effective cover of other gay women who do not want to speak up. Each Lesbian who comes out publicly helps to eliminate the stereotype truck-driver image of Lesbians that protects closet Lesbians, who have a vested interest in its continued existence.

Among straight women at the congress, reactions varied. Some felt the conference had been ruined, smashed. Others thought a major issue—sexism within the movement—had been raised. The Lavender Menace had presented the oppression of the gay women as the predictable response of the social system to rebellion of women against their assigned role. Society's attempt to crush the independence of the Lesbian was presented as a paradigm of women's oppression.

After the congress, New York Feminists held a meeting, which was not advertised, to determine what they could salvage from the congress. Lesbian groups were not notified. The new Lesbian issue was discussed, but reportedly only a minority of women spoke vehemently against it.

Meanwhile, unknown to New York Lesbians, three Lesbian groups in California officially held a panel on Lesbianism at the second congress out there. The lid was off, and the Lesbian involvement in Women's Liberation was now blatantly apparent.

The Lavender Menace, which had written the *Woman-Identified Woman* and taken over the congress, began to meet regularly under the name Radicalesbians. A militant Lesbian group, the core of the Radicalesbians was made up of women from the Gay Liberation Front who had been charging gay men with sexism. But the organizational break was triggered by the favorable response of women at the congress to gay women, which gave recognition and support to the idea of a new gay women's group. The Radicalesbians was the first East Coast all-Lesbian group since Daughters of Bilitis had been formed as a homophile organization some fifteen years earlier.

As a result of these actions, myths were being shattered. At first, as women in the movement talked among themselves, rumors of Lesbianism were confined to masculine-looking women, according to the prevalent stereotype. Next, as it became apparent that the stereotype could not hold up, many women were suspected of being Lesbians. This process is frightening to Lesbians who feared discovery. It was even more frightening to straight women who felt safe as long as a queer could be identified by special clothes, acts, and behavior. When these boundaries are shown as false, fear sets in, then paranoia. They no longer know who they are talking to, who they are sitting next to, or who it is safe to share their fears with.

During this time the discussion was fed by accounts of other encounters between Women's Liberation and Lesbians. The Gay Liberation Front women and Radicalesbians were rapping with straight women at dances, not advertised as Lesbian dances but as *all-women's* dances. The dances were publicized through Feminist as well as gay organizations. Lesbian leaders were invited to meet and discuss the issue with certain Feminist consciousness-raising groups and Feminists in the media.

A cross-fertilization of ideas was beginning. Awareness of common goals also began to be reflected in Women's Liberation periodicals, which published more and more articles on Lesbianism. New anthologies coming out on Women's Liberation all planned at least one entry giving the Lesbian point of view. Likewise, *The Ladder,* the nationwide publication originally directed primarily toward Lesbians, issued a statement of policy change indicating that it was now "the only women's magazine openly supporting Lesbians."

Formalized interactions were also taking place. Daughters of Bilitis invited several key Feminists to talk to its membership. A limited dialogue had begun.

Ti-Grace Atkinson was the first Feminist theorist to speak to DOB New York. Her paper, which she called a draft of a major theoretical piece, in part questioned whether Feminists and Lesbians could work together on the deepest levels. "Feminism is a theory; but Lesbianism is a practice."

Feminist writer Susan Brownmiller was asked to speak at the 1970 DOB convention in New York, but she did not appear. A kind of stereotyping of the Lesbian was evidenced in a letter she wrote to the convention. Gay women had made passes at her, she said; they were overconcerned with sex and were generally oppressive in their maleness. Come march with us if and when you want to, she continued, but our fight is not the same. You have bought the sex roles we are leaving behind.[*]

Members of DOB who had sat quietly through countless putdowns by psychiatrists and other straights speaking at their meetings, took these allegations calmly. More radical gay women visitors were incensed. Role-playing was a vanishing part of Lesbian life, they felt, disappearing much faster than the roles in heterosexual life.

The surprise was Caroline Bird, author of *Born Female,* New York N.O.W. member, and member of their advisory board. Asked to speak at the DOB convention, she at first refused, pleading her lack of suitability as a straight woman, and her ignorance of the deeper aspects of the topic. But later she agreed to speak, even blaming herself for nearly missing the point initially. She said that what she had been talking about was alternative life-styles and that this was an

---

[*] Both Ti-Grace Atkinson and Susan Brownmiller changed their attitudes about Lesbianism later and openly spoke out against Lesbian oppression.

alternative life-style, a legitimate choice. She was the first well-known Feminist to validate the Lesbian life-style.

Later Kate Millett spoke before DOB and gave a moving, personal statement.

The only encounter that took place at N.O.W. during this period was a Lavender Menace zap of the New York Councilwoman Carol Greitzer in 1970. Councilwoman Greitzer had begun to be known as pro-Women's Liberation. The Gay Activists Alliance had approached her, both publicly and privately, with data on homosexual oppression, which she had not dealt with. At N.O.W. the Lavender Menace asked her to include in all her bills on sex discrimination a clause on discrimination based on sexual preference, but to no immediate avail.*

Then came the summer. In late June, 1970, the first Christopher Street Liberation Day march for gay people was held, and a few straight Feminists joined the historic event. One Feminist marching behind a Lesbian banner was later questioned by a neighbor and did not take the opportunity to say she was not a Lesbian, a reaction which would become more common among Feminists who were not particularly threatened by homosexuality.

On August 26, 1970, the first Women's Strike and march demonstrated for the first time the numbers of women interested in Women's Liberation and their spirit and seriousness. Lesbian activists arrived and Martha Shelley fought her way onto the speaker's stand. Her talk was unscheduled. She spoke spontaneously, with great anger, and the reception was good.

Although the Strike committee was called together by Betty Friedan, it now involved every women's group, and a Women's Strike Coalition was formed to organize other mass demonstrations. The coalition, though heavily staffed by Socialist Workers Party women, showed some receptivity to the Lesbian issue and actually sought out Lesbian activists to participate in later events. This was a first for Lesbians and seemed to indicate some political respectability, but Lesbians, wanting to work outside any political party, shied away and did not accept SWP support, even though they were still *persona non grata* everywhere else in the women's movement.

On November 5, 1970, three officers from New York N.O.W.,

---

* A year and a half later, in the fall of 1971, Councilwoman Greitzer was friendly to a New York City bill providing civil rights to homosexuals.

including the president and a candidate for president, also went to speak at DOB. The New York president welcomed gay women to the women's movement and invited them to join N.O.W. "to work on our shared problems together and to get to know one another." Later she said: "One of the other speakers was most probably going to be the next president of New York N.O.W. With this in view, I had kept her informed on all the issues, including the Lesbian issue. We had had several conversations about this and I thought we agreed that it was relevant to the women's movement on humanistic grounds.

"Then she was up there, pretending she didn't know what it was all about, saying that homosexual women could work on women's issues, but not openly as homosexuals. It was not the time. The Lesbian issue could not come up now; it had to come later."

Then a progression of events began that was to end in a second and even more vicious power struggle, that wound up using Lesbianism against New York N.O.W. officers, committee heads, and so-called Lesbian sympathizers.

The seeds for the event were sown at Columbia University on November 12, 1970. Gay People at Columbia sponsored a Forum on Sexual Liberation, featuring Gay Liberation and Women's Liberation members and activists who had been or were Columbia students or professors. As the panelists waited to go out onto the stage, Morty Manford, chairman of the panel and a member of GPC, approached panelist Kate Millett. He introduced Kate to a young woman, a stringer from *Time* Magazine who had a tape recorder casually draped over her shoulder. They talked Women's Liberation. Then on to the stage and the discussion.

After the initial presentations, a third-world gay revolutionary woman approached the open microphone in the middle of the auditorium. She challenged Kate: "Why don't you say you're a Lesbian, here openly? You've said you were a Lesbian in the past, at DOB and other times and places. Then in *Life* Magazine it was printed that 'you were not into that.' Are you or aren't you? We get one story and another." Ms. Millett had already quietly stated in her remarks that she was bisexual; she was exhausted from a series of speaking engagements, but she repeated her statement.

Another Lesbian activist, known in the movement as Wendy

Wonderful, jumped to the mike. "I'm bisexual, but I've realized something. I can tell my friends I'm bisexual and they say how groovy, as long as I'm having a relationship with a man. If I say the same thing and introduce them to a woman I'm having a relationship with, they are very cool about it. I'm bisexual, but it is for my homosexuality that I'm oppressed. Therefore I say I'm a Lesbian as a political statement."

Kate Millett agreed. "Yes, I understand that. I too am oppressed for being a Lesbian, not for being heterosexual."

All the time, somewhere in the audience the spindles of the *Time* stringer's tape recorder were turning. No one knew that night that a tape had been made. It disappeared into the bowels of Time Inc., and all seemed calm and quiet.

The N.O.W. president made the next effort to bring this crucial issue to the membership and scheduled a panel on Lesbianism for November 24, 1970. The president: "It was said that the panel was rigged, and that everyone on stage was a Lesbian. That was untrue; two of the women were not Lesbian and said so. I had no idea that *all* the panelists, however, were pro-Lesbian until they had spoken. People said that the title 'Is Lesbianism a Feminist Issue?' had implied a debate and there had been none. Also, I believed that the audience would ask taxing and demanding questions following the presentations. I expected a lot more to come from there. But the audience was quiet."

During the evening one speaker suggested that all the women in the audience who had felt erotic or strong emotional feelings toward another woman stand up; easily two-thirds of the room rose.

Soon after the panel word flashed through Women's Liberation and Gay Liberation channels that *Time* Magazine was going to reveal Kate Millett as a Lesbian and that the article maligned Ms. Millett as a theorist on the basis of her sexuality. Among Lesbian activists there were mixed feelings: depression at the personal and emotional cost to Kate, elation that the Lesbian issue was being broken open nationally.

The *Time* piece appeared in the issue dated December 8, 1970, in a section titled "Behavior," which one would assume would have a scientific bias. In that issue it just had bias. Called "Women's Lib:

A Second Look," it opened with a few choice selections from Irving Howe's lengthy review of *Sexual Politics* that had been printed in the December issue of *Harper's*. This review does not miss a single opportunity to call names, to the point where it is almost not a review at all. Even *Time* dubbed it an attack. Then followed a list of the eminent intellectuals who had written their attacks on "Women's Lib" in the short period preceding the article. The editor was gleeful as he counted women among the attackers. But the crunch came in the second paragraph:

> [They] raised some provocative questions. Can the feminists think clearly? Do they know anything about biology? What about their maturity, their morality, their sexuality? Ironically, Kate Millett herself contributed to the growing skepticism about the movement by acknowledging at a recent meeting that she is bisexual. The disclosure is bound to discredit her as a spokeswoman for her cause, cast further doubt on her theories, and reinforce the views of those skeptics who routinely dismiss all liberationists as Lesbians.[2]

At about 8 P.M., December 10, Wendy Wonderful and a friend were taxiing to a party. Wendy's mind was on the *Time* exposé of Kate Millett, which had just hit the stands. The malicious intent of the piece in relation to Women's Liberation and Gay Liberation enraged her. She asked the taxi to go to the Church of the Holy Apostles where the Women's Strike Coalition was meeting to make final plans for a December 12 march. She remained there for over twenty-four hours.

Wendy's presentation to the Women's Strike Coalition swayed them, and they voted to respond to the attack on Kate with an action during the march to Gracie Mansion (Mayor Lindsay's official residence) for child care and abortion. Flyers explaining the divisiveness of the issue as it was raised in *Time,* press releases, and a large number of lavender armbands were made up.

On December 12, 1970, the icy cold, wet weather, and the long march route planned kept marchers down to a few hundred. When they arrived at a park near Gracie Mansion, the president of New York N.O.W., whose job was to introduce speakers and events that day, waved lavender armbands over everyone's heads from the top of a sound truck and joked, taking the fear out, making it all right.

"O.K., O.K., get 'em on," she said, "get your armband. I want to see a lavender band on every arm." At the same time leaflets were handed out to members and the press:

> You discredit a movement by calling a visible member a name designed to strike fear in the hearts of all respectable citizens. . . . On Tuesday, December 8, *Time* Magazine decided to try this time-honored method of intimidation on the Women's Liberation movement by publicly attacking Kate Millett for her courageous statement that she is bisexual. It is not one woman's sexual preference that is under attack—it is the freedom *of all women* to openly state values that fundamentally challenge the basic structure of patriarchy. If they succeed in scaring us with words like "dyke" or "Lesbian" or "bisexual" they'll have won. AGAIN. They'll have divided us, AGAIN. . . . *Time* Magazine wants us to run scared, disown Kate and all our gay sisters. . . . That's why we're all wearing lavender Lesbian armbands today—to show we all stand together as women. . . . They can call us all Lesbians until such time as there is no stigma attached to women loving women.

A woman from Gay Liberation was a scheduled speaker at the Coalition rally. Her speech, the armbands, the flyers—all possible only because of Coalition support—represented the first time Gay Liberation and Women's Liberation worked together. Yet the media ignored this important show of solidarity, in spite of its newsworthiness. The fact that virtually every woman present was wearing a lavender "Lesbian" armband was generally not mentioned to readers or viewers.

Not all was harmony at this march, however. There was public disagreement. During the speeches Betty Friedan said again that the Lesbian issue was a "lavender herring," a "diversion" from the women's movement. Kate Millett had never talked about Lesbianism at any Women's Liberation events. This time she devoted her entire talk to the oppression of homosexuals. She spoke in the third person, but with the kind of force that made the homosexual's struggle the dominant theme of the event. Nothing was said publicly about the obvious conflict between these two respected leaders.

The real confrontation took place after the scheduled events when marchers sought food and warmth in a small Irish bar and grill filled with rough and ready males watching a football game on television. Betty Friedan spoke to Kate Millett. Ms. Friedan's message was clear: "Kate, drop the issue of homosexuality and turn off your followers or you will destroy the movement." Kate, a long-time admirer of Ms. Friedan, answered quietly and somewhat reluctantly. At parting, her stand was defended by friends. In the end the two women shook hands, possibly realizing that the issues had now gone beyond them. It was not a personal argument but represented two distinct and apparently irreconcilable schools of thought.

Because the press did not give any coverage to the Coalition's support of Kate, it was necessary to do something more dramatic which would not allow the press to be evasive. A press conference was planned.

About forty women met. It was agreed that a statement would be written, and it was worked on collectively by gay and straight women from several groups. It was read to the meeting and approved. The statement was carefully worded to show that all were speaking as individuals who were part of a large, diverse movement called Women's Liberation. The speed was vital since it was necessary to counter *Time's* statement immediately. There was no time for the various organizations to meet and discuss the press conference if the blasts of media scandal were to be used to launch their own paper war.

On December 17, 1971, the press conference was held with wide support. Women's Liberation theorists and writers were there, including Ti-Grace Atkinson, Gloria Steinem, Florynce Kennedy, Sally Kempton, Myrna Lamb, and with an apparent change of attitude about Lesbians, Susan Brownmiller. The recently elected Congresswoman Bella Abzug sent a supporting statement:

> The capacity of women to create the conditions for the liberation of others who are oppressed depends on the capacity of society to respect their freedom to do so. Those literary critics who seek to limit this freedom by sniping are contributing to a limitation of freedom that in any other context they would normally reject. It is time these critics liberated themselves from our common oppressors.

Radicalesbians and Gay Liberation Front women were there, along with Ruth Simpson, President of DOB. National and New York N.O.W. provided massive support for their sister Kate.

Author Caroline Bird, N.O.W. member and advisory board member, wrote an angry statement against discrimination in employment on grounds of sexual preference. She closed with "My sexual preference is none of my employer's damn business!" Wilma Scott Heidi, behavioral scientist and N.O.W. National Board Chairman, wrote, "So all people are bisexual, so what else is new!"

123

To acknowledge this is not a confession but an affirmation of something few people have had the courage or information to share. The full broad range of our human sexuality and our potential for heterosexuality and/or homosexuality is just emerging to the public and private consciousness. The imperative for the profound humane liberation of women's liberation is dramatized, not diminished, by the emerging insights of oppressed men and women.

N.O.W. national president Aileen Hernandez wrote in part:

The National Organization for Women, Inc., has no formal statement on Lesbianism. We do not prescribe a sexual preference test for applicants. We ask only that those who join N.O.W. commit themselves to work for full equality of women and that they do so in the context that the struggle in which we are engaged is part of the total struggle to free *all* persons to develop their total humanity. . . . Let us—involved in a movement which has the greatest potential for humanizing our total society —spend no more time with this sexual McCarthyism. We need to free *all* our sisters from the shackles of a society which insists on viewing us in terms of sex.

Kate Millett read the joint statement:

As members of Women's Liberation we are concerned with all forms of human oppression, including the oppression of homosexuals. Therefore, we deplore *Time* Magazine's malicious attack on the movement, operating from the premise that it could malign or invalidate us by associating us with Lesbianism. Far from being vulnerable to this clear appeal to prejudice, we take this occasion to express our solidarity with the struggle of homosexuals to attain their liberation in a sexist society which oppresses them legally through the penal code, denies them economic security in employment, and subjects them to every manner of social and psychological harassment.

Women's Liberation and Homosexual Liberation are both struggling toward a common goal: a society free from defining and categorizing people by virtue of gender and/or sexual preference. "Lesbian" is a label used as a psychic weapon to keep women locked into their male-defined "feminine role." The essence of that role is that a woman is defined in terms of her relationship to men. A woman is called a Lesbian when she functions autonomously. Women's autonomy is what Women's Liberation is all about.

Media coverage was excellent. Despite some fear of ridicule, Feminists and Lesbians found reporters and editors fair. Some New York area feature journalists later told activists and N.O.W. people that in their judgment the press conference was a brilliant response to what could have been a bad situation. It virtually halted media dyke-baiting.

However, when various individuals returned to their organizations, they were told they had acted wrongly in participating, that participation should have been decided by the organizations. They replied that it had been an emergency and pointed out that no names of organizations had been used, and that the participants had only identified themselves as members of Women's Liberation, the umbrella name for all women's-rights and Feminist activity. Betty Friedan reportedly called up Caroline Bird in a huff and during the conversation asked her if she had consulted her husband before supporting the conference.

Before the next New York N.O.W. meeting a National Board Meeting was held in Houston, Texas. Lucy Komisar asked for a closed Executive Committee discussion on Lesbianism. "The issue was so touchy, especially in Houston, where people don't even use the word, that a closed meeting seemed to make sense," comments another National Board member. Thus, board members who had come from all over the country were not allowed to participate.

The next day the board member quoted above described the people attending as "up very tight." She said that the session "had been very heated and people were very angry."

The N.O.W. Executive Committee was split down the middle and could make no decisions.

At the first New York chapter meeting following the press conference and the National Board meeting, the president gave a rundown of the events of the preceding month. Necessarily the December 12 march and the December 17 press conference consumed a part of the report. Then, in the closing moments of the meeting, a motion was introduced. The essence of the motion was to link Lesbianism insidiously with other negatively charged words like "communism," "infiltration," and "diversion," and to propose that anyone who spoke on the Lesbian issue could not identify herself as a member of N.O.W.*

* The individual who introduced this motion came out in support of Lesbians and the Lesbian issue in the fall of 1971.

One member present that night said it was like the old cries of "Commie-Pinko-Queer." The timing was perfect for presenting a proposal without opposition. There were only seven minutes left before the room had to be cleared. There was no time for debate. The motion was voted on that evening, in spite of an appeal by the president to wait for discussion pro and con. It was defeated by a very narrow margin. The event was the first open show of strength on both sides of the issue in New York.

In January 1971 came the New York N.O.W. elections. The feasibility of running a more progressive candidate for president than the one chosen by the nominating committee—the woman who at DOB had advocated that gay women remain closeted—was discussed at two meetings attended by a small number of Lesbians who were also interested in introducing issues of race and class. All knew that the president would be going out of office and was running for chairwoman of the Board. They sensed trouble because the president had supported Kate Millett and was under great criticism for doing so. But the president said at that meeting, "I know N.O.W. members are fair. They know I have done a good job. I don't need any heavy politicking."

Word of the meeting spread. Scare rumors began to fly—"Lesbian plot," "Lesbian takeover." A few days before the election, several of those who wanted to protect the outgoing president heard things they found hard to believe.

Rumors had gone way beyond who was or who was not a Lesbian or Lesbian sympathizer. Numbers of N.O.W. members were being called and told that women in positions of responsibility made passes at younger women; in short, their morality beyond a mere sexual preference was in question. One rumor was that the then-current president had made a pass at the nominating committee's presidential candidate in order to implicate her in the Lesbian issue. Another rumor was that the Lesbian "bloc" was going to blackmail the presidential candidate through use of a photograph taken at a party showing her with a woman rumored to be a Lesbian.

There was a pathetic and shocking element in the behind-the-scenes plotting against Lesbians in New York N.O.W. Two Lesbians from the organization worked against their friends, perhaps to protect their own straight façades. They may have thought, "If we point out other Lesbians, we will not be purged ourselves. We will be allowed to stay and work in N.O.W." They seem to have reasoned that a caucus of Lesbian women concerned with the advancement of the New York chapter on several issues was dangerous to the chapter.

"The night of the election was unbelievable," one woman recalls. Women had been asked to join that night to vote the Lesbians down. Others had been contacted by a telephone tree and came to the first meeting they had attended in a year. Through manipulations, members coming in the door were given one slate only—which was not the original slate chosen by the nominating committee. Lesbians and Lesbian supporters were left off. It was made up only of people against the Lesbian issue, people who were for "the original goals of N.O.W.," a phrase which was to become a byword during the elections. Thus, members, the majority of whom knew nothing of the goings-on, made up an "uninformed constituency" for candidates interested in burying the Lesbian issue.

Among those who went down over the issue—which was never named during the entire meeting—was the outgoing president, who was running for chairwoman of the Board. She had been criticized for supporting Rita Mae Brown and later Kate Millett. She was defeated by a relatively unknown woman.

"There was no doubt in my mind that I had been purged, and that anyone who had supported me was in for a very rough time," she said. Just as the president was "purged," so were the supporters of the president, and the friends of her supporters were under suspicion.

Feelings ran high. After the elections twenty-five disillusioned N.O.W. members who felt that the election had been unethical to the point of being invalid met with Eileen Hernandez, the national president of N.O.W. Many felt that Lesbianism had again been used as an ax in a power struggle over many issues and many personalities. Only two women in the room were admitted Lesbians, and yet all had been called Lesbians or Lesbian sympathizers. Even a young man who was co-chairman of a committee felt he was ousted for being involved in some way with Lesbianism. The word blackmail was in the air. One woman referred to the victorious as "hard hats in white gloves." Mrs. Hernandez said that she was not in a position to do anything. The meeting left all present in still more pain and frustration.

Living the Future

An open letter printed in *Now and Then,* a publication for the dissenting point of view, reveals the anger at human destruction.

> *On and About Lesbian Purges*
> Subtitle: ". . . for the Good of the Organization"
>
> Well . . .
>
> The house has been cleaned. Once again.
>
> Your enemies?? Practically all gone.
>
> *But here's something to contemplate on your way to equality:*
>
> Human beings deserve to be held in higher esteem than half-decade-old goals. As strange as that principle may seem to you, sisters and brothers, I assure you that it *will* crop up again.
>
> If I understand you correctly, now that the political battle (I know you don't like the word "purge") for 1971 is over, we can once again get back to the business at hand. Or, as the letter I have in my home from one '4-star general' states, "If I've hurt a few people it is because I think in the long run, it will all iron out . . ."
>
> What has happened is that N.O.W. has one-upped *Time* magazine. *Time,* in essence, tried to purge one woman from the movement by attempting to discredit her because she had "confessed" to being bisexual. N.O.W. *successfully* purged people for allegedly being "Lesbian sympathizers." (This is the familiar tactic of guilt-by-association that flourished under Joseph McCarthy in the anti-Feminist 'fifties. The only difference is that the red herring of communism has been replaced by the lavender herring of Lesbianism.)
>
> Why are we here? Is it simply because we want more lady legislators? More lady cops? More lady Milhous advisors? If so, what ladies? Any ladies? Just so they're ladies? That's not why I joined N.O.W. I wanted us to teach everyone in this whole damn screwy world we live in how to —and *not* to—judge people. Feminism means more than electing women to office; it means accepting and treating all women and men as full human beings.
>
> In the meantime, I cannot belong to an organization that does the same thing, behaves in the identical fashion, as that society it wishes to change. . . .
>
> Carol Turner
> February 12, 1971

The former president, looking back, said, "On a gut level, the women's movement has to be about sexuality. Otherwise, it's just another civil-rights movement and that's not dealing with the problem women have to face. If sexuality is at the base, then Lesbianism is totally relevant. It's about being an independent woman . . . You can't have sexual freedom only for heterosexual women. That's ridiculous, you know. You either have freedom for all women or you don't have freedom for any. I've seen some weird fights, but this was the worst, the most insidious.

"They [some people on the national level] are starting to see the dangers of using this label as blackmail, of exploiting women's fears and making this a thing of fear and panic and they're trying to stop it. It must be stopped because this is how all movements are destroyed—how they destroy themselves. . . . It's terror tactics that cause the most destruction to any movement.

"You see, when statements are made that a woman is Lesbian, the accusations don't just strike at the person they're made against. That would be too simple. That the average person can deal with. The accusation 'Lesbian' hits everybody who hears it. There is an underlying fear, I think, in both males and females of their own latent homosexuality.

"And when a heterosexual woman makes that initial step into the women's movement, she is frightened because she is constantly being put down by her friends, her husband, and male acquaintances. The people she works with make fun of her. People are constantly saying: what are you doing working with a bunch of man-haters? Or, what are you doing working with a bunch of dykes? Neither of which is necessarily true.

"But she's faced with these statements. So that once the Lesbian issue comes up in her own organization, it's more than she can handle. Then she is suddenly forced to face the fact that there *are* Lesbians. She feels a gut fear: What does this say about her Feminism?

"Society says you shouldn't challenge your sweet domestic role that you're supposed to be deliriously happy in. If they say you shouldn't challenge it and you do, then, they say, it means you're homosexual. I mean one seems to follow the other in society's mind. After a while you work out of that. But the average woman when she first comes into the movement can't handle it.

"The only women who have been able to come through without a lot of fear are either those women who are Lesbians, or those who say: 'Yes, I recognize I have some latent homosexuality. That's not where I want to be, but I understand how someone can feel this way and I'm not going to put her down.'

129

"The weird thing is that recognition of Lesbians as human beings, totally equal women, will do more to free the straight woman than it will the Lesbian woman. If a woman can say I accept my Lesbian sisters, or I accept the fact that people can be homosexual if they wish, she is saying: now you can't scare me out of the women's movement. I mean that would be the ultimate. If the straight woman can come to grips with this, then society can't touch her anymore.

"They can't touch her anymore on equal pay for equal work. They can't touch her anymore on the abortion issue because it's legitimized. They can't touch her anymore on illegitimate children because society has begun to accept that. They can't touch her anymore on divorces. They can't touch her on alimony.

"So, if we can get the Lesbian issue together, we got a movement. But, if we don't get it together, we ain't got no movement no more. We're going to have a civil-rights cause. We're not going to have a humanistic movement, and that's where it is.

"But I think the fear, panic, and blackmail aspects are inherent in the issue itself, though they're hard for me to understand. . . .

"I saw the two basic kinds of reactions where I worked that day after the press conference for Kate. The reactions of some of the more sophisticated feature writers, male and female, were one thing. They said great, it's about time the women's movement dealt with this issue. You've got to meet it head-on or you're dead. As opposed to a couple of secretaries who were shocked to think I would even be at the press conference. How could you go, be in the same room with—wow!—it's like you're going to get something. Don't sit on the toilet seat. That kind of thing. The average person never uses the word Lesbian, never even recognizes that there are any.

"This issue is making people recognize something—something they have somehow sensed in themselves for a long time and refused to recognize, perhaps that we are all, men and women, sexually repressed in some vital way.

"But, I think, havoc is probably a healthy sign. This had to happen. I mean, this panic, this fear, this purging, vilification, all of these things had to happen before the organization could begin to deal with Lesbianism. We may have won by losing."

In the next months, she was to be proved right. Word spread around the country and speeded up things going on elsewhere. The West

Coast Regional Membership passed a resolution in April demanding the acceptance of Lesbians and Lesbianism and voted to present the resolution to the full N.O.W. membership in the fall of 1971. A workshop on Lesbianism was planned for the Labor Day Weekend convention in Los Angeles. The workshop was originally to be called "alternate life-styles," but after much discussion it was agreed that the title was a cop-out. The issue was really Lesbianism; and the word was included. It was agreed that the workshop would be on Lesbianism, Human Sexuality, and Feminism. The West Coast contingent planned to take the issue from the workshop to the floor of the convention, but they were ready for trouble.

Nobody expected victory. It was only the first time the National Organization for Women discussed the issue openly. This was progress and some consolation to gay women in New York. Intimations of a tide of change were felt when it was learned that Atlanta also brought to the convention a proposal to change sex laws and give women the right to their own bodies. Other chapters too had come through the problem. At the workshop a strong resolution was called for. There was no argument. The resolution even recognized N.O.W.'s culpability, stating that "N.O.W. must reassess the priorities that sacrifice principles to image."

What happened on the convention floor seemed even more miraculous. N.O.W. did a complete turnabout and voted, almost unanimously, to support Lesbianism legally and morally. They accepted Lesbianism as a valid life-style.

The breakthrough on this issue seemed very sudden; however, changes must have been taking place more gradually and naturally in the minds of individuals around the country than in New York. The same few national officers who had prevented the issue from being aired nationally had also used their influence to stifle discussion in New York. With national headquarters in New York through 1970, just a few strong personalities dead set against the Lesbian issue were able to keep the issue bottled up until it exploded.

Why did N.O.W. move so dramatically? Was the resolution a political triumph, or did it represent profound attitudinal change? The answer probably involves both elements.

A number of things had happened during the three years of controversy that could not be reversed; they had had a profound effect on members. Leaders may have been more sensitive to the fact that recently the press has been asking some hard questions about discrimination against Blacks and Lesbians within the movement. Press coverage in Los Angeles during the convention, for example, featured Lesbianism as an issue within the movement. Most important was the no longer deniable reality that there were valued people in N.O.W. who were Lesbians.

What happens when respected and valued people become identified with negatively valued ideas? During 1970, N.O.W. members had learned that an important movement theorist (Ms. Millett) and a few national, regional, and local N.O.W. officers were Lesbians. Such a tense situation potentially is a powerful one, tending to produce change.

Since people strive for consistency, and cannot rest easily until any such division in the mind is settled, they are forced to move. It seems a general law, recognized in psychology as the theory of cognitive dissonance, that people have to associate ideas they respect with people they respect, and disapproved-of ideas with people that they believe are evil or stupid.[3] Were some of N.O.W.'s valued members less valuable or trustworthy simply because of their unusual sexuality? Or was Lesbianism all right after all? The two elements—genuine commitment to the women's movement and Lesbianism—had to be made compatible: they clearly existed together.

Facing a truth that is neither acceptable nor escapable produces great tension. Such a predicament was created by Ms. Millett's acknowledgment of bisexuality. Her credentials as a Women's Liberation leader were stamped and sealed. Believing at first that Ms. Millett's popularity could help the movement, Feminists in and out of N.O.W. had readily promoted the association; they asked her to speak on panels, at conventions. Committed by their actions to Kate, Feminists were forced, following the *Time* exposé of her bisexuality, to search for a new equilibrium. A large number of Feminists obviously decided to confront their prejudice.

By chance, Lesbians fell into the right tactic to gain acceptance. If one wants to reduce discrimination it is not necessary to first make attitudes more favorable; according to social theory, if prejudiced people can be induced by external pressures to take a favorable stand (on Lesbianism) they may then change their attitudes.[4] Feminists found that their own past actions forced them to break through the barriers of myth and confront the issues.

Looking at the situation from another point of view—solidarity was vital at all costs. It was important for everyone concerned with N.O.W. that N.O.W. keep its unity in order to combat outside forces.

The whole struggle over the Lesbian issue was particularly painful in that each division felt its stand represented the good of the whole. Each group wanted harmony and wanted to get on with the business of fighting the real enemies of women. The ultimate goals were the same for both elements.

However, people against the issue felt that airing it represented a danger to the movement; supporters felt that denial represented a danger to the movement, because it left the movement vulnerable to Lesbian-baiting and media exploitation and left one group of women unrepresented. Both sides also agreed that Lesbianism *should be* a private issue, but the supporters made the point that it could only be a private issue *after* Lesbianism was accepted and protected. On the other hand, the opponents' time horizon was immediate. These people were being practical and political. The proponents were thinking of the future. They were asking for justice and a humanistic approach.

In the midst of arguing, both sides were contributing to what was least wanted: the squandering of strength that should have been channeled into societal change. The mutual exhaustion of forces that resulted did indeed endanger the organization's effectiveness.

For a time it looked as though cooperation was not possible. Lesbians in New York N.O.W., some of whom had left and some of whom remained, talked about breaking away and forming a separatist organization of gay Feminists.

However, while it looked as though the issue was irreconcilable in New York, some chapters, particularly in the West, were quietly working to free the energies of the organization for a higher purpose: the liberation of all women (this time with explicit understanding that Lesbians were included). Regaining a sense of solidarity was of primary importance. Similarities and not differences would have to be emphasized. It was finally decided then not to let the Lesbian issue split N.O.W. down the middle, which in a larger sense was a victory for all Feminists, and not just the Lesbians.

Hostility within a group of like-minded people is more bitterly felt than when it arises between separate entities.[5] After experiences in both the Black movement and Women's Liberation, Flo Kennedy refers to such in-fighting and trashing as "horizontal hostility."

The greater the parties' similarities, the greater the hostility.[6] The many shared similarities among Feminists—goals, interests, and feelings—heighten the importance of any discrepancies and sharpen the antagonisms. Thus, people who have many common features often do to each other worse harm than they would to complete strangers.[7] The last official words of the out-going president in New York were: "I find it hard to believe that one who has worked with you on every issue since the beginning of N.O.W. could be discredited on the basis of just *one* issue."

The decision to liberate Lesbians within the movement might have had something to do with expectations for the future, a kind of feeling for the spirit of our times; N.O.W. may have felt it wiser to vote in favor of forces apparently already at work. Furthermore, it was becoming clear that the Lesbian issue would give N.O.W. no rest. Trying to expel members was impossible and destructive: the N.O.W. New York purge, which had drained the chapter of vitality and spirit, had proved it. So heavy had the fight become that everyone wanted to start out fresh. Knowledge of the New York purge alone may have guided some toward a new system of values.

For any or all of these reasons, N.O.W. passed an historic resolution ending with:

> BE IT RESOLVED THAT N.O.W. RECOGNIZES THE DOUBLE OPPRESSION OF LESBIANS;
> BE IT RESOLVED THAT A WOMAN'S RIGHT TO HER OWN PERSON INCLUDES THE RIGHT TO DEFINE AND EXPRESS HER OWN SEXUALITY AND TO CHOOSE HER OWN LIFE-STYLE AND
> BE IT RESOLVED THAT N.O.W. ACKNOWLEDGES THE OPPRESSION OF LESBIANS AS A LEGITIMATE CONCERN OF FEMINISM.

6 LESBIANISM AND FEMINISM

For Lesbians, Women's Liberation is not an intellectual or emotional luxury but a personal imperative. Living without the approval or support of men, Lesbians desperately need women's rights. For Lesbians, independence and responsibility for self are lifelong realities and not merely interim needs between support by father and support by husband. Lesbians are therefore vitally interested in greater educational and employment opportunities. Since many Lesbians have been married, they may also need child care. And, because societal pressure may induce them to try heterosexuality several times in their lives, they may also need abortions. Finally, the strain of isolation has left an unfulfilled desire to belong to a unified community of "real" women.

In the beginning, the highest aspiration of most Lesbians in the women's movement was just that—to be included. For the first two years of the second wave of Feminism, this desire to be included was the perspective from which Lesbians viewed the women's movement. In the midst of fighting for Women's Liberation, they continued to submit to oppression by hiding so that they could be included, or worse, defensively trying to prove the obvious—that they were also "real" women.

Then came Gay Liberation. Gay women who had a women's consciousness suddenly found that they had no gay consciousness. They may have dealt with their root anger at being discriminated against as women, but as homosexuals they still had no self-esteem. Under the impact of Gay Liberation, they began to see the issues differently. With their new Gay Liberation perspective they saw that their expanded behavior was not unnatural for women, it was simply unacceptable. Some Lesbians consciously and analytically began to associate their past and present rejection of restricted female behavior with the Feminists' grievances.

A few Lesbians came to understand that they were much more than a despised minority to be heard, more than a troublesome problem in public relations, that Lesbian Feminists might actually be the spine of the movement.

Women's Liberation means independence. Feminists demanded control over their own bodies and over the decisions that shape their lives. They demanded freedom from sex-role stereotypes. With independence foremost in their minds, Feminists arrived at a turning point in the history of women only to find that Lesbians were already there.

It is now clear that the lives of Lesbians provide an example of Feminist theory in action.

The startling fact is that Lesbians already meet the criteria that Women's Liberation has set up to describe the liberated woman, while many straight women—even some of those in the movement—do not. Lesbians have economic independence, sexual self-determination, that is, control over their own bodies and life-styles. Daily they defy sex roles by freely combining any human behavioral characteristics they desire as individuals.

A number of Lesbians' life-styles seem in retrospect to anticipate Women's Liberation. Out of some inner necessity, many Lesbians choose to become more than sex objects, dictated to and dominated by men. They create their conditions for work and pleasure; they must work out their entire purpose in life. The choice of an unauthorized love partner is only *one* way, and often one of the last ways, in which they break the assigned female role. Lesbians choose autonomy even in the face of incredible hostility.

Alone and ashamed in the past, Lesbians have been unaware of what today is called Women's Liberation philosophy. Each Lesbian may have thought her life was highly personal—even insignificant. If she was probing a new way in the social wilderness, she was usually unconscious of it—and focused more on coping with daily stresses. Under the spotlight of Women's Liberation, her own solution to oppression—never to yield her independence and to refuse to call the male superior—should come to have wide-ranging repercussions, and help to redefine what it means to be a free woman.

The full impact on the movement of the new perspective on Lesbianism is yet to be revealed. However, it now appears that Feminists who have been running to get away from the Lesbian image in the movement are, in effect, running *after* it. For Lesbians live what Feminists theorize about; they embody Feminism.

The idea sends shivers through conservatives in the women's movement, who find their beautiful ideal so inseparable from the object of their deepest fears.

For Lesbians the realization of their meaning to the movement has been a long time coming. Lesbians find it as difficult to cast off socially instilled inferiority as feminists find it difficult to shake off their own fears. The truth turns Women's Liberation around and puts Lesbians in the forefront. It means that Lesbians need no longer ask for acceptance in the Women's Liberation movement because they are its natural leaders.

Here and there, from both Feminists and Lesbians, one hears that Lesbians are "the revolutionary vanguard of the women's movement" and "the most liberated women." This is essentially the position put forth in *The Woman-Identified Woman,* the important Radicalesbian position paper. Ti-Grace Atkinson, Feminist theorist, considers Lesbians the "front-line troops" of the women's movement— the women most harassed because they are by definition a threat to a system that subjugates women.

In trying to rid the women's movement of Lesbians, straight women nearly undercut their own support. They were in danger of damaging the very thing they need and wish to protect—the Women's Liberation movement.

However, Feminists are under great pressures from the world outside the movement. They constantly have to defend, explain, justify. Accusations of Lesbianism, ranging from the subtle to the obscene, are one of the common forms this pressure takes. Such accusations have been damaging to the Feminist image, as they seem to explain away the movement in terms that satisfy the movement's critics. It is still very hard, therefore, for Feminists seriously to consider what is most threatening, the point-by-point substantive links between Feminist theory and Lesbianism.

Those Feminists, at least, whose interest is limited to specific issues, seem to want only a little bit of independence, defined as relief from housework, a day-care center, promotion on the job. What the lives and writings of Lesbians tell them is that real independence means fundamental, even drastic societal change, and that this change begins with their own lives and the way they see themselves.

The more radical among the Feminists, that is, those who have begun to attack the core of the sacred role assigned to women— to obey men and be secondary to them—are themselves in danger of losing male approval and support for being unwomanly and un- natural. They are already linked with gay women damned as masculine. The press and the public, by jumbling Lesbians and Feminists together in their minds even before they understood the relationship were telling Feminists they, too, were living outside the sociosexual system as outcasts, defying their role as caretakers, and were therefore very much like Lesbians.

Looking at Lesbianism and Feminism historically, one sees that the Lesbian issue, which has sometimes been put down as the squab- blings of a few malcontents, is in fact a genuinely important issue. The common denominators of Lesbianism and Feminism have always been recognized though usually in a negative way. Although men harassed America's first Feminists with terms like "mannish" or "unnatural," and Lesbianism had been mentioned in the English and European counterpart movements, at least among social sci- entists of the time, Lesbianism did not surface as an issue in America until the current movement.

An English writer on homosexuality, working near the turn of the century, broadly hinted at Lesbianism in his remarks on the Feminist movement: "The women in the movement are naturally drawn from among those in whom the maternal instinct is not especially strong . . . Some are rather mannish in temperament."[1] Writing about that period, Arno Karlen in *Sexuality and Homosexu- ality* relates that "Several scientists and reformers admitted that there were a large number of masculine women and even Lesbians in the movement."[2] He notes that Magnus Hirshfeld, writing on sexuality in 1935, claimed that "among English and German Feminists, the percentage of Lesbians was high—somewhere under ten percent."

Furthermore, Feminism itself is often cited as having increased the number of Lesbians. Noting this position, on the part of some observers, Dr. Frank S. Caprio, after summing up the early Feminist movement writes: "Some authorities fear that the defeminization trends [in work, clothing and recreation] . . . more than likely [have] influenced the susceptibility of many women to a homosexual way of thinking and living . . . [they say] this new freedom that women are enjoying serves as a fertile soil for the seeds of sexual inversion."[3]

Despite the hysterical note on the part of the men quoted above, they all document an observed link between Feminism and Lesbianism and suggest that this relationship is neither new nor temporary.

Most contemporary Women's Liberation theorists, writers, or anthologists have recognized homosexual oppression, male and female, as somehow related to women's movement issues, if only because homosexuals are harassed and repressed in the society for their sexuality as much as women are for their sex. Sometimes Feminist writers go a great deal further than that.

In *Sexual Politics* Kate Millett said that a sexual revolution would require ending sexual inhibitions and taboos, particularly those that threaten "patriarchal monogamous marriage." Among these she listed the taboo against homosexuality.[4]

Shulamith Firestone, in *The Dialectic of Sex,* called for total freedom. The bans against homosexuality would be lifted in the scheme she outlines at the end of her book . . . "all forms of sexuality would be allowed."[5]

In *The Second Sex,* a classic for Feminists, Simone de Beauvoir writes that "Homosexuality is one way woman solves the problems posed by her condition in general, by her erotic situation in particular."[6]

Chapters on Lesbianism were included in the first four Feminist anthologies—*Sisterhood Is Powerful, Women's Liberation: Blueprint for the Future, The New Woman,* and *Woman in Sexist Society.*

Writers dealing with Lesbianism have also noticed important links. Donald Webster Cory, author of the classic *The Homosexual in America,* in his companion book *The Lesbian in America* (1963), says: ". . . One must ask whether Lesbianism is a wail of protest against masculine domination, a socio-sexual defiance of the male-dominated culture."[6] Cory concurs with Simone de Beauvoir's earlier work, and develops similar views from his perceptions and knowledge of the homosexual world:

> It is entirely possible that, for some women, Lesbianism is an expression of freedom from male domination, an effort to divest themselves of the quality of being sex objects for men, of being subservient to males in both sexual and non-sexual life. . . . No doubt, the frustration of modern woman, promised freedom and equality but finding herself handicapped at every turn in life, is, in a few instances, a contributory factor in the development of Lesbianism.

Jess Stearn, in his book about Lesbian life-styles published in 1965, recognized the Feminist consciousness in Lesbians although not in these terms. After interviewing hundreds of Lesbians: "Most significantly, perhaps, I do not recall a single Lesbian who thought of the male as the superior sex."[7] He points out, however, that a number of Lesbians "acknowledged a liking for some males, but based their liking entirely on the individual's charm, wit and intellect—not specifically masculine attributes."[8]

Like Cory, Stearn in his own way predicted the emergence of the Lesbian that is happening today. Linking his statement to "the continuing drive of women all over to share a place in the sun with the male," he says, "it was obvious that Lesbianism was not only here to stay but, on a tidal wave of new feminine self-appreciation, might be openly professed. . . ."[9]

Given the sexually based power hierarchy of society, wherein decision-making and leadership are the prerogative of the male, people were bound to associate the Lesbian's autonomy, self-actualization, and ability with masculinity. The label "masculine" has stuck because of the nature of their role-breaking socially, psychologically, economically, and politically. The same people interpret the Feminist's desire for independence as masculine—since dependence is seen as feminine.

A woman desires more than femininity. According to Simone de Beauvoir, she "spontaneously chooses to be a complete person, a subject and a free being with the world and the future open before her; if this choice has a virile cast, it is so to the extent that femininity today means mutilation."[10]

Studies show that while women are being thought of as being childlike, Lesbians have had to develop some of those qualities of spirit and mind that have been traditionally called male but have also been associated with adult status.

Evidence that to be a woman in this society means to be somewhat less than adult and that the term adult connotes *male* adult, is given by a study done on the mental health profession in 1970 called "Sex Role Stereotypes and Clinical Judgments of Mental Health." Dr. Jessie Barnard summarizes the findings: ". . . in one experiment male and female clinicians were given identical lists of traits. On one they were told to specify those that characterized a healthy adult, sex unspecified on the list; on another those that characterized a healthy adult male; on still another, a healthy adult female. The clinicians proved more likely to attribute traits characteristic of healthy adults to men than to women. They showed they believed:

> Healthy women differ from healthy men by being more submissive, less independent, less adventurous, more easily influenced, less aggressive, less competitive, more excitable in minor crises, to having their feelings more easily hurt, being more emotional, more conceited about their appearance, less objective, and disliking mathematics and science.[11]

This constellation seems a most unusual way of describing any mature, healthy individual. Pointing this out, the authors of this study called for definitions of mental health for both sexes that would include self-actualization, mastery of the environment, and fulfillment of potential.[12]

The experiment's findings are not unexpected, seeing that the traditional role of woman, in its economic, and presumably emotional, dependence, is similar to the position of the child. Like a child she does not control the resources but is the recipient of them. Willingly for the most part, she remains under the protective custody of the male.

What happens when such adult behavioral standards as those listed in the mental health study above are applied to Lesbians and straight women? A recent British study gives a clue. Published in the

141

British Journal of Psychiatry, and reported in the (London) *Times,* the study compared the personalities of a group of Lesbians with those of a comparable sampling of heterosexual women. The *Times* said: "It shows how untrue is one of the traditional preconceptions about Lesbians. Far from being neurotic, Lesbians emerged as more resilient, more self-sufficient and more composed than the matched group of heterosexual women." (November 2, 1970)

Simone de Beauvoir writes,

> To define the "masculine" Lesbian by her will to imitate the male is to stamp her inauthentic. The truth is that man today represents the positive and the neutral—that is to say the male and the human being—whereas the woman is only negative, the female. Whenever she behaves as a human being, she is declared to be identifying herself with the male.[13]

Women are not yet sure of their potential for strength, intelligence, and independence, qualities Lesbians have not feared to develop. The understanding that the Lesbian is not 100 percent feminine, not all "woman," is therefore positive in its implications. It means that the Lesbian is more than feminine, is more than a woman is allowed to be in the culture.

If Feminism were to define a Lesbian as a woman, as a mature being—as it has begun to do—it would be a radical step, a step freeing all women from servitude to what may be outmoded criteria, and introducing an element of choice into how all women conduct their lives. Women should be able to choose criteria under which they wish to lead their lives.

Male and female homosexuals are in many ways prototypes of what Feminists refer to when they speak of people freed from confining sex roles. Although Feminists may not agree with all the choices made—specifically sexual preference—they cannot ignore the fact that the homosexual exercises choices, not only in sexuality, but in *all* areas of behavior. The homosexuals' rebellion centers around a rejection of the tyranny of genital identity and a decision to open to themselves the entire range of human characteristics, drives, attitudes, expressions, and behavior.

Ironically, past accusations of masculinity leveled at Lesbians and accepted by them have to some extent freed Lesbians from the psychological restrictions dumped on women and have allowed them to participate in the "male" world of community and world affairs—to the extent they were allowed to as women.

Feminists first reacted against learned sex roles when they objected to society's programing girls not to try certain kinds of work or achievement. They quickly realized that the other side of this coin is the positive programing of traits that direct women to focus exclusively on home and family. Discouragement from involvement or achievement in activities allows a woman to give selflessly and endlessly to a man's personal needs. Thus the socialization into sex roles goes far beyond disapproval of women's success, which has put a brake on women's entry into world affairs; women have been positively socialized to love men and to be subservient to them.

The stereotyped male can only play his role in relation to the stereotyped female, whose behavior at all times reflects back at him his dominance and superiority. This means that the first condition for the success of the heterosexual system is that woman abdicate any role other than the assigned one, withdrawing from any competition with man. The system will be shaken by the advent of a woman practicing self-determination. As such women increase in numbers, the structure of sexual hierarchy necessarily will rock on its foundations.

Another breakthrough by Women's Liberation, and one that is allied with the demand to end sex-role stereotyping, is the demand that women be allowed to control their own bodies. Feminists fought, with some success, for the right to abortion on demand and the end of restrictions on contraception. Since the biology of women has been the primary means of their oppression, biologic aspects deserve first consideration. Without the attainment of these practical ends, much of Women's Liberation rhetoric would be empty rhetoric.

However, once again a kind of myopia sets in when the Lesbian is brought up. Freedom of sexual expression is imperative if one is to have control of one's own body. It is, like abortion, a decision by which the individual woman assumes a responsibility once left to the rules of the male-dominated society.

When Feminists deny Lesbians the right to sexual expression, they are, in effect, denying Lesbians the right to control their own bodies—a fundamental of the Feminist platform. In contradiction to their statements, they are still defining women in relation to men, not as independent entities.

The accusation that Lesbians have rejected their biologic role as females merely reflects the battle cry of the Feminists: We want to be identified as people, not only as sex object, wife, and mother. In holding out the word "woman" (as in "the movement is for all women") as an award for those females who relate to men and fulfill their biologic function, Feminists have acted exactly like the society they are striving to change. They are saying that the word "woman" does not simply mean an adult female. This major inconsistency has weakened the Feminists' theoretical position.

Feminists' exclusion of Lesbians seems stranger still in view of Feminist writings on sexuality. An early piece of women's-movement writing that is widely read, anthologized, and reprinted is *The Myth of the Vaginal Orgasm,* which proclaims the clitoris as the location of the greatest sexual pleasure for women. Its author, Ann Koedt, suggests the enormous ramifications of this knowledge:

> Aside from the strictly anatomical reasons why women might equally seek other women as lovers, there is a fear on the men's part that women will seek the company of other women on a full, human basis. The establishment of clitoral orgasm as fact would threaten the heterosexual institution. For it would indicate that sexual pleasure was obtainable from either men or women, thus making heterosexuality not an absolute, but an option. It would thus open up the whole question of human sexual relationships beyond the confines of the present male-female role system.[14]

Feminists rejoiced at the publication of Master and Johnson's work, since they had already been talking about primacy of the clitoris and the efficacy of masturbation. Feminists were seeking to define their sexuality in relation to their own bodies and not in relation to the penis. This tends to minimize the hitherto unchallenged claims that men are essential to women's pleasure.

Lesbians have always known the secret of the clitoris. The clitoris is important in Lesbian lovemaking, though the vagina is not ignored. The secret of the clitoris was the mysterious power by which that stereotypical predatory Lesbian of the myths could steal away that stereotypical sighing, unsatisfied housewife. Indeed, if Feminists are using contraception, having abortions, and asking their partners to focus on the clitoris, what is the difference between their lovemaking and that of Lesbians? Both express affection and love without the goal of producing a child.

Feminist Alix Shulman, in an article called "Organs and Orgasm," published in 1971 in *Women in Sexist Society,* not only maintains that the truth about the clitoris was long known by scientists and the information denied to women, but she implies that the sex of the love partner is relatively unimportant to female sexuality:

> The clitoris may be stimulated by a hand, by a tongue, or particularly if the woman is free to move or control the man's movements, by intercourse. No one way or combination of ways is "better" than any other though some women may prefer one way or another.[15]

Alix Shulman explains that the pleasure to be derived from the clitoris has been concealed from women. Now that they know, they need not regard themselves as frigid because they could not conform to a male definition of their sexuality.

The author concludes this section with:

> There are actually laws on the books in most states that define as unnatural and therefore criminal any [sexual] position other than that of the woman on the bottom and the man on top; laws that make oral sex a crime though for many women it is the only way of achieving orgasm with another person; laws that make homosexuality a crime, though for some people it is the only acceptable way of loving.[16]

Now that the Puritan ethic forbidding pleasure and decreeing biologic functionalism is cracking, and fears of overpopulation are intensified—and with the "new" physiological evidence on female pleasure—grounds for discrimination against the Lesbian seem to be disappearing.

Not only may lovemaking not lead to child-making for the Lesbian—her major crime—but maybe not even to orgasm. Lesbians have been exploring women's sensuality as well as sexuality. Tenderness and affection—holding and touching—may be the goal for some women some of the time, and not orgasm, which has more emphasis as a goal for the male.

Feminists also seem interested in destroying the myth of passivity,

145

which misleads many women. Lesbians have known that passivity is not necessarily a woman's natural role in life or in sex. If it were, two women could never make love. Although Edrita Fried of New York Medical College holds traditional views about Lesbianism, as "a lag in development," she fully recognizes woman's natural assertiveness, sexual and otherwise. At an Eastern Psychological Association conference on women in the spring of 1971, she pointed out that "any type of [exclusive] passivity is pathological. . . . Passivity is a condition due to organic illness or circumstances of environment. . . . Woman is anything but passive."[11]

Sexually, emotionally, and economically independent of men, Lesbians have been free to give energy and devotion to the women's movement.

Numbers of successful Women's Liberation projects have been launched by Lesbians, and Lesbians have held highly responsible posts as elected or appointed officers in the more traditionally structured women's-rights groups. Kate Millett has recognized this: "Lesbians have carried the women's movement on their backs for six years." Lesbians have contributed enormously to the work of the women's movement not only because women's issues are paramount in their lives, or because their abilities have been developed independently of men, but also because it was harder for heterosexual women to develop the habits of assertion and leadership.

The first loyalty of most heterosexual women still goes to their husbands and children. Other demands on their attention, especially those of Women's Liberation, are in conflict with those primary loyalties and can make their commitment to Women's Liberation a source of stress. Women are often fearful that full dedication to women's issues might jeopardize their relationships with men. They know they can go just so far and then they will have to choose. No matter how free heterosexual women feel they are economically or socially, if they are still bound to men for their erotic or emotional life, they are handicapped and their allegiance to other women necessarily runs in second place.

Lesbians who wish to dedicate themselves to the emancipation of women have no such personal conflicts. They have already lost or jettisoned male support and approval and are therefore not threatened by male tactics of withdrawal.

Lesbians have thus been able to act as a unifying force in the formation of a new bond among women. This potential among Lesbian women has been recognized by thinkers like C. G. Jung, who comments:

> In Anglo-Saxon countries it seems . . . that female homosexuality means rather more than Sapphic lyricism, since it somehow acts as a stimulus to the social and political organization of women, just as male homosexuality was an important factor in the rise of the Greek polis.[17]

Women's Liberation often speaks of sisterhood. At an emotional level it can mean that every woman has suffered: "I will back women. Every woman is my sister."

However, sisterhood by itself is only a small step from the traditional way married women have related to each other. This attitude was most apparent among wives a generation or two ago when childbirth was much more dangerous and when women were even more economically dependent on men. The feeling that it is the fate of women to suffer can draw women together. Traditionally women have felt closeness to other women based on an awareness of problems common to all. This feeling is basically an attitude of acceptance of the problems; it has produced no program, no plan of action.

The concept of a bond among women is key if women are going to work together in a steady and organized fashion to reshape society, but emotional "sisterhood" alone—awareness of common suffering— is not sufficient, based as it is on recognition of a common powerlessness, and may reinforce powerlessness.

The female bond is more than women suffering together. It is more than working together on simple tasks as women have done for years. It goes further, to involve a basic trust and reliance, a feeling that women can be powerful and effective, and it requires that a woman take herself and her life seriously. Once this bond has been firmly established, a sense of common commitment makes possible projects of increasing importance and complexity, involving planning over years and across geographical and socioeconomic distances.

The importance of a female commonality cannot be underestimated in light of the history of all male solidarity with reference to women, in all aspects of community life.

The presence of a male bond, a cohesiveness enabling men to accomplish complex projects and build civilization, was put forward by Lionel Tiger in *Men in Groups.*

Tiger states flatly that "Women do not form bonds."[18] He puts forth male bonding as a near-biologic trait stemming from food-gathering habits of the preanthropoid apes and later from the need to hunt; this proclivity for cooperative activity enables men to form task-oriented groups and accomplish the work of society. Male bonding patterns, he contends, reflect and arise out of man's history as hunter. Over time, the male-male link becomes programed. Yet he amplifies his statement on women with sociologic reasoning: "Dependent as most women still are on the earnings of men, they break ranks very soon," says Tiger.[19]

In the very next paragraph he points out that there may be "analytic and practical profit in seeing male homosexuality as a specific feature of the more general phenomenon of male bonding."[20] But what of female homosexuality? How are sexual and friendship groups made up exclusively of Lesbians related to bonding?

The political explanation of the phenomenon he describes is that males are able to *choose* to work and spend time together and so can form and administer governments, judicial systems, and so forth.

Apparently the primary function of the isolation of women—whether in the harem or in the single-family suburban home—has been to prevent access to other males. Today, there is another side to this: that the husband has priority on all the wife's time, which limits her access to other women as well.

Before Women's Liberation, women associated with each other mostly to fill time in the absence of their men. They related to volunteer work, to luncheons and bridge parties; friends took courses in art history at the university, participated in flower-arranging, gardening, or cooking, or went to the beauty parlor to enhance their image for the men. Interest in themselves was always secondary to husband and family. All this is still true for a large percentage of American women. But with the advent of Women's Liberation, gay women and straight women have begun to demonstrate an ability to bond. Lesbians are the key to this.

Lesbians bring a new kind of strength to sisterhood. The Lesbian is a woman who takes bold steps to make the life she wants. She may suffer from the drawbacks of Lesbianism under a sexist society, but it is a life she has chosen and knows she must answer for. She does not accept that it is God's will for women to suffer. She challenges society. Lesbians understand that sisterhood does not consist only of warm feelings for another who has suffered too; it means working together on specific goals; it means solidarity. In relationship to Women's Liberation, Lesbians provide the element of strength necessary to form a community of women. Lesbians are faced with a new role: to act as a cohesive force in the female bond.

Lesbians were forced to master the essentials of bonding in order to survive in an alien society just as males did to survive in nature, although lacking an open community has meant this quality is hard to transmit over generations. Lesbians who have been beaten and persecuted have had a need to bond together. While bonding is weak or nonexistent in the bars, it is evident in friendship groups and the Lesbians' own liberation movement. Lesbian women, whose loyalty is instinctively to other women, come to the women's movement with strong linking potential and move quickly and naturally into it.

Tiger showed the relationship between male bonding and aggression. He said that aggression is an intensely cooperative process and is both the product and the cause of strong affective ties between men.[21]

Although women, happily, have been excluded from organized violence, they have found it necessary to be assertive, and bold in their efforts to change institutions. Feminists are militant instead of passive. They encounter rather than wait and suffer. Dangers inherent in their struggle have strengthened their commitment to each other.

Tiger points out that the kind of solidarity experienced in male bonding has as a concomitant the exclusion of women. Whenever social change demands the admittance of females to male work or political activity, the locus of male power simply shifts to a more protected spot where females would still not be welcome.

For example, political decision-making to a large extent still takes place in all-male clubs, smokers, bars, "back rooms," or on the golf course where women are not welcome. The political process thus remains in male control. Most women, on the other hand, are delighted when a man honors them by attending an all-female function. The presence of men at women's groups is a sign of the attention and possible approval of the ruling group. On the contrary, the presence of women at a men's group is a sign of disintegration. Evidence of this is found in the abundance of women's auxiliaries and affiliates to male organizations and the lack of male auxiliaries and affiliates to women's groups. The women's groups almost always have a lower status than the men's groups.

Things are beginning to change after several years of Women's Liberation, and the change indicates the presence of a new bond. New all-women's political caucuses and professional groups seem to have more strength and purpose than they had before Women's Liberation. Women are beginning to value women more. Obviously they are no longer as concerned with male approval, particularly when that approval conflicts with their own growth.

Much to the surprise of men, Feminists have consistently enforced the official *exclusion* of men from some meetings and entire organizations. That men are excluded is a sign of the emergence of true female solidarity.

Once women decided to *choose* the company of women, the women's groups they enter take on a *valued status* as a preferred activity. As another sign of the new female bond, there are now men's auxiliaries to Women's Liberation. Men's Liberation groups around the country are springing up, made up largely of men whose wives or lovers are in Women's Liberation.

Man-hating as a part of Women's Liberation has received much attention in the media. This comes primarily from the radical groups.

It is considered, especially in radical circles, apolitical or antipolitical to relate to men, unless any relationship with a man can be demonstrated to involve equality. While the number of men willing to enter an "equal" relationship may be increasing, there are still precious few.

An early paper published by The Feminists is entitled "Man-

Hating." Pointing out that women too often wind up despising other women and cottoning up to the male oppressor, they say "If it is a choice between woman-hating and man-hating, let it be the latter."[22] Anger at men is defined as coming from "that part of you which turned you on to Feminism in the first place," as from "that part which is really human and cannot submit."[23]

In their papers The Feminists defined love as the attraction of the powerless to the powerful, that is, of women to men. As such, love was oppressive. They were the first group to take a public stand against marriage, which they termed "slavery for women." They went on to call marriage "the model for all other forms of discrimination against women."

It is hard for Lesbians to relate to these problems. For them, men are not to be hated, though they may seem irrelevant. Lesbians love other women, but do not usually hate men. It is unnecessary, since they do *not* struggle with men to achieve their own identity or independence.

> I don't have to fight to keep from hating men, because I don't hate them. I no longer have to resent them for my need of them and I am much freer to see them as people instead of tormentors/lovers, and most of all, judges of my validity.[24]

Traditionally sex with males calls on the woman to fantasize being helpless, being taken. A woman in Women's Liberation cannot accept this.

In an article on "Female Sexual Alienation," Linda Phelps points out that "the fantasy world of sex which veils our experience is the world of sex as seen through male eyes. It is a world whose eroticism is defined in terms of female powerlessness, dependency, and sub-mission. It is a world of sado-masochistic sex. . . ."[25] "Like the symbolic world of the schizophrenic, a woman's fantasy life—her desire to be taken, overpowered, mastered—allows her to play a passive role, perhaps even to enjoy it if she fully accepts the world as defined by men."[26]

But the Feminist who is aware of her oppression can no longer fully abandon herself to a man. Submission is in direct opposition to her struggle for independence. Straining for autonomy, she cannot be subordinate any longer, even in bed—especially in bed. Her new awareness that submission in bed is at the roots of the total cultural hierarchy, brilliantly analyzed in *Sexual Politics,* can prevent her from having sexual relationships with men any longer. Submission now goes against her philosophy and grates on her nerves.

A Lesbian sums up the feelings of many Lesbians in the movement: "I know homosexual relationships can get messed up by the dominant culture, by being repressed, by playing man and woman. I guess I have a thousand million hang-ups left, but the important thing is, I would have even more than that if I weren't a Lesbian."[27]

Although the Feminist arguments are clearly designed to change heterosexuality, they incidentally build a case for Lesbianism. In light of the exploitation by men, which Feminists document thoroughly, some may find it difficult to endorse heterosexual relationships at this point in time. Lesbian relationships have always offered at least an opportunity for a peer relationship, and that point of contrast with heterosexuality seems quite attractive today. Under present conditions, a Feminist may well ask: Is heterosexuality a valid life-style? Feminists who cannot tolerate traditional male dominance have good reason to see heterosexuality as masochistic and Lesbianism as rational.

And in view of the conflict heterosexual Feminists experience in trying to escape male domination while still depending on male approval, Lesbians often seem more comfortable in Women's Liberation than straight women do.

Within the women's movement and the gay women's movement, one hears the term "political Lesbian," which has come to have more than one meaning. First, a political Lesbian meant a woman who becomes a Lesbian as a result of Feminist theory. She sees Lesbianism as a separatist, alternative life-style, for her a revolutionary step.

Ti-Grace Atkinson has modified and extended this definition by saying that women who live a total commitment to women, even though they have never had sexual relations with women, are Lesbians in a political sense.

Finally, of course, a political Lesbian may be a Lesbian who is politicized, that is, she has analyzed her situation in society according to the theory of sexism and the nature of sex roles. She sees her views as part of both gay and Feminist theory.

Women who become Lesbians in the movement do so in a spirit of joyous self-discovery and affirmation of themselves as women and as revolutionaries. However, they tend to be regarded with suspicion by both heterosexual and gay women. Some of the young women who enter sexual relationships with other women as a result of the promulgation of the idea of sisterhood and the philosophy of equal, not power-based, relationships, feel betrayed. One young woman wrote a poignant letter about her feelings of rejection by straight women, which was first published in *It Ain't Me Babe:*

> We have all said in our leaflets, to our friends, in our screams in the night: what we want is equal, open loving relationships where each person can see the other as an individual human being. . . . So why when I affirm all this do you see me with strange eyes? Why when I talk of my feelings do you look away? . . .
>
> I may love my sisters with my mind and heart, but my body belongs still to men or to none; or you say it belongs to me but the love I express with it must be limited, by tacit command "You may love your sister— you may not make love with her. If it really can't be helped we won't shut you out, but of course you understand we can't have you speaking for Women's Liberation anymore; your feelings are too uniquely your own, too personal. In short, you are the second-class citizens we need to keep us from hitting bottom, to keep us from completely losing men's approval . . .[28]

Lesbians are both surprised by, and leery of, women with little or no sexual experience with other women who call themselves Lesbians. The woman who has become a Lesbian because of her political beliefs or who wants to become a Lesbian because they are "the most independent women" and "the vanguard of the women's movement" has trouble communicating with Lesbians because she lacks a gay consciousness. Lesbians hear her happiness, but they do not hear any recognition of society's hostility toward homosexuals.

For this reason, the political Lesbian who comes to Lesbianism through theory alternately delights and annoys premovement Lesbians. The political Lesbian's simplicity and joy in loving women are invigorating, spontaneous, and unburdened, but her inability to identify with homosexual oppression lends an air of unreality and a feeling of emptiness to her statement.

In fact, when a straight-identified woman comes to feel she wants to have a Lesbian experience to advance her politics, she can be most oppressive to the gay women:

> Another variety of a political Lesbian is the straight-identified woman who is interested in having a Lesbian experience. Necessary to this is an experienced Lesbian, to whom the woman comes on as a potential sex object, laying the male trip on the Lesbian. This is the most oppressive of all women's movement routines to the Gay Feminist, who is personally diminished to the state of "manhood."[29]

Far from being driven by lust for straight women's bodies, Lesbians are not always happy with the kind of attention they get in the movement.

Lesbians can stand as symbols of self-actualization among women, even—or especially—when Feminists do not actually know they are Lesbians. Feminists who have been dependent on men sometimes unconsciously look to Lesbian women as surrogate males. Lesbians have come to feel that at times they are the men of the women's movement.

Because most Lesbian women find loving a woman beautiful, they think it strange that other women might seek it as a political experience. They do not want to preach Lesbianism; they want others to comprehend why *they* are Lesbians, which is often interpreted as proselytizing.

Lesbians in the women's movement and the gay movement resent being told they are proselytizing when what they feel they are doing is being positive about their sexuality for the first time. They remember just a few years ago when it was not unusual for Lesbians in the women's movement to veto the appointment or election of a Lesbian sister on the grounds she "looked too dykey" to appear in public.

A few women do try Lesbianism, but that is not the only sexual alternative. There are also bisexuality, masturbation, asexuality, and revolutionary heterosexuality.

There is a sense of desperation among some straight women in the movement. "I am worried and saddened by women bragging about masturbation and by the joy in revenge shown by women trying role-reversal pickups."

A few straight feminists have found immediate release from anger by what they call role reversal:

"I picked up a man at a cocktail party. I took him to my apartment. We made love. I complimented him on his lovemaking and his body. Then I made it evident that I had other things to do and he should leave." Another woman arranged for a hotel room. She ordered drinks and flowers. She invited a man, went and got him and brought him to the room. She talked to him, gave him his favorite drink, and seduced him. The next morning she left the hotel to go to work and never returned.

Bisexuality is sometimes seen as a cover-up for homosexuality. Some women in the women's movement do seem to use the label bisexual as a cop-out. Others may sleep with women to somehow atone for relating to men. However, some women, more or less protected within the security of a heterosexual (that is approved) relationship may be moving into and developing a true bisexuality. Very little is known in the movement about the bisexual's views.

It may be true that numbers of women who will develop into true bisexuals, or who are true bisexuals—that is, able to enjoy total relationships with both men and women—are today calling themselves Lesbian, since despite all the controversy there is a theoretical basis for it as well as an aura of radical chic surrounding Lesbians in the women's movement.

According to straight Feminists, an increasing number of women in the movement—especially those who have tried revolutionary heterosexuality, whether as promiscuity, a long-term peer relationship, or role-reversal, and become embittered—move to masturbation.

Masturbation is becoming as much a Feminist demand as abortion and contraception. Masturbation is one way a woman comes to know her body and to know that her sexuality is her own, not the gift of a man, not derived from the penis.

Many Feminists believe they must be prepared to be self-sufficient sexually if they are to be fully independent. *Rat,* the women's revolutionary paper, suggests that masturbation is something that every woman must be able to do, like changing a tire, or defending herself.

155

If loving oneself is related to ego and narcissism, which is usually seen as a negative correlation, perhaps women are entitled to a little of this self-love. That masturbation is commonly accepted for men and is still not talked about or admitted by women may relate to male ego strength and a relative lack of ego strength in women.

Concentration on masturbation is often experienced by some as a phase leading to relationships with others. As an end in itself, as part of a negatively conceived "asexuality," it tends to lead to a mechanical, genitally oriented sexuality, too close to that of many males for political comfort.

Some women openly proclaim asexuality, apparently putting aside sex until after the revolution.

What emerges from all this is that sexuality in the women's movement is more diverse and more complex than the polarity between homosexual and heterosexual made visible by the media. If the true range of sexuality in Women's Liberation was made apparent by a number of caucuses representing all the options, the oversimplified battle between heterosexuals and gay women would cool off. The more complex picture would also be a more realistic one.

But until such groups form and members begin to discuss sex in general among themselves and between groups, Lesbianism will continue to be thought of as dangerous to the movement. And yet continuing to approve of only one way of gaining sexual and emotional satisfaction—that is, relating to men—or in effect asking that women in the movement deny themselves any sexual life, are alternatives that involve the risk of betraying basic principles. A revolutionary movement, especially one based on the deeply personal area of the member-group's sex life and the values attached to it, cannot espouse the traditional and remain revolutionary.

Bisexual women, who have been caught on both sides and in the middle of the heterosexual/homosexual argument, have a unique contribution to make to open discussion on sexuality in the movement. Their experience is nearly as hidden and difficult to weigh as a factor as that of the possibly prevalent asexuality in the movement. An "asexual" or a bisexual flying the flag of a practicing heterosexual gives an inaccurate picture of the movement's components

by increasing the apparent numbers of heterosexuals and concealing the options.

Clearly, most women will not become Lesbians, but more may experiment with bisexuality under the influence of Women's Liberation
(indeed, that is often what they are doing when they have a
"Lesbian experience"), the most important group yet to speak up in
the women's movement on the whole topic of sexuality may well
prove to be the bisexual women. Given the tendency noted by some
observers for some adolescents today to be bisexual or to try bisexuality, and with the opinion forming among some scientists that
free of societal restrictions everybody might be bisexual, it is amazing
that there is no bisexual caucus in the women's movement. One reason
for the omission may be that bisexual women bring out fears of
homosexuality in straight women and also fears of heterosexuality
in women who live as Lesbians.

The woman who has learned to be self-sufficient, perhaps by
developing masturbatory techniques, also has a political contribution
to make. She also shows a path of sexual and emotional independence
from men that may be more amenable than Lesbianism to women
who, temporarily at least, need this. The woman who masturbates
consciously for pleasure rather than relief is also making the statement that sex, for her, is for pleasure and not for reproduction.

Heterosexual women who have found satisfaction in multiple
relationships—or even promiscuity—with men, where no one man,
or no man, has control should speak up loud and clear. Women who
live in communes should let other women know more about their
experiences.

Thus, Lesbianism is only one possibility for a Feminist—but it
should be an accepted, even valued, one for those women who elect
to try it.

The best estimate on the number of Lesbians in the movement—
up to twenty percent in some groups—appeared in *Psychology Today*
in March, 1972. It is based on a survey of 15,000 women on women's
issues, and the largest sample of Feminists to date is among the
respondents.

Vivian Gornick wrote a dramatic and reasoned statement published in the *Village Voice*, which was widely read by those associ-

ated with all the movements. Her article called "In Any Terms She Shall Choose" said:

> Hundreds of women in the movement are Lesbians . . . They probably have more to gain from Feminism than any other single category of women, both in the more superficial sense and in the more profound one. Certainly they have more to teach Feminists about Feminism than has any other single category of human being—man or woman . . . disavowal [of Lesbianism] strikes at the bottom-most roots of Feminism, attacking the movement in its most vital parts, threatening its ideological life at the source . . . The whole point of the Feminist movement is that each and every woman shall recognize that the burden and glory of her Feminism lies with defining herself honestly in *any terms she shall choose.* Sexual self-definition is primary to the Feminist movement . . . the point is that whatever a woman's sexual persuasion, it is compelling, and she must be allowed to follow her inclinations openly and honestly without fear of castigation in order to discover the genuine self at the center of [her] sexuality.
>
> That, for me, is the true politics of the Feminist movement. It is woman recognizing that she is a fully developed human being with the responsibility to discover and live with her own self . . . [Hiding Lesbianism] encourages us to remain afraid of ourselves and to inflict injustice on one another in the name of our fears. And is that not what sexism is all about?[30]

If Sappho literally could be regarded as the archetypal Lesbian, much of the concern about the Lesbians in the women's movement would disappear. Sappho was an educated woman at a time when most women could not read or write, a political exile, a mother, and one of the finest poets who ever lived. When virtually all women apparently lived to serve the male hierarchy and died anonymously without leaving a trace of their uniqueness, she said her name would live through history, and it has. Today she would be called a Feminist.

7 THE REALIZATION
OF INNOCENCE

No politician, psychiatrist, or minister, however liberal, however sympathetic, can give Lesbians or gay men the self-respect they desperately need to create for themselves. What is required is a profound change within, a revolution in self-image.

This change began with rebellion. Propelled by long-suppressed rage over intolerable conditions, gays fought against police in June, 1969, after a raid on the Stonewall, a favorite bar in the Greenwich Village section of New York. For the first time homosexuals struck back. Street queens, despised and ridiculed by straights and by many gays, courageously battled policemen armed with clubs. Gays and straights were stunned as more homosexuals, and more kinds of homosexuals, rushed to the area during the several nights of the encounter to fight against the inhuman treatment that homosexuals had passively assumed to be their lot.

Gays have gone stark raving sane. Rebellion changed passive suffering into action and a negative identity into a positive one. The Stonewall generated a new philosophy of pride and activism for homosexuals and gave a new perspective to the exploration of the homosexual's problems by homosexuals.

Few who were there realized that the Stonewall riots and the reaction to them were irreversible, a really new beginning. The effects were far-reaching and permanent for Lesbians as for their gay brothers. Working together in those days, gay people found a new self-respect. They liked themselves, and they liked each other. They felt proud to be who they were. They also began to discover they were no longer alone and isolated. They had a community. Fighting on the streets, they started to overcome their overwhelming feeling of insignificance and helplessness. The problems that exceeded their powers as individuals were less threatening now. As they grasped their first opportunity for collective expression of their deep and long-standing discontent, feelings of puniness were transformed into an instinct for politics: Together they could be very effective.

"Gay Liberation is the realization of innocence." Marty Robinson made this statement at a rally a few days after the Stonewall riots. The words, which came to him only as he spoke, were to be one of the most profound statements of the Gay Liberation movement.

Innocence, bursting forth after centuries of suffering and guilt, brought a miracle of dignity and solidarity to an oppressed group that had been divided by self-hatred into bitter camps.

The simplicity of the historic event, and its revolutionary effects, were bound to prompt the questions: Why did I so willingly accept guilt for so long? How does this realization change my life?

Too many homosexuals, men and women, had spent thousands of dollars and many years in psychotherapy trying either to attain heterosexuality or to adjust to a subservient position in society. Others had channeled energy unendingly into building and maintaining façades or making apologies. Still others, paralyzed by fear and guilt, had become loners, asexual almost. They had denied themselves full expressions of emotion for so long, they now seemed like zombies.

For older homosexuals particularly, a realization of innocence was to accept that much of their lives had been spent (wasted!) in voluntary psychological imprisonment for a crime never committed.

Homosexuals learned that they must no longer accept society's definitions. Much of what was considered sick for the homosexual came to be seen as a direct and logical result of society's own sick attitudes and oppressive institutions. Realization of this is the essence of a gay consciousness.

It is not so strange that queens and street people started the homosexual revolution by rebelling at the Stonewall, nor that they are active and honored participants in demonstrations and marches.

Logically, those gays who have been least able to hide and thus have suffered the most are often in the forefront of the Gay Liberation movement. As Frantz Fanon perceived in the struggle for Black nationalism in Africa, the most despised of humanity, the downtrodden and ridiculed, enter fearlesssly into militant and decisive action.[1]

With no need for caution, they throw themselves into the struggle, often ahead of professionals and the middle classes. The downtrodden cannot be tempted by society's baits and are therefore unafraid and uncompromising. They know they are not candidates for tokenism. They take for granted the impossibility of their acceptance in society as it is. Propelled by rage, their demands are often purposely excessive and unreasonable, frustrating officials who try to reason a peace. Through the revolution "they are rehabilitated in their own eyes and in the eyes of history"[2] and walk proudly in the front ranks of gay marches and demonstrations. "All who turn in circles between suicide and madness . . . recover their balance and once again go forward. . . ."[3] Their color and enthusiasm have always attracted the sensationalist appetites of the press; thus, this small atypical minority is mistakenly thought of by the public as representative of the majority. Since the public feels confirmed in its beliefs by their presence and has no interest in believing otherwise, the image remains constant.

Psychologically the gay activist might be considered a mutant form of homosexual, who sees as essentially positive a life that has appeared essentially negative. "When we hated ourselves, we saw everything we were and everything we did as more or less bad. Now we are looking into things and realize that what we are and what we do is not bad, just different, and even beautiful." In so many ways the Lesbian looks back on what was in the past and what is now in the present and says, "I've been here before, but my head was in a different place."

The activist drops much self-consciousness and develops a social consciousness.

Instead of guilt, the activist experiences pride.

Instead of accepting the concept of "can't change," the activist refuses to change her sexual preference.

Instead of accepting homosexuality as a failure in development, the activist sees that she has been successful in resisting strong social forces toward heterosexuality.

Instead of deviant behavior, the activist sees homosexual behavior as creative and individualistic.

Instead of being defined by others, the activist now defines herself.

161

Instead of accepting the concept of disturbed patterns of gender identity, the activist talks of new and expanded human behavior transcending societally set boundaries.

Gay Liberationists are not only characterized by a reversal in perspective, but a release of energy, or more simply, not only a change in thinking but in behaving.

Instead of passively accepting oppression and surrendering to it like a vegetable, the activist confronts society.

Instead of hiding, the activist declares herself.

There has been much said by gay activists against apologetics. Baited into proving that they are not sick, insane, criminal, don't molest children, and so forth, the Lesbian is asked to prove her maturity and humanity. Gay Liberation strategy number one is openly to confront the opposition in an aggressive fashion so as not to be constantly on the defensive.

A Lesbian on a panel responded to a predictable question with: "I am very interested in *your* problem and would like to know just what caused *you* to become heterosexual."

Another Lesbian, who was told by a heterosexual that homosexuals proselytized, responded, "Heterosexuals don't proselytize of course, they just try to force heterosexuality on us."

The parents of another Lesbian accused her of flaunting her sexuality and she wanted to respond: "Perhaps your wedding rings, constant talk about the children, Mr. and Mrs. printed on everything, and the need to always be seen together flaunt heterosexuality."

A kind of Gay Liberation humor is built on this: a gay activist and mother of two children sighs deeply and says, "I don't know what I did wrong. I'm so afraid I have failed my children. They're growing up heterosexual."

Another Lesbian: "In the past, when people accused me of being a Lesbian, I said, 'Oh, no, I'm not'; now, ironically, some people are trying to slander me in the gay movement by saying I'm not a Lesbian, and I say quickly, 'Oh, yes, I am.'"

The Eastern Psychological Association conference held in New York City in the spring of 1971 was attended by a group of Lesbian activists. One, chosen by the group to speak, went to the lectern to respond to a male heterosexual psychotherapist who had just given a talk entitled "Lesbians Emerge as People," and had included statistics on Lesbians who had had heterosexual experiences or who had been raped by men.

Working with phrases that had been gathered from the various talks by members of the society—to point out the "vocabulary of denigration" used for Lesbians—the activist read a list of counter-conference topics:

> "Heterosexual male psychotherapists emerge as people"
> "Heterosexuality: Disease or way of life"
> "Can heterosexuality be treated?"
> "Heterosexual women: How their mothers failed them"
> "Heterosexual women who have had bad Lesbian experiences or who have been raped by women"

The audience of nearly 2,000—including several hundred members of EPA—held their breath, then began to laugh. The members described the action as "consciousness-raising."

Activists look for opportunities to bring up their sexual preference. On campuses, students wear buttons saying "Gay is Good," or "Lesbianism is revolution," or tee-shirts decorated with two linked female symbols. On marches Lesbians carry signs that read, "I am your worst fears and your best fantasy," and "Hi, Mom," or sing "I enjoy being a dyke." One woman, filling out a questionnaire for a five-year reunion at Mt. Holyoke crossed out the line "Husband's name" and wrote in "Lesbian."

Jill Johnston is always poking fun at society's fears: "Special from the White House. The President announced last night the appointment of a Lesbian to the Cabinet. It's nice if you can invite them in. They usually come in without knocking."[4]

Counteracting years of invisibility and hiding, Lesbians find it necessary to make noise and attract attention to reach the prejudice that has become so profoundly entrenched. They recognize that they must force themselves into the nation's consciousness. They break the silence. They no longer speak in whispers. They proclaim their sexual preference in the home, on the streets, and in the legislatures.

Some Lesbian activists feel they must now counteract centuries of invisibility by becoming apparent. Overlooked as women and as homosexuals, Lesbians are nearly totally invisible. At marches and demonstrations, straights have been heard to ask, "Who are these women?" or "I didn't know there were women, too." One Lesbian activist's father was stunned when she told him she was a homosexual. "But I thought only men were homosexuals," he blurted out.

Gays, particularly Lesbians, have been overlooked for so long that some feel they should "flaunt" their sexuality. Although at one time this may have appeared even to homosexuals as exhibitionism, the acts are now seen by some as political, to gain attention in society. There is political significance to "acting as gay as possible."[13]

The idea of making a point of it is to show clearly that Lesbians are not guilty and fearful any more. There is no political gain in silence and submission. In fact, sanctioned by silence, oppression is likely to increase. Male and female homosexuals know now that they are not making a mountain out of a molehill, as those who wish to silence them insist. Society has built a mountain by making homosexuality a factor in employment, government work, social situations, renting an apartment, college, everywhere.

The case against society is clear. A cautious Lesbian succeeds in life by establishing ties with the community, seniority on the job, financial security, respect from colleagues and neighbors over the years. But perhaps she finds the outward appearance of well-being unsatisfactory. She has forgotten something essential: herself. If, with the support of Gay Liberation and Women's Liberation, she finds the courage to step forward without her disguise and say, "I am a Lesbian," the whole setting of her life changes around her.

Ties with the community, acceptance, respect, security may disappear. She realizes that every gain in life was related to that superstructure, a straight façade; taking away the burden of the feigned identity also means risking the loss of most of the things she has worked for over the years.

The Lesbian's maturing necessarily differs from that of her straight sisters. Most women when they take on the responsibility of marriage and children automatically attain status as mature adults. Many heterosexuals simply muddle through to adulthood as more and more responsibility is transferred to them and as they fulfill routine societal expectations.

The Lesbian's situation is different. Unless she marries and has children, she is responsible primarily for herself. No children depend upon her, and no husband. She is not responsible to a husband's good name, does not share in the management of a husband's property nor take on substance from it, does not serve a husband in his career nor represent a family in the community. These are the factors that are seen to promote mature behavior and a mature image in our society. Defined in heterosexual terms, a Lesbian is seen as a sort of perpetual adolescent.

The Lesbian, as she comes out of hiding, finds herself stripped of whatever adult credentials she has accumulated through hard work and obedience to the system. She is reduced to adolescent status. Responsibility may be withdrawn gradually or at once. She is humiliated by family pressures more appropriate to childhood.

Obviously she can no longer define maturity in society's terms, for she is beyond the pale of mature adulthood—womanhood—in society's eyes.

At this painful time the Lesbian understands that society has forced her out of the system. She sees the futility in her desire to be included. For the first time she grasps the reality of her situation, that society's definitions do not include her, and this is the first step in her maturing.

She sees truths she had not perceived before, recognizes facts that were always there, acknowledges relationships between herself and society that had always existed. The understanding, gradual or sudden, that she will probably never satisfy agreed-on signs of maturity are essential to her personal growth.

And she is no longer confused about the origins of her conflicts. She has grasped the problems and the reasons that her search for individual solutions has been largely fruitless.

Through the various instruments of the movement—raps, consciousness-raising, reading, action, and introspection—she relives the past experiences that created her guilt, to the time she incorporated society's negative opinions of her. She tries to isolate the moment when guilt hit, and comes to see how guilt has spread, like ink, through her psyche.

Gay Liberation went instinctively to the core of the problem by encouraging and supporting homosexuals in the difficult task of being honest with their parents. Activists realize that establishing independence from parents is essential for growth. In particular, parents tend

165

to keep Lesbian daughters, no matter how old, in an immature status because Lesbians lack a family of their own. Telling the parents gives the Lesbian release from their expectations and an opportunity to live freely without parental restraints on her behavior. She discovers that parents may tolerate her or—more rarely—they may accept her or reject her.

But even rejection, though it is a sad and difficult experience, may show that the real experience is not as painful as the imagined one she has lived with over the years. Toleration, acceptance, rejection—each is more real and easier to deal with than fantasies issuing from her guilt.

Rejection may relieve the Lesbian of an impossible situation—that of remaining in her parents' favor by lying and denying her identity. At its best, telling parents gives the "child" a chance to begin dealing with her guilt on a real basis; it enables her to be free of a situation that tends to create more guilt. For clinging parents, telling them is a way of showing that their daughter is autonomous and intends to make her own life, assuming responsibility for herself —these, of course, are characteristics identified with maturity. Parents can even be reassured about a daughter whose behavior has worried them because they saw *no* reason for it.

Parents often seem to know or sense more than they admit to consciously. Often they have a perception of their daughter's homosexuality on some level—but try to suppress it. "If you really are a Lesbian don't tell us." Discussion can be painful—but honest—for both parents and daughter. Having things out in the open can be the beginning of reality—whereas before, all was lies and hiding on both sides.

Reckoning with oneself, and surviving any negative consequences, going on to grow and change, can be the start of a real relationship to society—as oneself, a homosexual woman—with freedom and advantages at this time in sexual and cultural history outweighing the painful disadvantages of rejection by segments of society.

New confrontations with parents and institutions bring new insight. It becomes clear that heterosexual society had arranged everything in its own self-interest, limiting attempts at a gay culture without accepting gays into the dominant culture. Heterosexuals have degraded and laughed at the old gay life and at the same time have permitted no acceptable way of life. Gays have had to explore the meaning of their own lives, to discover just what was forced behavior and just what was natural, what, if anything, was truly sick, and what was simply made to look sick.

Was there something of value in the old gay subculture? In the dominant culture? What about marriage, multiple relationships, roles, social resources, and the rest? Homosexuals began to rethink their needs and motivations and experiment with new ways of living. The new perspective of innocence demands a thorough re-examination of every aspect of daily life—as well as of life goals.

Now that homosexuals can exchange vows in some churches in an unofficial ceremony akin to marriage, is marriage such a good idea after all? Do homosexuals want marriage because they have never had it? If homosexuality becomes acceptable, and marriage is the only acceptable situation for a love relationship, will a binding marriage become the only acceptable life-style for homosexuals too? Even heterosexuals are beginning to question the validity of exclusive and eternal sexual contracts. Heterosexuals often feel trapped because of consideration for the children, joint property, and social expectations.

Some gay people who accept the traditional values of marriage— or the newer ideas like time-limited marriage contracts advocated by some Women's Liberationists—may try homosexual marriages when they are possible. Others may try marriage in the future simply because they have been denied it in the past.

For those gay people who want a life-long relationship with one person, but keep failing, there is a new understanding of the difficulties. Problems in living with another individual as an equal, the burden of past guilt which poisons love, the constant force of social indignation, and the learned necessity of becoming psychologically and emotionally self-sufficient, make monogamy a real challenge for gays at this time. With such obstacles it is beyond reasonable expectation that a gay couple could survive—and yet many do. In the future, if and when pressures ease, expectations of a life-long love will be more realistic.

Toffler, in *Future Shock*, points out that as homosexuality becomes more socially acceptable, we might even begin to find families with adopted children based on homosexual marriages.[5] Innovative minorities will experiment with many new family forms, Toffler says, including childless marriage, professional parenthood, postretirement child-rearing, corporate families, communes, geriatric marriages, homosexual family units, and polygamy.[6]

As gay men, who, like males in general, seem to have a drive toward multiple sexual contacts, begin exploring new ways of living together in love relationships, so gay women, who were taught to value monogamy, are beginning to explore the values of multiple relationships. Both marriage and promiscuity with their present meanings seem to be unacceptable to many gays.

Comments by Lesbians in the movement on monogamy:

"Monogamy is fantasy. We don't want to give up multiplicity for this monolithic thing called monogamy. Monogamy for heterosexuals or homosexuals is trying to stay together no matter what, for the idea of 'our marriage' or 'our relationship.' One sacrifices everything for an unobtainable ideal."

"We were two minds with but a single thought. We just kept arguing over what that thought was."

"If we must get our identity from another individual, which monogamous marriage—with another human being possessed as a form of property—implies, then there is something lacking in us. There is always the feeling that when the other person leaves, something—our identity—is pulled away too."

The idea that monogamy could totally consume a person was a major point for some, and especially younger Lesbians. Lesbians interested in multiple relationships felt that multiple relationships made it possible to comprehend people, not acquire them, or own them. Some voiced frustration at the feeling of stepping on someone's property when they were attracted to someone already in a couple relationship, and spoke of couples as being exclusive or excluding.

Some Lesbians have begun to explore communes to get free of confining and emotionally draining baggage of jealousy, fear, possession, and dependence.

Theory and practice are two different things, however, and women who advocated multiple Lesbian relationships were not always able to make them work. At a consciousness-raising meeting one Lesbian confessed with a smile that she thought she had "monogamous tendencies." Multiple relationships sound ideal, but they are difficult to live. Simply put, they are impractical: multiple relationships take multiple time, multiple emotional energy. But the primary problem seems to be the difficulty in escaping women's socialization, which teaches and reinforces single binding relationships. Even in group situations there is a tendency to focus on one individual and feel twinges of jealousy and possessiveness. Observing friends struggling with multiple relationships, one Lesbian observed that to her it looked more like "multiple monogamy" with all the troubles just compounded.

A Lesbian couple trying to live the revolutionary life-style ran into problems when one could not emotionally accept multiple relationships. Luckily both received support from peers in the gay movement, while the Lesbian who could not live the new politics went through a period of agony. Several couples say that they fled the movement in order to protect their relationships.

As Lesbianism gets closer to acceptability, some Lesbians choose to take on the added burden of justifying multiple relationships for women. To what some Lesbians sincerely exploring different relationships see as valid, straights will certainly say, "I always knew Lesbians couldn't make a relationship work."

One psychologist comments on the universal conflicts in monogamy:

> Of the thousand or more different societies that have been carefully studied, less than five percent claim to expect monogamy. Ours is one of them. There are no societies on record, including ours, that can demonstrate working monogamy. Where both parties, for moral or any other reasons, practice real monogamy, it kills the spontaneity. The quantity goes down, the quality goes down, and sex becomes routine. The non-sexual parts of the relationship suffer as well.[7]

But other Lesbians in the gay movement fear that the emphasis on multiple relationships will become a new tyranny to replace the old dictatorship of absolute monogamy, a new sexual commandment. To them the purpose of a sexual revolution is to make possible a wide range of choices in life-styles, all equally valued. Their greatest criticism of the present society is not that it is monogamist but that it is not a pluralist society. They feel that discussion on monogamy in consciousness-raising groups or organization meetings can become a way for a few to tell everyone how to live.

The far-out political heads seem to be going to bed with theories. They have so much anger against the oppression they suffered in so-called monogamous relationships in the past, whether with women or men, that they don't stop to try and find out what is human, what really is female. Often their liberated relationships cause pain in the women they relate to.

Reasonably enough, Lesbians have to fight blind acceptance of any value, no matter who lays it down. Gay women may need to experiment, at this stage anyway, to find out more about themselves, to understand what is societal programing and what is natural and desirable for women on a deeper level.

In discussions, values tend to be bundled together in one way only, when in fact they can be combined in many different ways. For example, any one-to-one primary relationship is called monogamous, but in fact it may not necessarily carry the understanding of "forever" or of exclusivity. Naturally a one-to-one relationship can include a profound recognition of the partner's otherness and independence. The two can want to relate in that way without wanting to own each other or without expecting to be together until the end of time. But this is seldom recognized by the most radical.

There has been a great deal of dependency in intense Lesbian relationships. But how much of this was because the lovers were isolated, ostracized, and weak in self-esteem?

March Hoffman, a theorist of the gay movement, points out that women are raised to be dependent. They are supposed to form an alliance with a being who is active, self-defining, with a strong identity—a man—and relate dependently to him. A Lesbian couple consists of two human beings, both of whom have been taught to be submissive in a dominant-submissive relationship. So there is often a kind of double dependency causing two women to cling together. Neither may have the self-confidence; each may lack a self. Yet both seek it in the other.

There is a movement answer to this, beyond banning one-to-one relationships. Both Women's Liberation and Gay Liberation provide ways for the woman to build the necessary ego and confidence not to want, need, or allow another to consume or smother her. Among women in the movement with a consciousness of women's problems, there is no reason either to oppress another woman in a relationship or be subservient to her. There is also no reason to deny a partner emotional or sexual satisfaction outside the primary relationship, if both partners can agree to this. Above all, today there is the possibility of having a Lesbian relationship in a context of many activities shared with a community, allowing many diverse kinds of friends and levels of friendship. There need be no more isolation. The content of a one-to-one relationship might be quite different now than before the movement.

The charm in the prevailing movement attitude about relating to many other women is the belief that women are valuable, important to get to know and to love on all levels possible. There is an underlying search here: gay women are looking for their identities as women and homosexuals. They are trying to resolve a basic conflict in these two terms. As women, by conventional definitions, they are expected to be ready to give care and support to one person. As homosexuals, they are supposed to be cool, daring, and promiscuous. The real identities of homosexual women are just beginning to emerge.

The problems of relating, of satisfying different needs with different people or with the same person, are true for heterosexuals and homosexuals alike. The same is true for the question of which needs are legitimate and which should be worked out in therapy or consciousness-raising.

"Homosexuality . . . has very minor differences from heterosexuality; the overlap is tremendous and the differences are essentially trivial."[8]

The one important difference is in the consciousness of gay activists. Floating around in a cultural void, having questioned the old culture and having not yet fully created a new one, Lesbians have an ideological thrust to examinations of relationships. Real questions as to what a human being is and what a woman is and what a gay woman is are brought up. The pains and pleasures of different relationships and different kinds of relationships are explored. This is far different from the old clandestine heterosexual affair or even the old-

171

style Lesbian extracurricular relationship, which remain hidden from view. Gay women have no contracts or traditions that bind them to any one way of acting and feeling with another human being, and thus they have a freedom to evaluate and choose.

What may evolve out of the different ways gay men and gay women are relating is a new value system for homosexuals. Gays have always had a mixed value system made up of some aspects of the heterosexual system and others of the old gay bar culture. The two sources are often in conflict, as with fidelity vs. promiscuity.

With a new ethic based on the value of an individual, which the young in general seem to embrace, and with the concept of sex as communication, sharing, between two individuals, a homosexual ethic without conflict is emerging. A new respect for the love partner and oneself indicates an important step toward more humanistic goals.

The practice of multiple relationships for Lesbians of course is not new. Being single in this culture commonly leads to short-term and multiple relationships. But the possibility that various kinds of relationships may be desirable in the future is new. Ironically homosexual women and men, who have lived outside the culture, may have unknowingly been living a life-style that will influence a future life-style for the heterosexual majority.

Experimentation with, and analysis of, newer life-styles like those of hippies and other groups who have also defied traditional structures are taken very seriously by gays and are seen as a part of the search for more creative and individualistic ways of living. The experiments of today—and even yesterday—may well become part of a larger variety of life-styles that will be accepted in the future and that promise profound societal change.

Heterosexuals are beginning to suffer from an identity crisis. Until now their solution to the existential problem of the meaning of life has been relatively simple. For most, having children has been their participation in the forces of nature, their portion of continuation, their extension beyond themselves. But with a need for population control, we see in heterosexual society manifestations of more sexual pleasure and room for self-definition not dissimilar to homosexual society. This is evidenced by the rising divorce rate and the fact that sex is approved of for pleasure as the widespread use of the pill and other contraceptives shows.

172

Heterosexuals no longer have a built-in responsibility to raise children. If population is to be curbed, family and children will have to be optional and not expected. More heterosexuals will be free to "invent themselves," just as homosexuals now are. Our culture does not train people to be free. There is a fear as well as an excitement in *choosing* a purpose in life. How is "my" life important? To make money? To have more pleasure? To seek a higher level of spirituality? In the past the goal of creating and caring for more lives seemed to answer the question "What are we here for?" Now heterosexuals as well as homosexuals are forced to confront the meaning of their lives beyond having children.

So it would seem that whether or not homosexuals and heterosexuals share a sociosexual philosophy, they are sharing a problem that promises to become universal in our culture: that posed by increased availability of love partners, quite apart from family, monogamy, and reproduction.

In light of their newfound innocence, Lesbians also have been critically re-examining sex roles. Instead of accepting the old explanation that was handed out to them that gay women were trying to be more male and gay men more female, they have identified cross-behavior as an important breakthrough, going beyond the confines of sex-role-categorized behavior. For the Lesbian this means that she is not trying to be like a man but that she is trying to be more of a human being. Because she will not stay in her woman's place, silent on a pedestal, she is capable of releasing more of her promise. In the same way a gay man's behavior can permit more feeling and expression of emotions, making him more human (if less of a man's man).

Most people have shown very little interest in understanding the full range of human behavior. They have divided behavior between males and females, fully accepting the biological-determination theory as people once accepted that the earth was flat.

Concepts of what is appropriately masculine and feminine have been of special concern to Lesbians, whose assertiveness has so often been labeled masculine. Psychologists have long understood that both boys and girls are assertive but that assertiveness is deliberately thwarted in the female. Referring to such conditioning, psychologist Roger Brown asks, "Does the daughter retain a desire to behave as-

173

sertively in new groups where the reinforcement program may be different?"9 We believe the answer is yes, and that Lesbianism provides an opportunity to release natural assertiveness. In this the gay community permits a freedom denied in heterosexual circles, which often causes married women to feel bored or frustrated. Denying to the public the knowledge that women are not inherently passive has inhibited straight women and made Lesbians guilty for their own feelings of assertiveness.

Loving another woman has been labeled by society as unnatural. But is it unnatural? It is accepted that the mother is the first—and natural—sensuous love object for girls as well as boys. Freud believed that in the maturation process, girls switch to the male for love because they want to acquire a penis. Freud believed strongly that our early experiences are powerful determinants to our present behavior. How far back does he take these experiences? To the infant's and toddler's experience of the mother? Many of those who go to clinics and mental hospitals are heterosexual women and homosexual men. Why? Could it be because both changed their love object from female to male, causing a basic insecurity, leaving a void forever? Homosexual women have been cited often by psychologists as seeking less help than homosexual men and showing less interest in change. Could it be because their first natural love object, a woman, is the same sex as their present love partner?

We simply do not know where biology stops and culture starts, but it is clear that culture dramatizes, ritualizes, and extends whatever biological base there may be, creating myths.

It is interesting that some leaders, especially religious leaders who have caused profound or widespread social change, have been androgynous figures. Gandhi is one example: he not only shed the prerogatives of his Brahmin caste, he did women's work such as spinning, for which he was often criticized. Erikson says of him that he undoubtedly saw a kind of sublimated maternalism as a positive identity for a whole man. "He almost prided himself on being half man and half woman" . . . and "so blatantly aspired to be more motherly than women born to the job."10

Jesus also broke rules of the sociosexual hierarchy. He was a care-giving and loving man, a maternal figure. He washed the feet of a prostitute and saw himself as a shepherd of men. He brought men together in close relationships conceptualized as noncompetitive, especially his disciples.

Today students of roles and behavior identify among the most creative people, who also tend to live creatively in their daily lives, men and women who are what is called cross-identified, that is, who do not hesitate to behave in ways that have been assigned to the opposite sex.[11] Most of the leaders who have really cared for their people have had to be both mother and father to their people, combining strength and sensitivity, authority with caring.

Gay men and women are also androgynous. They claim all human qualities as theirs or as within their realm of possibilities. Gay men and women want to relate to any emotion or task, whether it is considered male or female. The activists who admit homosexuality relinquish sociosexual caste and become untouchable, because their ideas as much as their behavior are banned.

It is unfortunate that so many men are uneasy about expressing gentleness or appreciation of the arts, and that so many women feel uncomfortable about expressing an independent identity or a desire for achievement. How many women's tombstones say simply "wife and mother," defining a woman's life only in her relationship to husband and children.

Often freedom of thought and action is suppressed to avoid ridicule or censure. The individual who seeks to act outside his or her role runs the risk of being labeled homosexual. "Faggot" and "dyke" have been used as social-control terms to keep men and women in their roles.

Bob Kohler, gay activist, comments:

> I have always been aware that women were allowed to do things I wanted to do. I came from a tough neighborhood in New York. I was an artist and that was considered sissy. At night I would go out and steal a car because that was considered non-sissy. My life was like a seesaw and I was able that way to stay pretty much on top with the other rotten kids in the neighborhood.

According to Jung, masculinity means knowing what one wants and doing what is necessary to achieve it. Once this lesson has been learned (by a woman), it is so obvious that it can never again be forgotten without tremendous psychic loss. The independence and critical judgment she acquires through this knowledge are positive and are felt as such by the woman. She can never part with them again. The same is true of a man who, with great effort and often at the cost of much suffering, wins that needful "feminine" insight into his own psyche. He will never let go again, because he is thoroughly aware of the importance of what he has won.[12]

One radical Feminist psychotherapist put it together politically when she said, "Women's Liberation and Gay Liberation should join forces and smash sex-role stereotyping forever."

The fact that male homosexuals are popularly thought of as female-identified and female homosexuals are popularly thought of as male-identified should create a common ground for communication between male and female gays. One Lesbian was even heard to say, "If you don't like gay men, you are anti-women, because gay men are criticized for doing what is considered womanly." In their efforts to grow into multifaceted, expressive human beings, gay men and women transcend stereotypes, contrasting sharply with the polarity inherent in the traditional male and female identities of their straight counterparts.

In the straight world, people deny that they play roles, but if you look around, you'll see. In her usual defiant manner, Flo Kennedy once exclaimed, "Here I am a woman attorney being told I can't practice law in slacks by a judge dressed in drag" (robes).

People have erroneously assumed that the choice of a love partner of the same sex means a confusion of basic sexual identity. Gays who grew up in the 1940's and 1950's believed this. The butch and femme roles are carry-overs from this belief, which has been discredited by most people in Gay Liberation.

Spoofing the old life-style, two women from Washington, D.C., wore butch and femme tee-shirts to a dance and then switched at intermission. Their joke confused some older Lesbians, who had learned to take these roles seriously.

Gay bars, other sanctuaries, and the total gay subculture also require re-examination in the new light of innocence. In the past, homosexual males felt they could only go to underground bars, baths, and side streets, while women felt confined to bars. Both went to the same beaches. Identification with other gays seemed to accent the negative, as all brought self-hate with them. Self-hate was more often magnified than mitigated by association with other gays. When isolation became intolerable, the gay subculture was a last resort for sanity, not a free choice.

Psychiatrist Irving Bieber, considered an enemy by male gay activists, nevertheless brings out this valid and alarming point.[14] Writing several years ago about homosexual men, he said:

> Homosexual society is neither healthy nor happy. Life within this society tends to reinforce, fixate and add new disturbing elements to the lives of its members. . . . Although the emotional need of humans to socialize with other humans keeps many homosexuals within groups, some find this life style incompatible with other held values.

With the emerging sense of pride, there has been a profound change in many parts of the gay culture. The word subculture connotes subordination and passivity in relation to the dominant culture. This is not the culture of the gay activists. For the gay activists a term like counterculture seems more appropriate. Gay activists are adversaries of the dominant culture and much of what it stands for. With a new feeling of self-respect and a new aggressive stance toward society, the Gay Liberation counterculture tends to reinforce and add positive elements to the lives of its members. Gay Liberation meetings and dances are held openly at colleges, churches, hotels, and homes, for example, instead of in depressing basements. They are advertised in newspapers. A rash of free schools, community centers, bookstores, counseling centers, and coffee houses, which are not principally sexual meeting places, greatly expand gay life. The fight for basic human rights and a place for gays in a pluralist society leads to a life-style that, for the first time, shows promise of being compatible with other held values.

The positive reinforcement that gays had been unconsciously seeking in the bars is now realized through Gay Liberation. Instead of banding together out of fear, homosexuals are coming together to

177

celebrate their love and struggle for a better, more humanistic society. They see, as the Blacks do, that returning to or staying with one's people brings spiritual renewal and enrichment—and courage for the long fight.

In addition to the importance of the gay counterculture as a source of identity and affirmation, there is an interesting phenomenon connected with the homosexual's separation from the dominant culture. Alienation gives distance and perspective, and these can be turned to advantage.

Homosexual men and women have shown imagination and insight in all areas of creative expression—painting, sculpture, movie-making, fashion, and particularly poetry, drama, and social interpretation.

The Advocate, a nationally circulated homosexual newspaper[15] published an article headed "Gay writers included world's most famous." It pointed out that some years ago a survey was made of the incidence of homosexuality as to profession, and topping the list, by a wide margin, were the writer and the poet. *The Advocate* states that researchers did not delve into the reasons for the finding, but contends that if one searches the lists of literary greats, the statement seems to have substance. In a series of subsequent articles, *The Advocate* then explored the works and lives of Walt Whitman, Hart Crane, W. Somerset Maugham, E. M. Forster, Rupert Brooke, Lytton Strachey, W. H. Auden, Arthur Rimbaud, Marcel Proust, André Gide, and others. No mention, however, was made of Lesbians in this male-oriented paper.

Benjamin DeMott, critic, essayist, novelist, and professor of English at Amherst College, seems to make a similar observation about homosexual males: "It is probable that most readers and theatergoers . . . will accept the claim that the most intense accounts of domestic life and problems in recent years, as well as the few unembarrassedly passionate love poems, have been the work of writers who are not heterosexual."[16] He too refers to men only, discussing the lives and works of Tennessee Williams, Edward Albee, and Allen Ginsberg.

But the association of homosexuality with creativity applies to women also. Cory talks about women of outstanding talent, perhaps genius, who have refused to be bound by conventions that dictate the norms of womanliness, and who were or who may have been Lesbian. He talks about the painter Rosa Bonheur and the writers Amy Lowell, Gertrude Stein, Emily Dickinson, Willa Cather, Charlotte Brontë, and others.[17]

It is natural that homosexuals should turn to social criticism and interpretation. Some will argue that a homosexual man or woman, simply because he or she is not heterosexual, is subjective and special. If we were living in an egalitarian sexual culture, it might end there. But the fact that gays are outsiders, looking at society from a removed position, provides a certain large view not available to the heterosexual who relaxes into the sociosexual system. Although homosexuals would like to participate more in the culture and identify more with the culture, the fact that they cannot creates a forced awareness of social parameters.

Homosexuals know there is torment in living as an outsider, but for some there is also value in it. DeMott refers to this seeming contradiction as the "excruciating value"[18] of more frequent and more intense encounters with society by outsiders.

Life for gay women and men is anything but humdrum and boring. In order to survive, the Lesbian or homosexual man must be perpetually alert. Life does not pass by unnoticed. Homosexuals must perceive subtle and not so subtle barriers ahead. Daily judgments of people and new situations are requirements if one is to make a place for oneself. Seemingly alone in a hostile environment, homosexual men and women live with an extraordinary intensity, burning a tremendous amount of psychic fuel on consciousness. If we look at these homosexuals in a slightly different way than in the past, and say that they are not self-conscious but conscious, we see that their survival information also provides insights into the human experience necessary for creativity.

To play the game of life, homosexual women and men consciously strive to achieve some measure of security; the struggle to belong makes them intensely aware of the dynamics of human behavior. Or, as DeMott puts it: "[Homosexual men] have been *provoked* into dwelling on the relative emptiness and unthinkingness of most men's commitments to the terms of their own lives. . . . They are people forced to face up to the arbitrariness of cultural patterns."[19]

Warning against overpraise, DeMott nonetheless comments:

179

With a few other poets and dramatists [homosexuals] are the only compelling writers of the postwar period who seem to know anything beyond
the level of cliché about human connectedness, whose minds break
through the stereotypes of existential violence or Nietzschean extrava-
gance into recognizable truths and intricacies of contemporary feeling.
They are not purveyors of situation comedy or Bond banalities or *Playboy*
virility or musical marital bliss (*I do! I do!*) or mate-murders.[20]

In Kate Millett, author, sculptor, and film-maker, we see a woman
whose outside perspective and provoked awareness acted as a stimulus
to important works of social criticism. The relationships between
this author's bisexuality, which caused a personal sense of alienation,
and the force and poignancy of *Sexual Politics*, which expresses
the fundamental alienation of *all* women, seems clear. As expressed
in *The Woman-Identified Woman:* "The Lesbian is the rage of all
women condensed to the point of explosion."

It is important to recognize that *Sexual Politics* achieved enormous
success (on the best-seller list) as a book expressing a universal truth
about all women. Then, when the author's bisexuality became known,
people typically assumed that Ms. Millett's insights were flawed. This
is documented by the fact that "sales virtually stopped." This series
of events indicates the public first proved what it refuses to believe:
that the human experience transcends sexual preference. If anything,
a different sexual orientation provides a reason for more intense
analysis of the nature of all human relationships, more sensitivity to
contradictions and complexities.

Lesbians and male homosexuals striving to define their identity
and life-style are much like the Blacks and other minorities who have
found that throughout history they have allowed themselves to be
defined by others. However, the fact that homosexuals are not a race,
color, or creed makes it difficult to define as well as to organize them.
The invisibility, the ease of concealment, makes it too easy on all social
and economic levels for them to hide their essential selves and adopt
a camouflage that perpetuates their own oppression.

The homosexual has no organized culture, no roots, no homeland
(although attempts were made to form a gay community in Alpine
County outside Los Angeles). The homosexual is, in a way, a kind
of wanderer, a person without a country, unacceptable, with no place

to go. Thus it is that some gays feel a closer bond to other gays than to anyone else regardless of race, color, creed, age, social status, or familial ties. They have little acceptance anywhere except in each other's lives.

Much has been learned about pride from the experience of blacks, who have demonstrated the importance of image reversal. In the 1950's winners of "natural standards" beauty contests had to show some signs of "racial awareness" and wear their hair in Afros. Black skin, full lips, and kinky hair became the standards for beauty, precisely at a time when women who possessed these characteristics were widely considered ugly. "Naturally" shows in Harlem in the early 1960's, which were designed to reclaim the values and heritage of the Blacks, were reportedly attended by those emerging as Black activists. The whole campaign toward "Black Pride" and "Black is Beautiful" was largely responsible for the increased value of black-skinned Negroes in contrast to the long-valued light-skinned Negroes who could "pass for white."

The awakening of Black pride provided a lesson to gays who had many of the same problems as Blacks: a poor self-image and a poor public image in an endless feedback loop. The concept of "Gay Pride" and "Gay is Good" closely parallels the Black efforts for a more positive identity. Though many homosexuals can "pass for straight," the GLF slogan "Be as gay as possible" has tried to counteract the impulse to hide. The gradual emergence of a "gay consciousness or awareness" on the part of gays increased the respect for gays who look gay. Some gay activists, who at one time might have felt embarrassed by association with dykes or queens, now value these individuals.

The new gay counterculture openly proclaims itself and its values, even arguing the virtues of freedom and autonomy against those of the heterosexual culture, that is, constraint and continuity.

Men and women in the twenty-year-old homophile organizations, which were essentially focused on civil rights and social services, were the first homosexuals to band together. Armed with facts and reasons, the homophile men and women donned the uniforms of the Establishment and went off to talk with, to petition, institutions and authorities. For many years progress seemed near zero on the legal, legislative, and regulatory issues. In dress, mannerisms, and life-style, its members seemed to want to say to heterosexuals, "We are like you."

The Gay Liberation Front is rebellious. Beaded, blue-jeaned, and booted, seething with ideas and energy, females and males are confronting society on basic humanistic issues in person or via the media in their own way. It is completely a product of its time. The Gay Activists Alliance shows promise of molding the two movements into one, combining work on civil rights issues with pride and activism.

However, neither the homophile movement nor Gay Liberation has mobilized widespread gay support. Certainly Gay Liberation is the more successful of the two, moving the numbers of those active in the homosexual cause from hundreds to thousands. But hundreds of thousands or tens of hundreds of thousands potentially could become supporters out of a population of millions.

Gays are integrated at every level of society. This is not an asset in reference to mobilization. In fact, according to political journalist Joe Casey, the acceptance available to hiding homosexuals is the movement's biggest *problem*. Blacks passing for white were never given much thought by the Black movement as potential recruits. They were a tiny minority. Gays passing for straight are the rule. Gays standing out front are the exception. What this means in political terms is that the gay movement, which has started out by mimicking the tactics used successfully by the Black movement, must analyze its differences and devise tactics that reflect the facts of life for the gay community, or the movement will eventually wither from its inability to make use of more than a small part of its potential forces.

In terms of organizing gay voters compared with organizing Black voters, Casey points out that Blacks are located in specific geographical areas of the city, and thus their potential wishes can be clearly charted by their votes for local candidates, for whom they are a majority of the electorate. Also, the candidates have to be responsive on a number of issues. But there are few elective posts for which gays, spread out and integrated into the society, constitute a majority, let alone all of the electorate.

Casey emphasizes that Blacks' economic problems, social problems, and everyday neighborhood problems are closely intertwined. Gays, however, are for and against welfare, urban renewal, state medical programs; they are Republican and Democrat, liberal and conservative. The politician who promises to end police harassment of bars and also wants to see space exploration curtailed or has a pet plan for halting inflation may or may not get the gay vote. Homosexual women and men lack sufficient homogeneity for gay tacticians to employ all the tactics of the Black movement.

At this time only a small percentage of gays have a strong positive attitude about being gay. Even fewer feel that their gayness is a primary factor in their lives. Most consider their sexual preference as a side issue, perhaps not an issue at all. Those who see it as a core issue realize that if most gays were visible, like most Blacks, they would lose the privileges gained by hiding. Then overt pressures would be so great gays would burst with anger and make their demands felt. Today only a few gays turn their realization of innocence into action. These few may or may not incur great losses, but they are free of the daily fear of exposure, the atmosphere of threat that many homosexuals live with.

For a Lesbian, who lives outside the culture, even the simple act of being oneself is often a powerful force. The taboo on homosexuality is still so strong that an example of pride on the part of a single gay woman can spread like wildfire from person to person, shocking both straight and gay people along the way. Those inextricably linked to the person by family, profession, or propinquity find themselves forced to reconsider their position on the subject. Involved against their will, relatives and friends may share their dilemma with others. Stories gain momentum and travel to friends of friends, relatives of relatives, and colleagues of colleagues—and to legislators—that a homosexual with pride exists.

8   CURING SOCIETY

We are used to enjoying the benefits of civilization and its offspring technology, and can broadly summarize them with relative ease. There is not only longer life, made possible by adequate food, shelter, medical care, and generally safer conditions; there is a fuller mental life and more goods produced to make life physically less strenuous. Most of us reason that these benefits are possible because of the underlying social order that prevents chaos.

Only recently have we begun to ask: What have we traded for these benefits? Freud theorized in *Civilization and Its Discontents* that for civilization, we traded full sexual and instinctual expression. He saw no way out of the bargain. He felt the trade was necessary, that to end repression was to end civilization. Others since Freud have worried that one result is that the possibility of natural love is already forfeited[1] and that consequently people must make the best of an unhappy fate.[2]

For example, religion, the law, and psychiatry have equated sex control with what is "good" and "right," and "healthy." So most people blame themselves when they are unable to meet societal demands for sex control or sex denial. Rather than question their environment, most people question their feelings, and in trying to solve their conflicts can become estranged from parts of themselves. The burden to fit into society is on the individual.

Jung writes feelingly of the individual's sense of powerlessness in modern society, and of the increasing control of society over the individual. Both, taken together, make it hard for individuals to discover and live their own life-styles, to sense the validity of their needs, and to be effective if they do undertake such a search.

It is small wonder that the individual judgement grows increasingly uncertain of itself and that responsibility is collectivized as much as possible, i.e., is shuffled off by the individual and delegated to a corporate body. In this way the individual becomes more and more a function of society. . . . In actual fact, society is nothing more than an abstract idea like the State. . . . The State in particular is turned into a quasi-animate personality from whom everything is expected. In reality it is only a camouflage for those who know how to manipulate it.[3]

Being gay is *ipso facto* a challenge of sex-control/sex-denial. But budding individual attempts at self-expression or self-assertion are usually crushed: Being naively, openly, gay is punished with ridicule, public condemnation and loss of job. As a result homosexuals have become a phantom population. Authorities usually suggest that the only way out of their pathetic state is personal cures. Robert Lindner, one of the first to write about antisexual social pressures as a reason for homosexuality, believed homosexuality was founded in rebellion against sex repression, and that the homosexual, because he cannot live happily and well in a hostile environment, fights a losing battle.[4] He reasoned that the best that could be done was to offer gay people psychotherapeutic intervention that would lead them to convert to heterosexuality.

Various psychiatrists and therapists specialize in such attempts at conversion. Very few claim any success, some of these behaviorists using electric shock where gentler methods of persuasion have failed. It is known that repressed feelings seek new outlets, and it must be asked whether individuals may not be plunged into violence, neurosis, drunkenness, or prolonged depression if they submit to societal coercion or punishment to change their sexuality?

Others point to another kind, or level, of solution. Neurosis, as defined by Jung, demonstrates the unsuccessful effort of the individual to solve personally what is essentially a universal problem.[4] Herbert Marcuse understood the problem when he said, "The cure of the personal disorder depends on the cure of the general disorder."[5]

Gay activists know that the only cure is rebellion, that their grievances are deeply rooted in social, economic, and political systems rather than in themselves.

Society, by some sleight of hand, has shifted the blame for its atrocities against homosexuals to homosexuals themselves. Hiding its own intolerance of difference, society, like a magician, makes those who try to live differently appear ridiculous, even insane. To create its own truth, society has built in misery, guilt, neurosis for homosexuals who attempt to exercise liberty outside certain authorized boundaries. Clearly, it is a clever trick when victims of injustice are made to look guilty.

As long as everyone believes what society has taught—that homosexuality is a private and personal problem—society is home free; it does not have to deal with the problem. But now that the issue begins to go public through national media, the homosexual's problems are being recognized as *sociological* problems.

A few liberal psychiatrists have supported gays in the sense of "giving permission" for their homosexuality. But support of the individual never completely solves the problem. Patients merely feel better about knocking their heads against the cultural wall. Without new attitudes in society and the opening of real opportunities, the cultivation of confidence and understanding in the individual does little in the end except increase frustration. When a Lesbian's fears are soothed while the real social barriers remain, she is in an unreal situation—like a fantasy.

Very seldom are gays given help in understanding that their unhappiness has its roots in society's hostility and that it indicates an awareness of real obstacles in *life*. Any "cure" logically and justly should be directed at society. There is no personal solution.

Gay Liberation began as an instinctive reaction against oppressive economic and social conditions. The street people at the Stonewall probably had not read Reich and Marcuse. They only knew that they hurt.

It is easy to see why a society attempting to survive and grow in numbers might place limits on homosexuality—or at least encourage simultaneous heterosexuality for reproduction. It is harder to understand the endurance of this taboo today, with a dangerously large population.

The continued insistence that a woman's place is in the home to care for one man and their children, and the homosexual's place is in the closet, perpetuates a system that no longer seems to require such restrictions. Those who try to justify their prejudice by saying "What would happen if all women were Lesbians; we would have no children," not only show a lack of understanding about Lesbians—since Lesbianism and child-bearing are not mutually exclusive—but also imply that Lesbianism is attractive enough to win over all women. This is flattering to Lesbians, but not very probable. Furthermore, it is a curious argument for *opponents* of Lesbianism.

Wilhelm Reich and Herbert Marcuse have written about the sexual dilemmas of modern civilization and proposed solutions combining aspects of Freudian theory and Marxian economic analysis.

While Freud maintained that culture owed its existence to instinctual repression and renunciation,[6] Reich departed from Freud when he said that sexual suppression forms the mass-psychological base only for a certain kind of culture—a patriarchal authoritarian culture such as ours.[7] Reich's analysis introduces the theoretical insight that women and gays have known instinctively: that civilization in its present form was designed for heterosexual men, and that its structure guarantees their authority within it. Thus, to change society by ending sexual suppression does not mean the end of civilization, but rather the end of civilization as we know it. If Reich is correct, a gradual release from sexual suppression means the emergence of a nonpatriarchal, nonauthoritarian society. However, Reich defined natural, unrepressed sexuality as heterosexuality—the end of sexual repression was seen as more and better orgasms in heterosexual couplings.

It was Herbert Marcuse who saw the critical function of homosexuals in ending repression. Simplified, his key argument is that much of repression today is "surplus repression" but that the very achievements of repressive civilization—technology and productivity—create conditions where the abolition of repression becomes possible. In theory then, it has been pointed out, modern civilization might be relieved of its repressive character without falling back into barbarism and chaos.[8]

Unlike Reich, Marcuse sees homosexuals as having an important place in history in helping to free sexuality, since he feels gay people have a more natural, totally erogenous sexuality.

Marcuse traces a historical connection between the genital tyranny of today and the "performance principle": "Libido became concentrated in one part of the body, namely the genitals, in order to leave the rest of the body free to use as an instrument of labor."[9] His conclusion is that only the resexualized, polymorphous perverse (the pregenital erogenic) body, resists transformation into an instrument of labor, and resists subjugation by the "performance principle."[10]

Marcuse finds that Western civilization has gone too far in suppressing eros—that is, love, the life instinct—with deadening and destructive results: when love is suppressed the forces of death occupy the cultural space made available. The death instinct can be defeated by the reintroduction of eros. The goal, Marcuse concluded, is freeing eros, a partial return to the "pleasure principle," via a non-repressive society, oriented around the life, not the death, principle.

Marcuse, unlike Reich, does not mean just intercourse when he talks of love. He refers to a whole way of life. A freed eros could function on a higher and broader plane than ever before envisioned, Marcuse felt. He describes an unbroken progression of love from the physical love of one person to the psychic love/respect/regard for many.

According to Marcuse, homosexuality needs to be reevaluated in an entirely different light. Martin Robinson, author of *The Freudian Left*, points out that Marcuse does not defend homosexuality in the sentimental and patronizing manner of liberal ideology. Instead, Marcuse emphasized the critical function of the so-called perversions: "The perversions . . . express rebellion against the subjugation of sexuality under the order of procreation and against the institutions which guarantee this order." Sexual deviance, then, represents a protest against genital tyranny. In a sense, Robinson concludes, the social function of the homosexual is analogous to that of the critical philosopher.[11]

> The perversions seem to give a *promise de bonheur* greater than that of normal sexuality . . . to reject the entire enslavement of the pleasure ego by the reality ego. Claiming instinctual freedom in a world of repression, they are often characterized by a strong rejection of that feeling of guilt which accompanies sexual repression. . . . In a repressive order which forces the equation between normal, socially useful, and good, the manifestations of pleasure for its own sake must appear as *fleurs de mal*. Against a society which employs sexuality as means for useful end, the perversions uphold sexuality as an end in itself; they thus place themselves outside the performance principle and challenge its very foundation. . . . They are a symbol of what had to be suppressed so that sup-

pression could prevail and organize the ever more efficient domination of man and nature.[12]

On the other hand, Reich's belief that homosexuality would be reduced by "establishing all necessary prerequisites for natural love life"[13] must be confronted. He says that homosexuality is solely the result of sexual repression and that the end of repression would bring an end to homosexuality. If Reich is correct, then homosexuals have a stake in repression: they would exist under sexual repression and disappear with sexual liberation. In fact, some officials worry that homosexuality is increasing with sexual liberation.

Reich's idea about homosexuality—a view shared by others—is that it is caused somehow when heterosexual instinct or expression is thwarted. He cites the army and the prisons.

Even though Reich is considered one of the first to recognize the influence of social factors on psychosexual development, he does not persist in his analysis when he treats homosexuality: he assumes heterosexuality is natural and homosexuality is unnatural. Heterosexuality—far from seeming effortless or natural—seems to be taught, reinforced, and rewarded from earliest childhood. Homosexual tendencies even in young children are punished.

Some psychologists have noticed this as well. "Various means of instruction are employed by the older members of society to get the younger members to perform just those responses which are most likely to be rewarded."[14]

Psychologists believe that what is true of the pigeons in their laboratories is also true of people: behavior that is rewarded is more likely to occur; behavior that is punished is less likely to occur.

It is plausible to assume that the reason strong social controls rewarding heterosexuality and punishing homosexuality exist is exactly that homosexuality is equally natural, and is therefore a real danger to a heterosexual social system.

A girl then who could have developed feelings of love for both men and women learns through reward-and-punishment manipulation that only a male is an appropriate love partner. Left on her own, she might have remained bisexual, or developed a preference on her own.

What prevents this natural process of discovery is several levels of social controls, which condition her rather than let her explore.

The most obvious level of controls are those that alert or alarm by speaking directly to the drive for self-preservation. These are the sanctions against homosexuals in employment and housing. Homosexuals essentially have no civil rights. They can live in great anxiety, fearing for their survival.

Economic security is an important incentive to be heterosexual, perhaps especially for women who may have bypassed educational or training opportunities because of expectations of a heterosexual marriage they held when younger. Later, they find themselves trapped. One woman, when she discovered she was gay, thought to get a divorce, only to find that she would be hard put to provide for herself, much less her three children.

The amazement straight people feel when they hear of a gay marriage seems to have something to do with reward-and-punishment. In a society built around the patriarchal nuclear family, marriage means obedience to its sociosexual rules and is highly rewarded: the blessings of God, tax breaks, inheritance benefits. Heterosexuals find it amusing or horrifying that homosexuals might expect the rewards without the obedience.

But most controls are not so obvious. Love and/or a sense of duty toward parents can be used manipulatively. Parents can punish simply by withholding love. Punishment does not have to be a negative act, it can be the absence of a positive act. The second can be as strong a control as the first. Indeed punishment as the absence of reward is common. Titles, promotions, honors, opportunities, or status can simply be withheld where homosexuality is concerned. In these conditions it could be said that homosexuality is not so much discouraged as heterosexuality is encouraged. In this way society does not look like a bully. Society has merely created conditions that make it more pleasant for a woman if she chooses its way.

Parents fall into society's grip and use their influence to convince a young woman to conform to society's models. They say they want the best for their daughter, and they usually believe they are sincere. But those who withhold their love until their daughter obeys may be deceiving themselves about their intentions. If they really want to give their love as a gift, they would not try to bargain with their daughter for her identity. To ask for such an unfair deal is to commit psychological violence on her; it is as if they were asking their daughter to find happiness by severing a limb. Parents who would inflict such unnecessary pain on their offspring must cherish their own fears more than their own child's happiness.

Attempts to squash their daughter's feelings seem to indicate much more concern about guilt for not bringing their daughter up properly (with enough controls). Society seems to have them under complete control. Unaware that their solidarity is really with the community and not with their daughter's interests, such parents are often blind to the fact that their love, when used to manipulate, can be destructive. They would be most baffled if their daughter committed suicide to avoid disgracing them.

Thus, what parents really mean when they say "It's because we love you" is "If you remain heterosexual, we will continue to love you," and what they really mean when they say "It's for your own good" is "You will be rewarded," and what they really mean when they ask "But haven't we been good parents?" is "You owe it to us!"

We must then consider that what is often called a "bad home situation" is one which permits the daughter freedom in self-determination, and a "good home situation" is one with effective psychological controls.

Because Lesbians are not arrested or beaten or murdered that often, and because of the subtle nature of some of the methods of control, liberal individuals can plead innocent to causing any harm to Lesbians or to being aware that substantial problems exist. But if liberals unthinkingly subscribe to conventional ideas or beliefs without making a plea for the existence of several life-styles, they too are guilty of consciousness-killing; that is, they endorse by silence the conditioning by fear that robs people of choice.

What in society persuades people of the Lesbian's presumed inferiority?

Basically, the Lesbian is seen as a victim, and a victim is always suspected of compliance in the process of victimization. There is something repulsive about a victim, some odor of weakness. Lesbians are said to be victims of bad homes, of early, traumatic sexual experiences, even of chemical or hormonal imbalances. A victim does not exercise free will, cannot make choices, or can only make limited choices. A victim is helpless before some greater force. However, Lesbians often perceive themselves as rebels who pay a price for some measure of psychological freedom. They feel that at some time they made a choice as to how they would lead their lives, and that they are mature, healthy, competent beings, members, however, of a minority group, and thus liable to legal and other harassments. Needless to say, the majority does not agree, and offer as evidence widely-known legal, moral, and mental health sanctions.

Laws, which are primarily an expression or effect of commonly held values, are not nearly such convincing evidence of the Lesbian's "failures" as are certain social traps into which even parents play. Effective control over attitudes toward Lesbianism comes more from the manipulation of values or standards to which we all subscribe, but which only certain groups can fully attain: mental health, rationality, morality, and maturity.

These characteristics, thought to be ascribed on the basis of personal achievement, are more often taught as part of a base of conformity. Authority, by seemingly innocent means, subtly directs the interpretation of commonly held values to its own ends. It is through such psychological design, more than anything else, that the superior qualities of those in authority (whites, heterosexuals, and males) and the inferior, or even odious, qualities of the powerless (Blacks, homosexuals, and females) are established. The game is psychological politics and it dazzles and intimidates Lesbians and straight women.

Lesbians and others who cannot or will not meet the norm, are permanently denied the standards of validation necessary for socioeconomic status in this culture. But there are at least two possible interpretations for each standard: one, always the most popular (and destructive to the Lesbian), not so mysteriously fits society's goals; the other, which puts more value on the individual, is a source of renewal to Lesbians, because it is supportive of their lives as healthy, rational, moral and mature beings.

Society calls Lesbianism sick. This raises two questions: what is mental sickness? And what is mental health? Mental illness, as argued by Thomas Szasz, is a mythical construct that serves covert social purposes. This psychiatrist has shown clearly in *The Manufacture of Madness* how society has methodically dismissed the homosexual —especially the Lesbian—as subhuman. For one thing, he says, the concept of mental illness provides "reasons" and "explanations" for individual behavior that is different, disturbing, and incomprehensible; for another, it furnishes an acceptable, apparently humane mode of controlling deviant behavior; for a concept that defines offenders as "ill" justifies locking them up until they are "well."[15]

Psychology has, to a great degree, become a tool of authority, convincing the governed that what is "normal"—what the majority does out of obedience to social conditioning—is also "natural." Those who are not obedient are "ill." A condition of "sickness" is created where none exists.

Prejudiced people can hide behind the quantitative definition when they say "deviant," but the fact that the word is used for unpopular individualistic behavior, like Lesbianism, and not for certain popular individualistic traits or behavior such as brilliance or talent, is not explained. "Deviance" almost always connotes inferiority. It is not commonly understood that Lesbians are social deviants only because the majority of women are heterosexual, much as Republicans could be called "social deviants" because the majority are Democrats.

The unpopular, the nonconforming, the socially unapproved, is called deviant or mentally ill. We need not quibble over words. "Nonconformity and mental illness have become synonymous."[16]

This interpretation is as good as official. The Public Health Service, when asked to give its opinion to the House of Representatives, included within its classification of psychopathic personalities "persons ill primarily in terms of society and the prevailing culture."[17] Szasz submits this statement as an admission that social nonconformity is considered an illness.[18]

The consequences for the Lesbian can be severe. Mental illness, when too threatening, justifies institutional commitment, and, because commitment is almost never voluntary, the Lesbian is powerless to defend her choice. She is, by definition, ill. In a mental institution, Goffman assures us,[19] she will be stripped of all rights, liberties, and satisfactions, and undergo a severe resocialization process in which the deviant is trained to obey simple commands to regain even a token of former status. The process would seem to require that she be cured of her "illness" (disobedience) before she can be released, lest she "harm" (by advocating independence) other "healthy" (obedient) people.

We must agree with Szasz that "our mental health practices represent a massive re-embracing of this collective and sadistic principle of social control. . . . Institutional psychiatry is, as it were, designed to protect and uplift the group (the family, the State), by persecuting the individual (as insane or ill)."[20]

Laing, too, recognizes that psychiatry can be a brainwashing technique to induce adjusted behavior by various forms of conditioning. He emphasizes that our "normal," "adjusted" state is too often the abdication of ecstasy, the betrayal of our true potentialities.[21]

A number of categories of concepts now emerge that put the Lesbian who believes in her life-style in a more positive framework.

Current definitions of mental health lean away from quantitative notions and toward the individual. Maria Johoda outlines several approaches that suggest that indicators of positive mental health should be taught in the attitudes of an individual towards herself.[22] Another professional group designates the individual's style and degree of growth, development, and self-actualization as expressions of mental health, while a third singles out autonomy or independence from social influences as most revealing of the state of mental health. (Dr. Marvin Frankel, a professor of psychopathology, in a more value-free definition, describes a person as being mentally well to the extent that [she] endorses her experience and/or actions.")[23]

Today, many accepted definitions free Lesbians from the social trap set around quantitative deviance and would seem to recognize her self-actualization as a sign of good mental health.

What about rationality? In his writing, K. Mannheim talks about the "social disproportion" in the distribution of rational capacities in society, and indicates that the uneven distribution is no accident, but depends on the problems set by the existing social order.[24]

Those close to the Lesbian who consider her "out of her mind" may consider Lesbianism a problem of ignorance rather than sickness and try to appeal to her reason. Since men have historically withheld

195

any recognition of women's reasoning powers, women are especially vulnerable to this approach, which they are supposed to accept as flattery. It works diabolically.

If we see that society sets out to reward heterosexuals and punish homosexuals and then consider that one definition of rationality is "roughly speaking, behavior designed to produce the most rewards and the least punishments,"[25] the hazard in accepting rationality is exposed. By appealing to the Lesbian's reason, the friend or relative is merely trying to persuade the Lesbian to heed controls. As Skinner notes, "Through a masterful piece of misinterpretation, the illusion is fostered that these procedures do not involve the control of behavior; at most they are ways of getting someone to change [her] mind."[26]

Mannheim calls rationality based on obedience "functional rationality," that which deprives the individual of thought, insight, and responsibility (abdicating them to authority). This seems to be the basis for what is popularly called "rationality." Another state of being, also discussed by Mannheim, involves "substantial rationality," which means self-observation rather than obedience. It is succinctly defined in terms which also describe the Lesbian's strongest characteristic— independent judgment.

The Lesbian, then, who has chosen independence, feels in control of her life. Those who do not make a choice and seem to follow tradition seem to be "out of control," relinquishing control to institutions or authority figures of the patriarchal society. With such a technique, which conditions women to eagerly seek submission and Lesbians to feel inferior instead of superior because they resist submission, male authority has little need for physical force.

In fact, the Lesbian has no reason to shrink from a rational argument about her life. Women's Liberation has provided her with clearer insights into her decisions. From her point of view she has many rewards and avoids many punishments. If the Lesbian says, "I wish to develop my own identity. I wish to choose my own life and control my own resources. I want a peer relationship, not *a priori* submissive to a partner for whom society sanctions a dominant role," she sees that a traditional marriage presents almost the opposite of this, a kind of confinement and submissiveness she cannot endure. From this point of view, which society does not encourage, a Lesbian is rational.

Morality, too, though seemingly personal, is political. Again, it is not surprising that morality is usually attributed more to whites, heterosexuals, and men, and withheld from Blacks, homosexuals, and women. It is "common knowledge" that Blacks are irresponsible, homosexuals promiscuous, and Freud, whose theories frequently are used to support tradition, attributed morality or conscience more to males than females.

Kohlberg called the kind of morality based on conformity and obedience "conventional morality," which determines most people's values. But he also outlined another kind of morality, considered a more advanced stage of development, called "principled morality," in which the individual transcends public opinion and makes independent criteria for morality. From this point of view the Lesbian is no longer immoral or amoral. Through this added, intellectual dimension to morality, any Lesbian who evaluates her own experiences and contructs her own set of principles to live by is moral.

Maturity is something every human being should be able to acquire. But why is it that society never quite considers Blacks, homosexuals, and women fully mature beings? Maturity for the male is defined in terms of independence, we see, but maturity for the female is defined in terms of dependence on a male. (Independence for her is considered not mature, but sick, as in Lesbianism.) The adaptation to sex roles is often a criterion for maturity.

Certain authorities on social systems have made clear that the maintenance of a social system is integrally bound to appropriate role performance. The role is recognized as "the smallest unit in the social system; the operation of the social system ultimately and most directly, depends on the proper performance of roles."[27]

Lesbianism, particularly, threatens the marriage system. Marriage depends not only on a woman's aspiring to the role of wife and mother, but on her viewing it as the greatest accomplishment of her life. The unmarried woman has traditionally been considered a failure, an "old maid." On the other hand, it is assumed that men select bachelorhood. The idea that Lesbians would *voluntarily* remain outside the marriage system is clearly threatening to the present system, which relies on women making marriage a goal.

The form of sexual expression practiced by Lesbians directly undermines the sex roles which the patriarchal, authoritarian system requires for survival. Lesbians, by certain standard psychological definitions, are said to be only in a state of "arrested development"; that is to say, they are immature. A woman can only achieve the label of maturity, then, when she serves the needs of the system and submits to a male. But if we take the male definitions of maturity—independence and responsibility for one's own actions—we see again that the Lesbian possesses the attribute of maturity.

Gay people, like all minority groups, handle their hurt and anger about name-calling through turning the tables occasionally, sometimes with humor.

In January, 1972, the Los Angeles *Advocate*, the respected nationally distributed gay newspaper, devoted an entire page, including an editorial, to serious questions about the majority culture. The paper asked, "Is *Heterosexuality* an illness?" Most of the page was taken up with abstracts of items—35 of them—found in the pages of the Los Angeles *Times* in the space of five weeks. Here are three of them, and not necessarily the worst.

> CINCINNATI, Jan. 5—Mrs. Eulalia Fuchs, 44, pleaded guilty to manslaughter in the fatal shooting of her husband, Sept. 19, during an argument over whether to watch football on television or listen to music.

> WASHINGTON, Jan. 6—A 57-year-old woman teacher was shot to death in front of her fifth-grade class after an argument with her estranged husband.

> GARDEN GROVE, Calif., Dec. 28—A Stanton man was burned to death early Monday as he was apparently attempting to set fire to the home of his ex-wife and her (new) husband—his brother—police reported.

The accompanying editorial, "Don't jail heteros; they need help!" read:

> The problem of the violence-prone heterosexual community is alarming to most homosexuals. Some dismiss the problem as an abnormality deeply rooted in heterosexual history; others advocate extreme oppression that has never worked in the past.
>
> One gay extremist, for example, regards all heterosexuals as being sick and will have nothing to do with them. He would seize on any

pretext he could to put them in jail. He attempted to justify his rigid attitude in a recent interview:

"Now someone who's unfortunate enough to be heterosexual and doesn't get into any trouble . . . has nothing to worry about. . . . But the vicious, violent, aggressive, recruiting-type heterosexual is a problem. . . ."

We share this individual's concern, but we think that his solution is no solution at all. Jails have been filled with heterosexuals since jails were invented, and heterosexual violence has increased steadily to frightening proportions.

So there is overwhelming evidence of a tragic defect in the heterosexual personality. Rather than jail them, however, we think it would be far more valuable to confine heterosexuals to hospitals at some stage in their early development so that those who are most afflicted with the virus of violence can be isolated and treated. Those who are no danger to themselves and others can be released to procreate the nonviolent human beings of the future, while the experts study those who are sick in a serious, all-out attempt to develop a cure.

Only when we find such a cure for this heterosexual madness will we achieve that long-sought goal: peace on earth.—DM

More often, though, expressions of negative feeling come from angry heterosexuals. Could it be because they have in some half-felt way sensed that they never chose their own lives and therefore feel anger toward Lesbians who have refused to be completely hooked into the system? O. H. Mowrer has very effectively warned us that conditioned fear is for human beings a major part of the socialization process,[28] and Roger Brown, elaborating on this, suggests the possibility that conformity to every sort of norm is maintained by the fear that follows any kind of deviance.[29]

If socialization is indeed a process of intimidation, as the above suggests, Lesbian activists, who will no longer be intimidated, have a right to be proud, for they are exposing, at great risk, the hypocrisy of a system that talks of freedom while it exercises controls.

In the context of intimidation, it is plausible that some housewives —those who did not really choose their lot—might be particularly uptight about Lesbians. The liberation message sensitizes them to their unexamined allegiance to conventional values and makes them aware of other options, perhaps too late. When Lesbians insist on happiness on their own terms, regardless of the opinions of others, those women who have, without question, succumbed to custom and are now bound to it by contract, might readily accept and promote anti-Lesbian prejudice to support their own shaky rationalizations. They cannot afford to believe their lives were not their choices but were imposed on them for social ends to their loss. Disgust for Lesbians makes them feel better about their role and, in terms of society's objectives, ensures the continuation of that role.

It does appear that pure heterosexuality in many cases is culturally engineered, but this is far from always being the case. The Lesbian's choice is not the only valid one; insistence on this point would be as fallacious as the contrary view. Freedom, liberation, consists of the awareness of alternatives—and the opportunity to act on them. Women should be able to decide without coercion whether or not they want marriage and children, affairs with men, or relationships with women. For this freedom to occur, we would have to teach that Lesbianism is a valid alternative life-style, in schools, and on television. Until this is done, society is still not giving women an alternative. Women will still not be in a position to shape their own destiny.

If Lesbians are viewed as a valued group of social innovators experimenting with developing a culturally accepted life-style, instead of as a control group functioning as social pariahs to ensure obedience through fear, then women would be truly liberated.

Surely any potential influence of Lesbianism is terrifying to those who stick blindly to tradition; for it is not only a sexual preference but a political stance against male domination. The message of choice would surely unchain the wishes of those women who do not really want to relate to men—or to men alone—but are held in check by ignorance and fear. Authorities have a motive for keeping Lesbianism a "private issue." They do not want large numbers of women to know the good aspects of this alternative. What would happen to the "healthy" patriarchal authoritarian system based on women's submission to men?

Some Lesbians have looked to other systems for their freedom. Given the prominence of Marxist theorists in the area of sex and society, we have to ask if communism or socialism have the answers. From what we know, women have been no better off, and, in some cases, homosexuals are worse off, under these systems of government. What the laws made just after the Russian Revolution promised for women and homosexuals was not to happen. Legislation, or any other formal change, according to Reich's analysis, has social significance only if the psychic structure of the people also changes.[30] Only in this way, he says, can an ideology or program become a revolutionary power of historical dimensions: if it achieves a deep-reaching alteration in the emotions and instinctual life of the people. The attitudes of the people were not changed; the laws, Reich points out, only indicated the revolutionary spirit of the early leaders.[31] In the end, gays were still persecuted and women were still dependent.

Hopes ran high among homosexuals in Cuba in 1959 with the triumph of the socialist revolution, which promised the end of traditional injustices. Gay bars were packed with people celebrating what they thought would be a new freedom. Within a few weeks the gay bars were closed. According to *Ecstasy,* the Gay Revolutionary Party publication in the United States, there were experiments in isolating gays that approached prison conditions.[32]

The First National Congress on Education and Culture held in Havana in May, 1971, and endorsed by Fidel Castro himself, included a strong antihomosexual statement. As published in the English edition of *Granma,* the official newspaper of Cuba, and reported in *Ecstasy:* "The social pathological character of homosexual deviations was recognized. It was resolved that all manifestations of homosexual deviation are to be firmly rejected and prevented from spreading."

Homosexuals living in Cuba wrote to *Ecstasy* and explained their situation:

> If, in a society of consumers—capitalists, and oligarchical—like the one you are living in, the life of a homosexual is discriminated against and suffers limitations, in our society—entitled Marxist, revolutionary—it is much more so . . . they have kept farms of prisoners who are exclusively homosexual. On the street we suffer persecution, aggression and constant abuse by authorities demanding I.D. cards, arresting us because of clothing, hairstyles or simply group meetings, which are rights guaranteed by the Declaration of Human Rights.

Life magazine reports a spokesman for Communist China—a land of 800 million—as saying, "We have no homosexuals."

No known political system or ideology accepts gays for long. Homosexuals can be accepted briefly during a period of upheaval. However, persecution is always resumed after a short time. In Germany, they were put in the concentration camps; in Russia, purged and persecuted; in Cuba, imprisoned. Homosexuality *per se* has become the grounds for being against the state as it once meant being against the church.

Gay people in the United States have realized that no existing political or social system fully includes them, neither capitalism nor socialism; so they have concentrated on trying to change the present monolithic structure of values, which promotes only one life-style, into a more accepting pluralism. They are trying to make a primarily social revolution and see what political adaptations follow from it.

Can Lesbians be free? Women's Liberation is an important factor. Here, efforts are being made by women to free women, and gay women are increasingly accepted and valued. By helping to eradicate masculine and feminine stereotypes, Women's Liberation is helping to free both male and female homosexuals and fundamentally change those concepts that make domination possible.

The sex-based movements in the U.S. constitute an uncontrolled revolution, happening internally, without one accepted ideology. This is exactly the opposite of the official Russian sexual revolution, which was passed down by decree from the top—and ultimately failed. Curiously, many of the social goals *declared* by the Russian authorities are the same as the goals being *demanded* in America today.

In America, then, with the revolution coming from spontaneous rebellion against social, economic, and psychic conditions, the environment for widespread social change is more promising.

The democratic system works on the assumption that the individuals who contribute their part to the whole benefit from the whole. But the Lesbian's situation is quite the contrary. The Lesbian participates in economic, political and social institutions that do not support, enhance, or protect her life in the same ways that they do for heterosexuals.

"I don't know why I vote any more. Why should I support a system that is destroying me? It just doesn't make sense."

There is potential, however, in a system at least designed to respond to new values. New values are appearing and the promise of the democratic system is that changes will occur when these new values are generally recognized. Thus, hope for the homosexual lies not in giving up, but in carefully thought-out protest against the idea of proscribing one life-style. Other groups rebelling against the current social system are helping to create new and more flexible definitions of masculine and feminine. Homosexual liberation would be impossible without the questioning of sex roles that has gone before as part of the work of other liberation movements. Homosexual liberation itself has emerged recently to pose the central issues. The homosexual liberation movement has brought the sexual identity questions posed by all the movements out into the open.

It is as if in the sexual dimension of the many revolutions—Blacks, poor, young men, women, homosexuals—the nation's unconscious is surfacing. Just beyond the more publicized legalistic demands of the massive social movements of the late 1950's and the 1960's are important questions of life-style, and hence of sexuality and sex role.

The Black movement not only demands equal education and economic and social opportunity for the Black race, it makes visible a way men and women can relate to each other that is different from the conventions of the white majority of the population.

Black family life can differ from the white model. Women play a strong role. Labeled a matriarchy in a key government study, this life-style was, in effect, put in jeopardy by much of the language or used by officials administering antipoverty programs, and the thrust of much talk was that the programs would elevate the Black male to his proper dominant position by providing him with training and jobs. Welcomed at first by all the Black community, the assumption of male primacy behind this kind of rhetoric is now being examined more carefully by some Black women—and men. Some Blacks are now defending the Black family structure as more advanced than the white, with more equal and flexible roles for the male and female. They are saying: Maybe you should learn from us.

The hippie movement and the peace movement were in many ways men's liberation movements. Hippie men broke with the approved male sex role in several ways. First, they rebelled against traditional ideals of masculine appearance and dress; they saw themselves as sexual, colorful, individualistic—and they dressed accordingly. Second, they seemed to question the idea that it is the role of the male to run a hierarchical society by rejecting the role of breadwinner, they dropped out of school or work and devoted more time to reflection. Caring relationships with others became as important to them as they were traditionally supposed to be for women. Third, they defied the social expectation that required marriage before sexual pleasure.

In the peace movement, young men renounced a central aspect of masculinity—the duty—the right—to deal violent death in specifically sanctioned situations. They rejected the concept that manliness depended on a willingness and ability to kill.

The ecology movement has zero population growth as one of its goals. New definitions of womanhood would help to alter patterns of reproduction. Children, and therefore marriage, are no longer necessary for every woman; women who choose not to relate to men must also be valued, not ridiculed. Dr. Evelyn Hooker says, "The big push for Nixon is population control. Now if I can only persuade him that there is a connection between [that and] homosexuality, we might get somewhere."[33] Just such a link was made by Paul Gebhard, Director of the Center for Sex Research at the Indiana University, world-famous as Kinsey's research center. He predicts, as a result of the population crush, a complete turnabout in sex laws, from repressing to encouraging nonreproductive behavior.[34]

Obviously, if the government were to take steps to cut down population growth, it would begin to subsidize the single person and hence the homosexual through tax benefits.

Options given by science also encourage women to begin to define themselves in other ways besides wife and mother. Science is separating sexual pleasure from procreation. In a world of artificial wombs and sperm banks, a man and a woman will no longer have to unite in either time or space in order to reproduce. Certainly with this in the future, homosexuality would be no drawback, socially or practically, even for procreation.

All these movements support one another and the gay revolution in a common direction: freeing people from stereotypical behavior based on gender.

That many movements besides Women's Liberation and Gay Liberation have at their root questions about sex roles is not surprising: the attempt to live within the confines of traditional sex roles has been a source of agony for people of all sexual persuasions, according to Phyllis Chesler, a radical psychologist. The results of a study Ms. Chesler has done on women patients in institutions indicates that sex role stereotypes are at the heart of much so-called mental illness.

One movement has not been any help. What has been called the sexual revolution has not helped women, or benefited homosexuals.

Sexual liberation so far achieved has essentially provided heterosexual males with more physical experiences and less responsibility; and the female with fewer polite outs. Linda Phelps describes how the traditional type of release of sexual energies usually meant by the sexual revolution has affected women:

> After the gang rapes at Altamont and Seattle, after the demands raised at People's Park for "Free Land, Free Dope, and Free Women," after the analysis of (male) rock culture, women are beginning to realize that nothing new has happened at all. What we have is simply a more sophisticated (and thus more insidious) version of male sexual culture. Sexual freedom has meant more opportunity for men, and not a new experience for women.[35]

The negative valuation of sexuality *per se* is central to the Lesbian's problem. Instead of being just another human being, whose sex life is an integrated part of her whole life, the Lesbian is viewed primarily as a sexual creature. Although she may have no more or no less sex than anybody else, society seldom recognizes any other identity.

The intensity and focus on the Lesbian's sex life gives her a special responsibility. If our society still thinks sex abhorrent, then the Lesbian must help to give a new image to sexuality before she can be free. The subject of sexuality still requires delicacy. There is little reason to expect parents who have trouble talking to their children about heterosexuality, for example, to feel comfortable explaining or discussing homosexuality.

To remove the restrictions around a natural and spontaneous love and create what Reich calls a "sex affirmative"[36] social atmosphere is desirable for both homosexuals and heterosexuals. Both Gay Liberation and Women's Liberation activists recognize that real sexual revolution entails fundamental changes in people's lives and the culture. Changes that will lift the independent woman and male and female homosexuals from the bottom of the culture must take place, perhaps on a grass-roots level in the small groups of both movements.

Changes in institutions, beyond tokenism, come slowly. Real and widespread progress seems delayed by the long-accepted idea of women as weak and empty-headed and homosexuals as sinful, sick, and criminal. The exclusion of Lesbians from positions in education or business on both counts is like a red flag signaling the need for action, but a forced acceptance of Lesbians at a time when people still tend to believe they are inherently and permanently unfit is next to impossible. As Franz Fanon understood about Blacks, "What counts is the frightening enemy created by myth."[37] It is very easy for myths to endure where there is little knowledge.

Breakthroughs in religion, law, and mental health are used by Gay Liberation activists to influence change in fields derivative in values like education.

Each breakthrough, however small, has effects far beyond itself. New precedents are set in motion. A change in city laws can be used to pry loose legislation at the state level. Legislation in one state prompts other state legislators to follow.

Religion. Religious sects can be competitive in their liberalism. If one sect welcomes admitted homosexuals, others begin to consider the issue. No one wants to be labeled unchristian.

Efforts in all these directions by homophile and Gay Liberation groups is paying off. The institutions of American society are moving, though glacially, in the direction of justice for the homosexual. Because of the empirical nature of our democratic system, this slow-moving change seems to be part of the psychic makeup of the people and the times: It is not just being handed down from above. The organized religions, the most ancient source of gay oppression, are beginning, hesitantly, to try to fit the change within their theological as well as social beliefs. Some denominations accept homosexuals—if not homosexuality as a valid life-style—and although the effect of increased religious toleration on law and other institutions is not calculable, it may prove significant.

A group of dissident Roman Catholic priests and lay workers in San Francisco have organized a new ministry to the gay community. One of the goals is to attempt to foster reconciliation between gay

Catholics and the Church as a whole. This ministry has the official support of the Society of Priests for a Free Ministry, a national group of some 900 Roman Catholic priests who feel the Church must be liberalized and modernized if it is to survive and have relevance in today's society.

Methodists in Minnesota support the creation of a state law providing equal job opportunities for homosexuals. Some 70 percent of the 800 delegates, representing 140,000 Methodists, voted for the resolution.

Two national denominations, the Lutheran Church of America and the Unitarian Universalist Association, have made public statements supporting homosexual civil rights. Of course, this kind of action does not constitute theological endorsement of homosexual life-styles. Lines in Genesis describing the one way to express sexuality as a monogamous union of male and female are proving hard to refute.

What might be considered a typical statement on homosexuality by religious leaders comes from the Presbyterians. From a report released in 1970 and published in part in *Look*.

> Homosexuality itself is considered incomplete and is not accepted as a valid life style . . . but no one is exempt from the experience of alienation from God, neither the homosexual person or the heterosexual person. Therefore presumably both are eligible for the experience of reconciliation to which all men are invited in Christ.

Though this paragraph on homosexuality in the Presbyterian report calls homosexuality an incomplete expression of sexuality and thus not acceptable, a more inclusive statement in another part of the report seems to lay the groundwork for a future, greater acceptance. Citing current official Presbyterian policy on sex, which opposes "adultery, prostitution, fornication, and/or the practice of homosexuality," the authors of the report respond: "All that may be necessary, but it does not attend to the equally Christian calling to glorify God by the joyful celebration of and delight in our sexuality." They go on to comment: "The attempts by some theologians to encourage Christians to appreciate the fact that our sexuality can be fun as well as functional has throw some of our fellow faithful into paroxysms of fear and guilt."

Various ministers point to one reason some of the denominations are having trouble with the homosexual issue. They estimate that up to one-third of ministers in this country are homosexual or bisexual. This obviously puts the churches in a hypocritical position. Within the clergies, the presence of a large number of homosexuals is speculated on, although individual homosexuals often are not known. The churches are thus in a position of tacitly tolerating practices within their own ranks that they forbid to their parishioners.

Thus, paradoxically, the very incidence of homosexuality within the clergy hampers honesty and a direct approach to the issue.

To discuss the conflict within religion with homosexuals, 70 representatives of church and homophile organizations attended the first national conference on religion and the homosexual held in New York City in March, 1971.

Because changes in the church are predictably very gradual, a few homosexual clergy have broken away and formed their own churches. The Rev. Robert Clement has started the Church of the Beloved Disciple in New York City; Troy Perry's original Metropolitan Community Church is now one of twelve in the Universal Fellowship denomination. A gay Jewish synagogue was formed in Brooklyn.

Law. Adopting what is called a consenting-adults law is usually considered the way to alter the criminal code. Such a law states that homosexual acts conducted by consenting adults in private are not illegal. Five states have so far added and/or eliminated laws so that a homosexual act that takes place in private between consenting adults is no longer a criminal act. The five are Illinois, Connecticut, Idaho, Colorado, and Oregon.

Prohomosexual legislation has been introduced in California and New York but has not yet made it into law. In New York State a total of seven bills were introduced in 1971, including a fair-employment-practices bill. Minnesota has a fair-employment bill in the works; New York City legislators are considering a civil-rights bill covering employment, housing, and public accommodations. The mayor of San Francisco supports the recommendation by the San Francisco Crime Committee for a consenting-adults law.

Other prohomosexual legal actions include the decision of a Federal court judge in San Juan, Puerto Rico, that homosexuality *per se* is not immoral. The point came up in a hearing to assign bail, when the district prosecutor asked that the moral character of a defendant be considered and introduced a line of questioning designed to show that the defendant was homosexual. A Federal District Court in New York City granted citizenship to an admitted homosexual in March, 1971, over the protests of the U.S. Immigration and Naturalization Service. The judge said that the applicant's private morality was not the concern of the naturalization laws. The applicant had never corrupted the morals of others, preyed on minors, or engaged in publicly offensive acts. Furthermore, the judge noted, he led a quiet, peaceful, law-abiding life and was gainfully employed.

Although these decisions specifically involve male homosexuals, the protection they offer extends to Lesbians and should encourage them to fight for their rights.

The old fear of being tainted in the public eye just for helping homosexuals is breaking down. In June, 1971, the formation of New Yorkers for Homosexual Rights was announced. Prominent politicians, religious leaders, including those of Jewish and Roman Catholic persuasions, municipal administrators, lawyers, union representatives, and writers are among the members. There are five women on the 27-person committee, three of them nationally known figures: Congresswomen Bella Abzug and Shirley Chisholm, writer and Women's Liberation leader Gloria Steinem. Recognition has also come in favorable statements made by several of the 1972 Democratic Presidential hopefuls, including Hubert Humphrey and George McGovern. The strongest statement was by George McGovern.

> Senator McGovern recognizes that in American society today—no less than in other cultures and as throughout recorded history—a substantial minority of women and men of all ages are identified with a homosexual life-style. He further recognizes that certain *assumptions* of the majority concerning homosexuals have been used as a rationale for harassment and denial of elementary civil liberties for millions of individuals. As for other oppressed and stigmatized minorities, Senator McGovern *pledges the full moral and legal authority* of his Presidency toward restoring and guaranteeing first-class citizen rights for homosexually-oriented individuals. (Authors' italics)

Although in most states the Lesbian mother can still lose her children if the judge decides to use the open-ended criterion of "fit mother" to exercise prejudice, there are signs of pressure to improve the situation. In an important step the National Organization for

Women passed a resolution at its national convention in 1971 to offer legal and moral support in a test case involving child custody rights of mothers who are also Lesbians (Resolution 129).

Not only Lesbians are arguing for full status as unmarried women. Women's Liberation has made this an issue. The National Organization for Women officially supports women who choose to remain single. For women to achieve full economic, social, and political parity with men, N.O.W. recognizes that women should be free to rear their own children or to adopt children without social, legal or political prejudice (Resolution 130). This means that large numbers of women, not only Lesbians, want the right to remain outside the marriage system and do not feel they must have fathers present for healthy child-rearing.

Another path leading toward full constitutional rights for Lesbians is through court fights for the right to Lesbian marriages. In 1971, there were at least two cases. One in Florida concerned two young women who applied for a marriage license. They were refused by a lower court and did not appeal. However, two older women in Kentucky who were denied a marriage license appealed to the level of the State Supreme Court, and they intend to try to go all the way to the Supreme Court. The case is especially interesting since one of the women has three children, with a teen-age son still living at home.

A potentially important indicator of change lies in the national meeting of radical lawyers in the summer of 1971. The lawyers agreed to fight against all laws discriminating against homosexuals.

Psychology. The entire work of psychiatrist Thomas Szacz centers around a single argument: that we have replaced a theological outlook on life with a therapeutic one.[38]

Myths persist even in the face of scientific evidence that there is no substance to them. Thus, even studies that do indicate that homosexuals are normal, operative, healthy people are ignored or buried.

The belief that the homosexual is sick is severely undermined by the results of the National Institute of Mental Health study conducted by Dr. Evelyn Hooker (final report submitted in October of 1969). If homosexuality as disease or symptom affects a whole life, then certainly signs of this disruption should appear on the projective tests administered by psychologists. In fact, Dr. Hooker showed, they do not. Mental health professionals asked to select homosexuals' test results from a stack of heterosexual and homosexual results did no better than chance. Their comments even showed a kind of reverse valuation—an intelligent or artistic man was sometimes labeled homosexual because the clinician linked those traits with homosexuality.

Dr. Hooker's final report recommended that laws against consenting adults in private be abolished and that blanket employment discrimination be stopped. Speaking in Los Angeles in 1971, she pointed out that NIMH has yet to publish the study or move to implement any of its recommendations, such as the establishment of a center for the study of sexual relations. She questioned whether interference by the Nixon Administration in the functions and purposes of the NIMH prompted the resignation of the director who had originally backed the homosexual task force and the report.

In San Francisco a Lesbian and a male homosexual have been named to the board of the San Francisco Family Service Agency. The agency is a private one, but has non-profit status, and is funded primarily through the Bay Area Crusade, making it in effect semipublic.

The San Francisco Association for Mental Health issued a policy statement, produced by a task force made up of gay and straight members, stating: "Homosexuality can no longer be equated only with sickness, but may properly be considered as a preference, orientation or propensity for certain kinds of life-styles." The chairwoman of the task force was the head of the San Francisco Social Services Department, suggesting that the association's statement has at least some support from those involved in forming and implementing public policy. California branches of the American Psychiatric Association may pass a strong prohomosexual statement in 1972.

Three cities are seeing an entirely new phenomenon: the emergence of numbers of homosexual and heterosexual mental health professionals to actively working with gay organizations and clients to help gay people. Boston has a homosexual clinic and health service, staffed primarily by homosexual professionals. Chicago has a group called Gay Shrinks, reportedly doing consciousness-raising prior to forming a therapy collective or clinic.

In New York City there are three gay counseling centers—Identity House, the Homosexual Community Counseling Center, and Gay Counseling—all of which grew out of the belief that the gay life-style is a valid one.

Perhaps the most innovative is Identity House. This complex of services has steadily grown since the winter of 1971–72, when a small group of professional therapists and members of Gay Liberation decided to meet the needs of gay and bisexual people looking for a new kind of attitude from psychotherapists. Professional therapists interviewed by the Steering Committee are screened as much for their attitudes about sexuality as for their professional experience.

Charles Silverstein, director of Identity House, explains its special function: "Our program of services is designed to offset the poor self-image of gays caused by the prevailing moral view of sinfulness and the medical view of sickness, and to provide the means whereby each person may decide his or her sexual identity without guilt."

In addition to a walk-in center for crises, Identity House has special therapy groups, including those for Lesbian mothers, Lesbian couples, and married gay men.

An extensive program is addressed to the families of gay people. "We understand that the revelation that a daughter or son is gay produces profound feelings of resentment, anger, and guilt in some family members. Just as a gay person must integrate sexuality into his or her personality, so too must the family restructure their perception of the child and reintegrate him or her into the family in a new role," says the director.

Beyond therapy, Identity House plans to conduct research, publish a journal, present papers at meetings of the various psychiatric, psychoanalytic and psychological associations, and send speakers to training schools. Such a center is an instrument with which to strike at the heart of the oppression of gay people—labeling and treating Lesbians and male homosexuals as sick or as sexually and emotionally retarded.

At least four mental-health conferences were zapped by gay activists in 1971. Frank Kammeny and Washington, D.C., activists caused pandemonium at the American Psychiatric Association Convention when they took over the platform for twenty minutes. Lesbian activists, invited and uninvited, spoke at the Eastern Psychological Conference in New York City in the spring. A psychological conference in Boulder, Colorado, was challenged on gay issues by student gay activists from the University of Colorado. And a conference of the archenemies of gays, the behavioral therapists, was disrupted and a session halted by Los Angeles Gay Liberation Front. GLF members described some aversion techniques as "primitive medieval torture" where an electric current is administered to "correct" sexual preference.

The *Radical Therapist,* a publication out of Minot, North Dakota, which is read by young therapists, has printed the Gay Liberation Manifesto, letters from discriminated-against Lesbians and, most recently, a Lesbian section. Editors called *The Woman-Identified-Woman,* which appeared in the section, possibly one of the most important articles ever to appear in the paper.

However, while the advances seem revolutionary, impressive, exciting, for every avant-garde therapist, radical therapist, or Feminist therapist backing the Lesbian as a full human being, there are hundreds of mental-health professionals who regard homosexuality as pathological. Many of them are treating female and male homosexuals every day, and either trying to create a change in their sexuality or condescendingly agreeing to help them adjust to and accept their illness.

Education. Students are openly organized into Gay Liberation groups on a great number of campuses, sometimes with official recognition. University facilities are often used for dances and conferences.

Although university professors are still fired if they are publicly found out as Lesbians, professors are not as frightened to come to the defense of a homosexual in danger of being fired as they used to be. There is cautious support of the idea that this is not adequate reason for dismissal.

In one area there is definite progress. Colleges around the country are offering courses on homosexuality, sometimes taught by homophile leaders or gay activists, and a number of others have added sections on homosexuality to existing courses. Colleges in Massachusetts, Kentucky, Nebraska, New York City, Vermont, Illinois, Florida, and California have independent courses on homosexuality, and courses are planned at the University of Michigan at Lansing, and Cornell University, Ithaca, New York.

A new kind of gay person will be emerging from the colleges soon. She or he will have been openly homosexual on campus—a member of a gay group, a participant in conferences and dances and a student in classes on sexuality and homosexuality. It will be interesting to see how this kind of person adjusts to employment and professional restrictions in the outside world. Hopefully, they will join in the push to end this kind of discrimination.

Where there has not been progress, there has been recognition. Even recognition may be a form of progress.

Today it is becoming clear that it is not homosexuals, or women, or Blacks, who are sick or deficient—it is society that has a sickness near its very center—fear and hatred and lack of understanding of sexual drives, feelings and needs. These seem somehow tied up with the way we generally dehumanize and brutalize each other and perhaps with our tendency to mistreat the environment.

The ravaging of nature—human and environmental—seems an integral part of the industrial age. Perhaps, in what Kenneth Boulding has called post-civilization, boosted by electronic technology, we are heading to new progress in ways of relating to people that will help to overcome our alienation from each other.

Young people today are uncovering society's hypocrisies and are questioning what other generations have blindly accepted: that money is of great value, that marriage means loving, that attack and aggression are natural, that multiple sexual relationships are shameful, that manliness means power, that womanliness means passivity, that homosexuality is bad, etc. All of this threatens the authoritarian, patriarchal, heterosexual-dominated society and provides hope for a fairly rapid change in individual attitudes that makes legal and legislative changes both possible and useful.

In trying to accommodate these revolutionary pressures, America may evolve toward real freedom, wherein a person can choose a life-style and be respected for it, or at least move toward tolerance of uncommon life-styles. The only truly revolutionary society would be a pluralistic one that recognizes that people are individual human beings, that they will grow and change in exciting ways.

The monumental task of awakening social conscience and a sense of justice for Lesbians will not be accomplished easily, especially when those who disapprove of homosexuality can still look to established institutions for support. The weight of ages and the attitudes of millions—dead and alive—are against homosexuality. People have been willing to call it sick, criminal, or sinful, whichever is most effective in a particular time or place. Gay activists, often young, idealistic, lacking position, authority, economic support, or the good-will of society, are nevertheless committed to the task. They are tire-less, sometimes awkward as they learn political ways, but confident and enthusiastic, and growing in numbers.

The accomplishments after just three years of Gay Liberation seem herculean when there has been little movement for centuries. Gay activists are living in a time of accelerated change when nothing seems impossible for those with the impulse to fight for freedom. They know they must find a way to change the culture, or else—like millions of other gay men and women—end up in danger of being crushed by it.

9 I'M A LESBIAN AND I'M BEAUTIFUL

If a Lesbian permits herself to be inundated with the standard opinions of psychiatry, law, and religion, she is in a very real sense doomed. If a Lesbian accepts that she is sick, sinful, a criminal, she will undoubtedly fail, and even seek ways to fail. Her environment is polluted with sexism: she will be given no boost from society, only discouragement in the themes "you can't do it" as woman and "we don't want you" as Lesbian.

Lesbians need to find themselves acceptable, to free themselves from emotional stress, guilt, and other automatic reaction patterns caused by society's negative evaluation. They have actively to challenge the basic beliefs that keep them down and to examine their own acceptance of these beliefs.

Thus, while purposeful, goal-oriented behavior is important for all people bent on achieving or affirming a more positive identity, this kind of effort is air and light for Lesbians whose egos have been damaged, if not destroyed. Before an activist can change the culture, she must change herself by doing what is necessary to liberate her vitality. The alchemy by which she transforms something mean into something precious is the power of Gay Liberation and Women's Liberation ideas and actions.

Women's Liberation and Gay Liberation meet in the gay Feminist. This woman has declared a break with the past and her life has a new beginning. She has found her divided state unsatisfactory at a gut level and, after much conflict, has come to rely increasingly on her personal values and convictions. She challenges the habit of hiding by reaching within herself for the strength to be honest and to take action. Her identity solution gives her courage to step out of line and be counted as an individual.

To transcend her circumstances, she may defy the reality of the present and purposely live openly as though the present were the future. By envisioning and demonstrating a new reality for and with Lesbians, she also *creates* it.

Pride and self-love are not permitted in the present; they are off limits. So an activist lives "as if" she were acceptable. Her unexpected attitude jolts those around her into new ways of reacting and sometimes into at least momentary acceptance. By assuming new attitudes and new modes of behavior, she helps to modify or overcome obstacles. She creates her own future simply by living it.

"Only in the change in the attitude of the individual can begin the change in the psychology of the nation."[1]

A Lesbian activist tries to achieve a new way of looking at herself and the world. She frees her ego from the crushing influences of society and considers herself the equal of men and heterosexuals. She resolves sane schizophrenia by withdrawing ego investment from her straight-identified component and investing it in her new identity as a total Lesbian woman.

At first there is considerable fear that the Lesbian identity is too small, too incomplete to build a life on. "I am more than a Lesbian" is a common statement. However, as gay women begin to think about sexuality, its place in a life as well as its relationship to cultural and political patterns, the term Lesbian begins to expand in scope and meaning. The Lesbian's growing consciousness is nurtured by insights and ideas from Gay Liberation and from the liberation movements of other oppressed peoples.

A Lesbian activist works within a special set of conditions called "the movement"; in this she usually benefits from an urban scene, which provides a degree of anonymity and the stimulus of Feminist and radical political ideas. But the pride and sense of wholeness attained by an activist involved in gay women's liberation is felt also by Lesbians living in relative isolation. Lesbians who may only have heard or read of "the movement" are developing a new respect for themselves and their ways of life.

What is at work in the activist, or any Lesbian who seeks a new view of life, is a quest for positive self-definitions that counteract society's negative definitions. Much has been written about the importance of self-image in psychology, and the term becomes part of the jargon in self-improvement articles and books. That amazing results come from changes in self-image has often been put down as a popular oversimplification. But, for a Lesbian, cursed with the double negative of weak woman and sick homosexual, creating a new self-image is imperative. A new mental, even spiritual, concept of self and a sense of purpose are at the core of Gay Liberation and Women's Liberation.

Consciousness-raising is the means to a new self-image and a new sense of purpose or focus. In a C-R group, members learn to identify the problems of Lesbianism with society rather than with self.

Consciousness-raising functions as an instrument for emotional, spiritual and political development.

It is done in a small group—usually six to ten women. It may take several forms: one prevalent and effective form focuses on topics selected by the group. The topic is addressed via individual testimonies, which should not be interrupted or judged by anyone present. Testimonies should be as personal and as expressive of the emotions as possible. A general discussion or analysis follows after each member has testified. Good consciousness-raising groups are noncoercive and encourage individual points of view. While there is warmth and concern between members of the group, there is usually no attempt to duplicate a group-therapy experience.

The unique contribution of consciousness-raising to a gay woman lies in the opportunity to evolve a personal set of ethics through obtaining a perspective on society in a reassuring environment where her experiences are revealed and shared. Here a Lesbian can sort out the various influences on her, from the pressures of conventional moral tenets, which may or may not apply to her, to those of the atmosphere of the bar, which encourage a kind of adolescent selfishness. She questions habits, explores beliefs blindly accepted, and peels off layers of assigned roles not useful, even intelligible any longer, when living outside the culture. One answer to the dilemma of what emerges in consciousness-raising is a self-determined morality. A troublesome situation is perceived and weighed by the individual from the twin points of view of her life experiences and her own ever-developing personal set of standards and criteria. This new ethical individualism can be more easily obtained by attending consciousness-raising meetings with others who are also raising issues.

219

Thus the primary purpose of gay women's consciousness-raising groups is to provide a chance for self-awareness and growth that is not duplicated for gay people anywhere else in society.

What happens here to Lesbians is decisive, although very few women can explain exactly what it is. An alteration in perception takes place which is both substantial and lasting. Although some attribute their new awareness to participation in marches, actions, and organizational work, as well as consciousness-raising, most feel their new cognitions started or grew importantly in c-r. In a paper entitled "Consciousness-raising and Personal Change in the Women's Movement," anthropologist Esther Newton compares the dramatic change in self-concept with a religious "conversion experience."

There are numerous ways of describing what takes place:

Consciousness-raising has been called a conversion experience from self-hatred to self-respect; it can also be called an intellectual awakening from ignorance of society's conditioning to awareness of the possibility of resistance; a moral transition from unexamined conventional morality to individual principles; a maturing process from dependence to independence; a recovery from sickness to health, from apologies to endorsement. To sum up, one could even say that it is a reconditioning experience designed to shed layer after layer of trained negative thinking and free the vital self which oppression has so effectively buried.

Although the availability of a consciousness-raising group, and of supportive friends or an organized political movement, helps create a new, more unified identity, her change of direction in life ultimately is felt and lived by the individual.

A Lesbian's new consciousness is reflected in her day-to-day interactions with others. Whether or not she ever marches or becomes politically active, she experiences a wider circle of friends, with whom she is more relaxed and open. She feels these friends really know her. Her isolation is ended, and she risks sampling the reality around her in better spirits. Many Lesbians, after some months of consciousness-raising, are no longer nervous or ashamed to be seen in public with other Lesbians. Older Lesbians find that role-playing—which they most always felt was artificial but which they participated in because everyone else in the bars seemed to—drops away or is greatly reduced or eliminated. Since they are more relaxed and comfortable with themselves and their sexuality, much less energy is used in self-monitoring and self-censorship, freeing it for more productive goals.

Lesbians can be more expressive in more kinds of social situations. Many come to feel that if someone in a restaurant or on a beach figures out that they are gay, it is the problem of the others to deal with. It is no longer the Lesbian's problem. Most tell brothers and sisters and straight friends—if not parents or employers—about themselves, and the result is that if encouragement or support for some endeavor comes from these people, it is really positively felt. For the first time, it is really for you, not for your façade.

New liberation attitudes and ideas pose a grave threat to the old unquestioned principles that have governed most Lesbians' lives. The new alternative creates ambivalence in Lesbians who may have solidified their life-style when there was no alternative, and who resist consciousness-raising. If a Lesbian has established a straight façade, she will probably want nothing to do with "crazy" ideas of liberation, which shake her carefully built superstructure. For this reason, Lesbian activists have often been accused of offending or alienating the very women they wish to liberate.

To Lesbians in hiding there is a disturbing element in the very presence of activists among them. At first the Lesbian activists' message seems remote to other Lesbians, who may even laugh at it. "Good luck with *your* liberation," a few have said.

Activists pose unwanted challenges to Lesbians who have, understandably and expectedly, cut themselves off from their own integrity in order not be cut off from society.

With stubborn insistence, the message of Gay Liberation strikes discord in many gays. Its theme is a threatening counterpoint to their current mode of existence. Talk of "coming out" publicly unearths that painful feeling buried since the decision to "come out" sexually. It threatens a new upheaval in one's life, the breaking down of established social and emotional structures.

Then, it is almost as if the activists awaken something in the nonactivist. Guilt and fear are brought out of a deep sleep and viewed again under a glaring light. The activists cause other Lesbians to focus on their unresolved conflicts.

221

While pointing out a new way of life, they are also, by implication if not directly, pointing out the humiliation and degradation in the old life that other Lesbians are still living.

At the beginning of a vacation weekend, a successful Lesbian psychologist was conversing with a Lesbian activist. The activist expressed some irritation that the psychologist seemed hostile in the city, where she was a practicing professional, and friendly in the country, where she socialized with other Lesbians. The activist jokingly told the psychologist she must be schizophrenic. The psychologist paused, then replied seriously, "I accept that diagnosis." During the weekend, the psychologist became increasingly agitated. She openly expressed anger at being "pressured" to come out publicly; guests and friends, however, agreed that there had been no real pressure. The activist was on vacation too. The activist's presence and that one conversation with her had "activated" the psychologist's consciousness of her own divided state. She was pressured, attacked, insulted by, her own conscience, not the activist.

Lesbian activists and their message make it impossible for those they encounter to enjoy the bliss of unconsciousness. Confronted with their own necessarily hypocritical lives, many Lesbians find themselves changing their values. Gay Liberation becomes a turning point, the beginning of a new direction.

At a party in New York City, two Lesbian activists in the movement were present among two dozen or more gay women. The Lesbian activists, who had been mentioned in the press and had acted openly in the women's movement, appeared as enemies to the "closet" Lesbians. For weeks after the party, one of the activists was accused of threatening to disclose the hostess' pseudonym, of wanting to break the "gay code" of secrecy. The activist fought back, denying the accusation but reminding the woman what the need for a code of secrecy meant in her life. Six months later the angry hostess, who had been so fearful that her true identity would be revealed, decided to use her real name for the first time at Daughters of Bilitis, where she had been known under her pseudonym for many years. Soon after she dropped her pseudonym, she marched up Sixth Avenue in New York with gay militants.

Lesbian activists, who know the questioning and suffering that go into making this transition, generally give warm support to others struggling to build a more honest life. When is the timing right for affirmation? Lesbians who have felt pressured to come out publicly have sometimes suffered emotional traumas, as well as social and economic losses they were not yet willing or able to handle. Furthermore, a fear-ridden or uninspired declaration of sexuality is easily watered down to a trembling confession. Confession works against the essential message of Gay Liberation: pride; more important, it sometimes severely damages the Lesbian, who was not acting out of choice or deep conviction. Commitment comes to each woman differently, and in its own time.

A declaration of honesty is not enough. When the Lesbian switches her focus from Lesbianism as immoral to honesty as moral, she makes herself vulnerable to external hostility. Once more she is in serious conflict.

Readiness to become an acknowledged Lesbian seems to involve a personal and emotional restructuring of values, often with the help of friends or a consciousness-raising group. A good deal of energy goes into this process. The Lesbian has accurately to perceive her motives and the consequences, and if she can get out from under the weight of old arguments and truly believe in the goodness of her love and the possibility of a rewarding personal life-style, she arrives at a new place.

The activist has a continuing battle against ambivalence in herself and in others who, in letting a conflict lie dormant, may come to believe it has gone away. The problems of choosing between known security and unknown integrity are universal among gays. At first, new activists hide their remaining fears or weak moments, their flashbacks to insecurity, until they feel confident in their message. Then they begin to talk about their new problems as well as gains.

The transition from a feigned heterosexual identity to a Lesbian identity may constitute a period of considerable confusion. There is a time when a Lesbian feels she is nobody, nowhere—on a bridge between an old self and a new self. During this time she is very vulnerable. The gains and losses of both identities push and pull at her. Her world seems chaotic. Even when she reaches the other side, she may still not be able to settle down. She may grow to feel strongly about herself as "good" or even "great," while at the same time she has to justify a compromise now and then. Society continues to demand this of her, and she sometimes weakens; for she cannot always risk everything to confront a heterosexual chauvinist.

It is a rare activist today who can act with perfect consistency. There are Lesbian activists who have still not told their parents or who still go under pseudonyms for some purposes. The process of change is not cataclysmic; it is gradual, though the initial insight can be a "flash." One has to learn to carry along the "psychic shelter"[2] found in consciousness-raising groups on visits with parents, to the office, to the dentist, or to the minister. There is great difficulty in acting consistently alone in a hostile environment; anyone may hesitate at times and cop out.

Other Lesbians ask: "Why do it? Why be public?" "What is the truth worth when you have to pay your rent?" "If I go into my school and say I'm a Lesbian, I'd be out of a job, and teaching is my life."

Not only financial security is at stake. One risks valued straight, and even gay, friendships. "Identity solutions can lead to the dissolution of friendships."[3] This is certainly true of the Lesbian who risks losing straight friendships built on the shaky foundation of lies, omissions, and half-truths. How can a person who thinks one way and acts and talks another way form a deep friendship? Friendships with other gays built on common guilt and mutual protection are also in danger. Family members also will probably weigh the Lesbian against their reputations in the community. The realization that some friends were never really friends to the Lesbian's true self or that the family is not necessarily a unit of unconditional love and protection is hard to take.

And yet the activist still chooses to take on the burdens of those who prefer to hide. She exposes her life to the public to be damned and ridiculed. She makes herself vulnerable financially and socially for this abstract thing called liberation. She risks virtually everything for an unsure future. Why?

Powerful memories claw at her conscience: One Lesbian watched her lover die in her arms and she did not say "I love you" because there were straight people present who would not understand; another tells of reading a news account of an Argentinian homosexual who, pushed by fear, jumped from the second story of a police station and landed on a sharp picket fence. The iron poles of the fence had to be severed with a blowtorch before he could be taken to the hospital—with pieces of the fence still inside him. Another talks about her constant vision of a thirty-five-year-old Lesbian in a small town, alone and in pain. Another Lesbian says she watched a gay march for hours and listened to the people chant "Join us! Join us!" until her stomach knotted.

One Lesbian who was an officer in N.O.W. during the discussions on Lesbians now regrets that she did not use her influence to facilitate understanding and avoid the purge.

Another Lesbian, a professor in a university, was asked by students if she would be the faculty advisor for a new gay organization on campus, and she declined out of fear. Another woman, not a Lesbian, filled the post and the Lesbian regretted her decision.

In still another case, a Lesbian was an editor on a national magazine doing a story on Lesbianism. Male heterosexual writers did the story with misconceptions and factual errors. She was afraid to correct them.

Numerous events, psychic or actual, in the life of a Lesbian may lead her to concentrate on the nature of her oppression and eventually to become a committed activist. Some were repelled by the old gay life-style; others are attracted by the prospects for the future. They know they have to build a new life, so they grab on.

"If someone throws you a life preserver, you're a damn fool if you don't take it."

In the end, it is relating her suffering to the suffering of others that connects the Lesbian's own experience with the meaning of homosexual oppression. She may have felt she could stand it by herself, but when she realizes there are millions of others, she knows it is not her problem alone.

Cutting through the reluctance of many Lesbians to face the identity conflict is a message of pride. Even if it is softly sounded, the message takes on a kind of resonance. Liberation pits the spirit, that animating and vital force in every human being, against external values of acceptability and material security.

For the Lesbian today, Gay Liberation as a philosophy, or

ideology if you will, seems to provide the one chance for harmony. The choices are to be in conflict with oneself and in harmony with the world, or in harmony with oneself and in conflict with the world Gay Liberation is committed to changing society so that both self and society can eventually work in harmony. At present Gay Liberation seems the only hope for a totally integrated personality.

The hiding Lesbian who feels good about her sexuality still may suffer greatly for her dishonesty. She may feel she is a sinner not because she is a Lesbian, but because she is a liar, and she longs for honesty. Gay Liberation offers her an alternative: coming out into the open. Instead of functioning in two different worlds, always dragging along one-half of herself that cannot participate, the Lesbian finally gets "her selves" together and permits her new integrated self to guide her personality. Having begun to overcome the societal forces that diminished and separated her, she may find a new excitement and joy in wholeness that few nonhomosexuals can appreciate. There are some things heterosexuals cannot appreciate, because they have never lived without them: one is living as a whole person twenty-four hours a day.

Love seems to flourish with the start of a new gay consciousness. The message of pride carries with it "permission" to be happy and enjoy love. It frees expressions curtailed by guilt. In proportion as a woman feels better about being a Lesbian, love gets better, stronger.

Lovemaking, once seen as final proof of her illness, becomes a celebration, an impetus to life. A Lesbian may feel free for the first time to abandon herself to another woman and experience total response that she has denied herself since her very first encounter with guilt.

Honesty may trigger a new feeling in the Lesbian reminiscent of the first time she ever made love with another woman. As the first Lesbian experience is the beginning of a personal journey from innocence to guilt, the first step toward living an honest life is the beginning of the journey back to innocence.

This Lesbian is so transformed that she is almost oblivious to criticism. Sneers, warnings, or threats glance off her. Accusations that she is a sinner are particularly futile, since her stand against deception gives her a new perception of goodness in herself.

However, any declaration of the truth about her sexuality is regarded by society as "advertising, broadcasting, or flaunting" what people think should remain a hidden part of her nature. People see no logic in the Lesbian's proclaiming her sexuality since she could very well remain silent and enjoy all the benefits of the system. One man said, "If I commit adultery, I don't tell people at the office." This is a totally spurious comparison, since adultery in no way alters his male identity, but may strengthen it. His social and sexual identity is safely lodged in his heterosexual marriage. His marriage is approved of; by some, his adultery is too. The Lesbian, on the other hand, who does not mention her sexuality, is merely in the no-man's-land of the single woman, nearly without a sociosexual identity; or worse, she is forced to inhabit one not her own. What the Lesbian is trying to do in being honest is to battle sane schizophrenia and its debilitating effects on her personality.

There had never been real tranquillity in her life, the emerging activist realizes, only the tension of her conflict. Eventually she must be grateful for her awakening, however painful, compelled by truth and dignity, which, as a homosexual, she has never experienced. She does not resent the struggle to achieve these gains or the consequences that may flow from them, for she now realizes that they are essential to her well-being. The rationale for obeying the golden rules of motherhood and wifehood never seemed clear to her, but she may have suffered for denying them. Now promises of fulfillment as woman and human outside the home seem profoundly clear. She has reached her inner self and experiences a new quality in life. She feels intensely alive. "The real me," which finally seems unique and valuable, is not to be hidden, but celebrated. Her new identity is a treasure that cannot be lost or stolen.

One Lesbian activist recalls trying to explain to a woman she used to know in the bars what Gay Liberation is all about. The woman was not interested. Ironically, she said, "I don't care about this movement stuff. All I know is that you're smiling and laughing for the first time."

The happiness activists find in their lives and work can be annoying to straights. Three activists were being interviewed for the David Susskind show. Suddenly the person screening them interrupted with, "You say your life is beautiful; you use words like happy. I wonder how you use them. I just get up in the morning and do what I'm supposed to do. It's just my life; I do what I have to do. I don't say my life is beautiful." She turned to one of the women. "You don't really mean your life is beautiful?" The activist looked back at her. "My life is very beautiful," she said quietly.

The heterosexual not only may not agree with certain choices of life-style the Lesbian has made, but seems to resent the Lesbian's ability to make choices. Lesbians, especially Lesbian activists, are taking their lives into their own hands, being responsible for themselves. They live, not so much according to a list of rules, but by the dictates of mind and spirit.

Once the level of consciousness has been raised or awakened, the Lesbian cannot forget the meaning of Gay Liberation in her life. She cannot go back into unconsciousness.

Accompanying her new attitudes are new actions. The Lesbian may join a committee or hand out fliers on the street or take part in gay marches. The idea of marching in public wearing a sign "I'm a Lesbian" or "Hi Mom" seems terrifying at first, but it is a natural extension of activities in keeping with the Gay Liberation ideas the Lesbian has accepted. Unconsciously or consciously, the Lesbian knows she is playing a kind of Russian roulette when she participates in a march. It has happened that photographers or writers decide that the Lesbian who seems most anxious to be buried in the crowd should be the focal point of a picture or story.

The moment of truth, that critical juncture between a private and a public life, between commitment and retreat, may come in many ways, but to some it has come on just such a demonstration on a bright, sunny day of joy and celebration. When the moment of decision comes, the Lesbian knows that, like it or not, she is not one in the crowd; she and the thousands marching are symbols to millions. She knows she has only two ways to go—forward with courage or back to fear.

The instant she is picked out by a photographer for what she frantically imagines must be at least a closeup to appear on the cover of a national magazine, she makes a split-second decision to hide her face or to smile and look into the camera with confidence;

if asked for her name by the press, to give her real name, a pseudonym, or no name. The women to whom this has happened say they had little time to ponder. Readers or viewers could be parents, employer, teacher, daughter, neighbor, grocer, superintendent, dentist, creditor, enemy. But most importantly, they include gay brothers and sisters who could not believe in a rhetoric of gay pride spoken by those ashamed to give their names or show their faces: To inspire courage in others, the emerging activist knows she must demonstrate courage. She says to herself: "I am what I am and I will not deny it; I'll affirm it no matter what. If I hide now, I am destroying myself and injuring all the others."

This may take place in a flash, but the Lesbian has been preparing for the decision since she joined Gay Liberation, and perhaps a long time before that.

One Lesbian, an attorney, tells of making an "instant" decision about the direction of her life at a Daughters of Bilitis meeting. When two police interrupted the meeting, she surprised herself by standing firm and saying, "I'm a lawyer." She then counseled the organization's spokeswoman on what she did or did not have to say. She demanded that the police produce a warrant or a definite complaint or else leave; they left. This lawyer holds a government position. She knew that she was putting her career on the line that instant. "I suddenly knew I could not live in fear again. I could not go back."

The decision to act can come about at any time or under any circumstances. Then a consciously felt encounter occurs to interrupt the habitual submission to old values. A Lesbian who tells her parents or who decides to take her lover home for a holiday regardless of the consequences, a woman who tells her lover to meet her at the office, a Lesbian who invites to a party both gay and straight friends and colleagues, or uses the pronoun "she" for her lover in a critical situation—all these women are making the new decision. It does not take a march or a raid by police.

Coming out publicly acts to force other people to confront their cognitive dissonance: either to accept the idea that Lesbianism is compatible with someone they like and value, or somehow to explain to themselves how the woman they like and value fits the stereotypical ideas of a Lesbian pervert.

229

Living the Future

More than anything else, Lesbians may hold back from joining the movement because joining sooner or later will entail telling their parents. They are unable to deal with the fear of losing their childhoods, their homes, brothers and sisters, and the continuity embodied in family relationships. The feared break with parents epitomizes the total conflict with society. They know that Lesbians who have told their families are sometimes never able to go home again, never permitted to see the children in the family or even to go home to claim their possessions. Even among committed activists, the problem of parents is frequently discussed. The encounter is emotionally loaded; the activist who is willing to talk confidently to thousands at a demonstration might crumble under parental pressures, which threaten to reduce her to a child. One Lesbian, divorced, with four teen-age children, said before being interviewed for a TV show: "I don't think I could do this if my parents were alive."

An activist who takes what others might call chances may really be taking a sound and needed step toward happiness. Others may say she is "asking for it," and in very positive ways she *is* asking for it. To her "it" is peace of mind. She has made a decision that others will say she "has to live with," but that she is eager to live with. Her act of defiance, which might be interpreted as self-destruction, may mean her liberation. It begins with a moment in which the Lesbian values integrity over acceptance.

Author Frank O'Connor once suggested that if you come up against a wall that you feel you cannot get over, you should throw your hat over so that you'll have to follow. Emerson said this in other words: "Do the thing and you will find the way."

When the Lesbian makes her "irreversible decision" by giving her name to the press or by some other act that could change her life, she is going out ahead of herself. She declares her identity, so she must find a way to live it out. The Lesbian is now committed to Gay Liberation because she willed it . . . but also because she can no longer go back to living as a feigned heterosexual. She has reached the point of no return. Her identity solution may also mean the dead end of the traditional kind of social respectability.

How does the Lesbian feel about her self-declaration? Doesn't her commitment, which brings new rewards, also make painfully clear possible new losses? And does this prompt her to strengthen her beliefs to justify her irreversible decision? Perhaps. But if we assume that initially she did struggle with the consequences of her decision, then we see that she would probably do it over again; although she is now aware on a gut level of what she already knew intellectually: the price the Lesbian is asked to pay for peace of mind.

Certainly the Lesbian may have experienced real, even severe, losses, since she became an out-front Lesbian, but she now views her stake in the system differently from the way she did in the past. Life under deception was as unstable as a house of cards. With honesty, the same losses which she feared most may actually happen, but self-esteem usually fills the resulting void. The Lesbian is no longer contributing to society's efforts to make her ill. Her previous fear and anxiety required her compliance.

Understanding of the Lesbian's success or failure must be determined by an understanding of her goals. A Lesbian activist's personal goal may be internal well-being. By this criterion any resulting problems are irrelevant. Her actions have been efficacious if she feels good about herself.

If a Lesbian has been seeing a psychotherapist before she becomes an activist, her new consciousness does not necessarily mean that she stops therapy. She may, however, switch to a more radical psychotherapist—a Feminist psychotherapist or even a Lesbian psychotherapist, who will give support to individuality and transcendence. As the Lesbian resolves her identity crisis and calms the turmoil within her, she finds a storm outside that was not there before, a storm that ironically is caused by her new assertiveness. The end of hypocrisy, the solution to her personal crisis, may bring havoc in her immediate environment. As she experiences relief in honesty, family and friends may try to persuade her to go back into hiding because *they* cannot stand it. Even if the Lesbian's sanity is at stake, others do not want her to break with convention. This serious game cannot end until society sees the Lesbian as she sees herself.

From the new good aspects of her life, she gathers strength for the long haul. Coming out one time is not always enough. The

Lesbian activist finds that even if she has had her most feared encounter, there are others daily as her gay identity grows and develops.

For the Lesbian activist, the liberating of herself and her sisters becomes a dominant aspect of her life. Her whole life becomes one driving force toward liberation. It is this focus that most distinguishes the Lesbian activist from Lesbians who have not yet had this experience. "In truth nothing characterizes us more than our field of attention."[4]

A commitment to the liberation of gay women means a rearrangement of priorities. Gradually a new hierarchy develops. What seemed important before—job, family, career, home—cannot compete with the compelling vision of liberation. Some activists withdraw from job, family, or university, not out of fear, but to use their time and energy to try to change conditions for homosexuals.

However, there is a democracy in the movement, an understanding between those who work daily for the movement and those who do what they can when they can. Some full-time activists are on welfare, either because they have been denied employment opportunities because they "look" Lesbian or because they refuse to work under circumstances in which they cannot be honest. Lesbian activists who are practicing architects, attorneys, psychotherapists, and the like, may decide not to give full time to liberation, but they especially value activists who devote their total energies and talent to the movement.

Lesbians who change their opinions of themselves and become positive about their homosexuality find it more and more difficult to hide. The idea of hiding is now repugnant to them. They feel good and can no longer justify sacrificing themselves to the fears and prejudices of others. So they may tell their colleagues or employers. Timing is important. To be most effective, a Lesbian makes her statement when a critical situation arises and not just as a function of expansiveness or euphoria.

Although they must be prepared for serious consequences, they may be surprised to find that everyone knew or that no one particularly cares.

Some Lesbians are lucky enough to be on their own, in independent jobs. These women find no need to tell anyone in their work situations, but seem to experience some kind of renewal that improves their work.

One activist, a reporter with an international news service, and another, a second-year graduate student, abandoned their career goals and are now driving taxicabs. They can no longer tolerate occupations that require them to conceal their identity and force them to live in isolation of mind and spirit. They would rather suffer alienation from society in terms of social and economic losses than give up their new unified selves.

Although she may feel that a demanding job requires too much of the time and energy she now wants to channel into the movement, a Lesbian activist may also find that her current position is not compatible with her new interests. In the first stage, activists who may have set out to be professors, businesswomen, or reporters, may start their own small businesses, drive taxis, or waitress, or go on welfare. The new options are limited to that type of work that does not require more than a superficial adherence to social custom.

At this time, when Lesbians find their great release from pressures that have damaged their egos, society may see them as going "downhill."

Whether such preoccupation and focus of energy—in this case, on liberation—is good or bad is not the issue: It is essential to the motivation and continuation of any new endeavor. If the goal were money, power, or family, the commitment would have social acceptability. Said one capitalist father: "If there was money in Gay Liberation, I'd back you 100 percent." But the fact that liberation has very little value to those who don't need it cannot be important to the activists. Her idealism may seem nearly fanatical to others. Nevertheless, it is such commitment and focus of energy that has led to the new things of life, inventions, new religions, the discovery of new worlds. When Newton was asked how he had been able to discover the mechanical system of the universe, he answered, "by thinking about it night and day."[5]

Some Lesbians say, "I'm beyond that. I am going on with my life." As individuals they may succeed, but if their success relies in part on a pretense of heterosexuality, they may have the burden of a new kind of guilt, which comes from not taking part in a decisive moment in history.

Psychotherapists report stress and anxiety among homosexuals that is being *caused by* the movement. This is especially true among some who cannot sacrifice what they have gained in hiding, but feel, at the same time, a kind of moral demand to do something.

Time and circumstances create almost an historical imperative for Lesbians to act now for themselves and all of their own kind in the favorable climate of a changing culture. "Identity becomes evident in unhesitating commitment—when the time is ripe."[6] The feeling is both momentous and fateful for activists, who know there is nothing behind but despair, and whatever is ahead can never be as bad. So they must risk the past, which is nothing, save for destroyed souls of friends and the reflected glory from a few homosexual writers and artists whose sexual preference, however, is considered to have left a "stain" on their biographies.

Like others dealing with contemporary issues, activists are aware that we are "in the twilight of the industrial age" and that a new age with new values, hopefully more humanistic values, is dawning. If Lesbians are to have options to live more freely and honestly in the emerging society, it is up to the gay activists to participate and explore, even to demonstrate models for the future.

A Lesbian activist seeks the meaning in society's demands and no longer responds unquestioningly to them. One by one, she cuts the societal strings that had her operating like a puppet. She is no longer culture-bound. She moves away from roles that no longer have any relationship to her growing self.

> We have left behind the authority of the past, the home of our childhood. We must find psychic shelter in our peer group. We must make each other's personalities satisfy the deep need within us for the psychic shelter of the home. We must be mother and father to our ourselves, and others.[7]

What the activist does appears excessive to others, sacrificial, risky, reckless, crazy. Well-intentioned straights and gays say, "Why don't you get out of this thing?" The question is not hard to answer. As her commitment grows, the wasted, broken life of one human being is enough to make her stay. The task of moving the culture just one inch is enormous, but in the individual who realizes that there is no other way, a process of conversion occurs. She realizes that the minimum she can do with her life is the maximum.

As the Lesbian gets more involved in her struggle, her life takes on greater intensity. She is constantly and consciously moving away from tradition and into her vision. The danger to the movement, however, is that she will become a solitary figure with little in common with other women and other nonactivist Lesbians. To do her job, she must remain grounded in reality. She is also liable to anxiety and depression, especially if she feels she is not being effective. She learns to recognize the danger of coming to live so totally within a counterculture that she can no longer reach out to her hiding sisters and brothers. Her consciousness must never become so "high" that she accuses other Lesbians of having no consciousness at all. For each Lesbian knows her own suffering, and that is the seed from which consciousness grows.

The Lesbian activist becomes more involved in Gay Liberation, Women's Liberation, or the less publicized but very much alive Lesbian organizations like Radicalesbians, or Daughters of Bilitis, where her two oppressions are linked. In all-Lesbian groups she validates her perceptions and gains solidarity with sisters. Work with other Lesbians provides a kind of home base for those who may also be active in the other two movements.

With her sisters she helps to unmask the forces behind oppression and publicly articulate the conflicts that have caused the Lesbian to struggle hopelessly against herself.

The gay women's movement also makes it possible to reach other Lesbians, to encourage the optimization of their potentialities. The Lesbian already in the movement has learned, and now wishes to tell others, not to compromise the integrity of the inner experience. The gay women's movement strives to inspire each Lesbian with the value of her own personality and to release the promise so far anchored by oppression.

The Lesbian activist is no longer a transgressor who has merely overstepped societal boundaries; she is a revolutionary committed to changing those boundaries. The anger and frustration that once corroded her life in the past is now directed toward changing society.

Fanon on Black oppression: "If the suppressed fury fails to find an outlet, it turns in a vacuum and devastates the oppressed creatures themselves."[8] The negative energy that can turn upon itself is reversed, harnessed, and multiplied, and becomes a positive force for moving society.

"The difference between a case history and a life history: patients, great or small, are increasingly debilitated by their internal conflicts, but in historical actuality inner conflict only adds an indispensable momentum to all superhuman effort."[9]

The movement as presented here is a kind of process. A woman is turned on to it, and to what it can do for her. She enters consciousness-raising or an organization. She participates to her level of expectation, which may, for a while, move on in front of her like a horizon as she has experiences she couldn't predict.

Then one day a Lesbian finds that she has devoted most of a year—or two years—to the movement. Marching, talking, writing, organizing, speaking. She has experienced emotional catharsis, growth, and self-integration. She has made self-discoveries and political discoveries and has formed deep friendships. But most of all, she has developed an appetite for challenge and perhaps a hunger for a new, useful skill. She may have pretty much dropped out for a while, and financial pressures may have built up. Coming out of the kind of darkness imposed by having to deal only with her own problems, which are now not quite so immediate or overwhelming, she finds she may have developed a new sense of what the human condition is for all people.

She may want to split her time between a worthwhile job or graduate school and specific goal-oriented activities in the movement —legal, legislative, or perhaps counseling others. She turns back to the bigger world and surveys opportunities. At every academic or employment interview, on every application or questionnaire, she has to account for her last year or two. She has to tell how she has gained skills at organizing or evaluating she may now feel she has. And out there, the world is pretty much the same as before she left. There are a few enclaves, but most people are anti-gay, and may in fact have been frightened by the movement. Ready to go, more fit to serve herself, the movement, and an employer, than ever before, a gay Feminist activist can feel hampered, constrained. She finds that she chafes at the practicality of concealment. Now she truly hates lies or even half-truths.

Psychologically, it is hard to go back into situations that have caused pain. Remembrance of them stimulates fear, and she may avoid what she now knows she wants. Her energy and productivity may be lost to the employer or university, since she may decide after some thought that she can never be comfortable in a straight job or in a classroom again, since she still will not be allowed to be herself there.

It may well be that it will be the younger gay women who put it all together and benefit from options beginning to open. Hopefully they will have fewer aversive experiences in their memories and will face occasional biting remarks with quicker anger and far fewer inhibitions.

"It is from need and distress that new forms of existence arise, and not from idealistic requirements or mere wishes."[10]

It is a set of unwanted circumstances that force activist Lesbians into an historical position, that of helping to guide society toward a new set of values that includes a totally positive approach to sexuality and a new concept of pluralism—the acceptance, not merely the tolerance, of others unlike oneself.

In her sensitive state as an outcast confronting society, the Lesbian activist is aware of the relationship of her struggle for expression and a new life-style with the struggles of other oppressed peoples. She sees the widening circles of issues that for her start with Gay and Women's Liberation but end with human liberation. Things that might pass unnoticed by those not forced to be aware, the subtleties of the oppression of many kinds of people and its effects, come to be recognized easily.

The activist questions the rigid structure of things that lock people into certain roles and give some people—white heterosexual males—dominance over other people—Blacks, homosexuals, and women. She may undertake a critique of heterosexuality that gives her new, sympathetic insights into the oppressor as victim.

She begins with what it means to be a Lesbian. To affirm the label is to understand that it encompasses being a woman in a sexist society. She seeks knowledge that springs from the roots of her womanhood. Lesbian issues, while distinct in part, also blend with issues common to all women, and with the liberation of gay brothers, heterosexual men, and with the problems of all people whose potential has been frustrated by binding societal structures.

Women in the usual course of events give the gift of care and nurturing exclusively to a husband and children, one family unit. The Lesbian, who may not have children of her own or who may not be presently devoting her energies to a family unit, is in a position to use her ability to love, be it conditioned or innate, as energy for the liberation of herself, her sisters, and others. Through Gay Liberation and Women's Liberation, she is looking for new and freer ways for everybody to grow up and live. She is independent and free to work in the world.

The Lesbian's problems of identity and assertion of a different life-style relate to everyone's feelings of suppresion, anonymity, alienation, and ineffectiveness. In these, everyone in society is oppressed. No one is allowed to be fully himself or herself. The Lesbian's need to find freedom for herself and her regard for the freedom of all men and women, propel her to explore the problems of many and to try to see how to extricate people from written and unwritten codes of behavior that weaken or curtail things unique in them. Thus, instead of silent outcasts, some Lesbians are becoming outspoken critics of the way things are.

"It just may be the Lesbian's job to help transform mankind into humankind."[11] It just may be that the Lesbian, far from being an odd kind of woman—tolerated, at best, by society—is a catalyst to a new culture. Far from being sick, she may be extraordinary, even heroic.

Heroic in what way?

Careful psychological conditioning over many years of a person's —or a society's—life plants the seeds which have kept many Lesbians passive, willing to accept ridicule and denial, and even to persecute other Lesbians. Lesbians who dig deeply enough into their consciousness may remember actively participating in—or at least condoning by silence—the degradation of another Lesbian. Analogies from history—most notably, the complicity of Jews themselves in the extermination of their own people, which at the time seemed not only necessary but unavoidable due to the conditioning by the Germans—show how powerful this kind of training is.

Like other women, Blacks, Puerto Ricans, and other oppressed groups of people in our society, Lesbians have been conditioned to feel somehow permanently incomplete, less than human. Until recently, these groups have remained, for the most part, in their assigned positions in society, believing this was, if not the natural, then at least the irreversible, state of things. Surely each such group felt constrained in its psychic and/or physical ghetto; along with this, though, each group sometimes found a kind of safety there—from the unknown, from insecurity or harassment.

The same society which visits its oppression on Lesbians as a group provides a *coup de grâce* for individual Lesbians in the form of the psychiatric "cure," compared some years ago by a president of the Mattachine Society to the "final solution" for the Jews.

In a society where this kind of psychic death has often seemed inevitable, and thus acceptable, revolt seems insane. Too often, the "most sensible" thing for the Lesbian to do has been passively to allow her identity to be executed, to allow herself to die inside, to lose a sense of her humanity. For her, inner destruction has too often been the norm, and rebellion unthinkable.

How then can the Lesbian activist be termed heroic? Her heroism lies in the proclamation of her identity. She faces the attempt to dehumanize her, when she declares herself. This individual, very human, kind of heroism involves dealing honestly with oneself, struggling against great inner odds to *act* honestly. It becomes a larger matter in the face of society's repressions. If the Lesbian is willing to commit herself, to revolt, to explode myths—and to suffer no illusions about the consequences—then the step from "willing" to "doing" does indeed involve heroism. She is very much aware of the reasons to keep silent, but she sees more reason to go ahead.

Lesbians are providing women with the psychological breathing space to invent themselves. They are helping to make it impossible to brush aside the importance of women who insist on total autonomy. In their personal as well as public lives, they are living Jung's admonition: "No one can make history who is not willing to risk everything for it, to carry the experiment with [her] life to the bitter end."[12]

NOTES

Chapter 1

1. Germaine Greer, *The Female Eunuch* (New York, Bantam Books, Inc., 1972), p. 32. Paper.

2. Statistic from an on-going study being done at the Post-Graduate Center for Mental Health, New York City, under the direction of Dr. Bernard I. Riess. Some early results published as "Self and Sexual Identity: A Study of Female Homosexuals," *New Directions in Mental Health* (New York, Grune & Stratton, 1968), pp. 205–229.

3. Marie Hart, "Women Sit in the Back of the Bus," *Psychology Today*, October, 1971, p. 66.

4. Roger W. Smith, ed., *Guilt, Man and Society* (Garden City, N.Y., Anchor Books, 1971), introduction, p. 18. Paper.

5. Smith, pp. 20–21.

6. Margaret Mead, "Guilt, Ritual, and Culture," *Guilt, Man and Society*, ed., Smith p. 124.

7. C. G. Jung, *Civilization in Transition* (New York, Bollingen Foundation, 1964), pp. 34–35.

8. Mead, p. 125.

9. Irving Sarnoff, "Psychoanalytic Theory and Social Attitudes," *Public Opinion Quarterly*, Vol. 24, 1960, p. 270.

10. Sarnoff, p. 270.

11. Anthony N. Doob, "Society's Side Show," *Psychology Today*, October 1971, p. 50.

12. Peter Pan (Pat Maxwell), in conversation.

13. Clarence Tripp, as quoted in "Can Homosexuals Change with Psychotherapy?" *Sexual Behavior*, July 1971, pp. 42–49.

14. Jung, p. 249.

15. Theodore Reik, *The Compulsion to Confess* (New York, Farrar, Straus & Cudahy, 1959), pp. 184–185.

Notes

Chapter 2

1. Hannah Arendt, "Organized Guilt and Universal Responsibility," *Guilt, Man and Society,* ed. Roger Smith, pp. 264–265.

2. Alvin Toffler, *Future Shock* (New York, Random House, 1970), p. 223.

3. Donald Webster Cory, *The Lesbian in America* (New York, Mac-Fadden-Bartell, 1965), p. 133. Paper.

4. Wardell B. Pomeroy, "Homosexuality," *The Same Sex,* ed. Ralph W. Weltge (Philadelphia/Boston, Pilgrim Press, 1969), p. 5. Paper.

5. Jane E. Brody, "More Homosexuals Aided to Become Heterosexual," *New York Times,* February 28, 1917, p. 47.

6. Hendrik M. Ruitenbeek, ed., *Sexuality and Identity* (New York, Dell Publishing Co., 1971), p. 204.

7. James Bossard and Eleanor Boll, *The Sociology of Child Development* (New York, Harper & Row, 1966), pp. 271–272; as cited in "The Development of Sex Differences in Behavior," unpublished paper by Emma Price, p. 7.

8. Kate Millett, *Sexual Politics* (New York, Doubleday, 1970), p. 26.

9. Millett, p. 32.

10. Seymour M. Farber, Roger H. L. Wilson, eds., *The Potential of Woman* (New York, McGraw-Hill, 1963), p. 55.

11. Lawrence Kohlberg, "A Cognitive-Developmental Analysis," Eleanor Maccoby, ed., *The Development of Sex Differences* (Stanford, Calif., Stanford University Press, 1966), as cited in unpublished paper by Emma Price, p. 19.

12. Toffler, p. 225.

13. Doob, p. 48.

14. Doob, pp. 47–51.

15. Jolande Jacobi, ed., *Psychological Reflections,* selections from the works of C. G. Jung (New York, Harper & Row, 1961).

Chapter 3

1. Cory, p. 154.

Chapter 4

1. Evelyn Hooker, "The Homosexual Community," *The Same Sex,* p. 32.

2. R. D. Laing, *The Divided Self* (Middlesex, England, Penguin, 1971), especially pp. 94–106. Paper.

3. Arno Karlen, *Sexuality and Homosexuality* (New York, W. W. Norton, 1971), p. 558.

4. Isabel Miller, author of *Patience and Sarah* (New York, McGraw-Hill, 1972), in conversation.

5. David M. Robinson, *Sappho and Her Influence* (New York, Longmans, Green & Company, 1924), p. 240.

6. Radclyffe Hall, *The Well of Loneliness* (New York, Pocket Books, 1966), p. 201. Paper.

Chapter 5

1. Donn Teal, *The Gay Militants* (New York, Stein & Day, 1971), p. 180.

2. "Women's Lib: A Second Look," *Time,* December 14, 1970, p. 50.

3. Roger Brown, *Social Psychology* (New York, The Free Press, 1965), p. 551.

4. Brown, p. 585.

5. Georg Simmel, *Conflict and the Web of Group Affiliations* (Glencoe, Illinois, The Free Press, 1955), pp. 87–123.

6. Simmel, p. 43.

7. Simmel, p. 44.

Chapter 6

1. Karlen, p. 208.

2. Karlen, p. 208.

3. Frank S. Caprio, M.D., *Female Homosexuality* (New York, The Citadel Press, 1967), p. 133. Paper.

4. Shulamith Firestone, *The Dialectic of Sex: The Case for Feminist Revolution* (New York, William Morrow, 1970), p. 237.

5. Simone de Beauvoir, *The Second Sex* (New York, Bantam Books, 1968), p. 398. Paper.

6. Cory, p. 62.

7. Cory, p. 63.

8. Jess Stearn, *The Grapevine* (New York, Macfadden-Bartell, 1970), p. 317.

9. Stearn, p. 319.

10. De Beauvoir, p. 384.

11. Jessie Bernard, "The Paradox of the Happy Marriage," *Woman in Sexist Society,* eds., Vivian Gornick, Barbara Moran (New York, Basic Books, 1971), pp. 94–95.

12. Bernard, pp. 94–95.

13. De Beauvoir, p. 383.

14. Ann Koedt, "The Myth of the Vaginal Orgasm," *Notes from the Second Year,* p. 41.

15. Alix Schulman, "Organs and Orgasm," *Woman in Sexist Society,* p. 203.

16. Schulman, p. 203.

17. Jung, p. 99.

18. Lionel Tiger, *Men in Groups* (New York, Random House, 1969), p. 216.

19. Tiger, p. 216.

20. Tiger, p. 216.

21. Tiger, p. 210.

22. Pamela Kearon, "Man-Hating," pamphlet distributed by The Feminists, June, 1969, p. 3.

23. Kearon, p. 3.

24. Anonymous, "Letter from Mary," originally published in *It Ain't Me Babe,* reprinted in the *Radical Therapist,* April/May, 1971, p. 12.

25. Linda Phelps, "Female Sexual Alienation," *The Ladder,* August/September, 1971, p. 34.

26. Phelps, p. 35.

27. "Letter from Mary," p. 12.

28. "Letter from Mary," p. 12.

29. "Realesbians, Politicalesbians and the Women's Liberation Movement," *Ecstasy* (New York, Gay Revolutionary Party publication), p. 10.

30. Vivian Gornick, "Lesbians and Women's Liberation: 'In Any Terms She Shall Choose,'" *Village Voice,* May 28, 1970, p. 5.

Chapter 7

1. Frantz Fanon, *The Wretched of the Earth* (New York, Grove Press, 1968), p. 130. Paper.

2. Fanon, p. 130.

3. Fanon, p. 130.

4. Jill Johnston, "Dance Journal: On a Clear Day You Can See Your Mother," May 6, 1971, p. 37.

5. Toffler, p. 219.

6. Toffler, p. 221.

7. Tripp, pp. 42–49.

8. Tripp, pp. 42–49.

9. Brown, p. 401.

10. Erik H. Erikson, *Insight and Responsibility* (New York, W. W. Norton, 1964), p. 402. Paper.

11. Arthur Jersild, *Child Psychology* (Englewood Cliffs, New Jersey, Prentice-Hall, 1968), as cited in unpublished paper by Emma Price.

12. Jung, p. 126.

13. A slogan of the Gay Liberation Front.

14. Irving Bieber, et al., *Homosexuality: A Psychoanalytic Study of Male Homosexuals* (New York, Vintage Books, 1962), p. 317.

15. "Gay Writers Included World's Most Famous," *The Advocate,* June 9–22, 1971, p. 15.

16. Benjamin DeMott, *Supergrow* (New York, Dell Publishing Co., 1970), p. 24. Paper.

17. Cory, p. 63.

18. DeMott, p. 29.

19. DeMott, p. 30.

20. DeMott, p. 25.

Chapter 8

1. R. D. Laing, *The Divided Self,* preface.

2. Philip Rieff, *Freud: The Mind of the Moralist,* as cited by Paul A. Robinson in *The Freudian Left* (New York, Harper Colophon Books, 1968), p. 148.

3. Jung, p. 254.

4. Robert Lindner, "Homosexuality and the Contemporary Scene," *The Problems of Homosexuality,* ed., Hendrik M. Ruitenbeek (New York, E. P. Dutton, 1963), pp. 52–79.

5. Herbert Marcuse, *Eros and Civilization* (New York, Vintage Books, 1962), Preface, p. xvii.

6. Wilhelm Reich, *The Sexual Revolution* (New York, Farrar, Straus & Giroux, 1971), p. 10.

7. Reich, p. 10.

8. Robinson, *The Freudian Left,* p. 203.

9. Robinson, p. 206.

10. Robinson, p. 206.

11. Robinson, pp. 207–208.

12. Herbert Marcuse, p. 46.

13. Reich, p. 211.

14. Neal E. Miller and John Dollard, "Four Fundamentals of Learning,"

Social Learning and Imitation (published for the Institute of Human Relations, by Yale University Press, 1941), p. 38.

15. Maggie Scarf, "Normality is a Square Circle or a Four-Sided Triangle," *New York Times Magazine,* October 3, 1971, pp. 16–17.

16. Thomas S. Szasz, *The Manufacture of Madness* (New York, Dell Publishing Company, 1970), p. 257.

17. Szasz, p. 258.

18. Szasz, p. 258.

19. Erving Goffman, "The Moral Career of the Mental Patient," *Psychiatry,* Vol. 22, 1959, pp. 123–142.

20. Szasz, introduction.

21. Laing, p. 12.

22. Maria Johoda, "Criteria for Positive Mental Health," *Psychopathology Today,* ed., William S. Sahakian (Illinois, F. E. Peacock, 1970), p. 39.

23. Marvin Frankel, notes from lectures on psychopathology, New School for Social Research, New York, 1972.

24. Karl Mannheim, "Rational and Irrational Elements in Contemporary Society," *Man and Society in an Age of Reconstruction* (New York, Harcourt, Brace, 1940), p. 43.

25. Howard Rachlin, *Introduction to Modern Behaviorism* (San Francisco, W. H. Freeman, 1970), p. 185.

26. B. F. Skinner, "Freedom and the Control of Man," *The Cumulative Record* (New York, Appleton-Century-Crofts, 1959), p. 9.

27. M. E. Spiro, "Social Systems, Personality and Functional Analysis," *Studying Personality Cross Culturally,* ed., B. Kaplen (Evanston, Illinois, Row, Peterson, 1961), p. 98.

28. Brown, p. 537.

29. Brown, p. 538.

30. Reich, p. 169.

31. Reich, p. 169.

32. *Ecstasy,* p. 20.

33. "Dr. Hooker Sees Nixon as Obstacle to Gay Law Reform," *The Advocate,* March 3–16, p. 1.

34. "Sex Law Turnaround Forecast by Researcher," *The Advocate,* Jan. 20–Feb. 2, p. 1.

35. Phelps, p. 33.

36. Reich, p. 15.

37. Fanon, pp. 5–6.

38. Szasz, p. 17.

39. Jung, p. 285.

Chapter 9

1. Jacobi, ed., *Psychological Reflections,* p. 137.
2. Linda Clarke, in conversation.
3. Erikson, p. 175.
4. José Ortega y Gasset, *On Love* (New York, Meridian Books, 1960).
5. Ortega y Gasset, p. 47.
6. Erikson, p. 169.
7. Linda Clarke, in conversation.
8. Jean Paul Sartre, preface, Fanon, *The Wretched of the Earth,* p. 18.
9. Erikson, p. 363.
10. Jung, p. 92.
11. Linda Clarke, in conversation.
12. Jung, p. 130.

BIBLIOGRAPHY*

Altman, Dennis, *Homosexual Oppression and Liberation,* New York, Outerbridge & Dienstfrey, 1871.

Bieber, Irving, *et al., Homosexuality: A Psychoanalytic Study of Male Homosexuals,* New York, Vintage Books, 1962.

Brown, Roger, *Social Psychology,* New York, The Free Press, 1965.

Caprio, Frank S., *Female Homosexuality,* New York, The Citadel Press, 1967. Paper.

Cory, Donald Webster, *The Lesbian in America,* New York, Macfadden-Bartell, 1965.

De Beauvoir, Simone, *The Second Sex,* trans., ed., H. M. Parshley, New York, Bantam Books, 1968. Paper.

DeMott, Benjamin, *Supergrow,* New York, Dell Publishing Co., 1970. Paper.

Eiseley, Loren, *The Unexpected Universe* New York, Harcourt, Brace, Jovanovich, 1969.

Erikson, Erik H., *Gandhi's Truth,* New York, W. W. Norton, 1969.

———, *Insight and Responsibility,* New York, W. W. Norton, 1964. Paper.

Fanon, Frantz, *The Wretched of the Earth,* New York, Grove Press, 1968. Paper.

Farber, Seymour M., and Wilson, Roger H. L., eds., *The Potential of Woman,* New York, McGraw-Hill, 1963. Paper.

Firestone, Shulamith, *The Dialectic of Sex: The Case for Feminist Revolution,* New York, William Morrow, 1970.

Fisher, Peter, *The Gay Mystique: The Myth and Reality of Male Homosexuality,* New York, Stein and Day, 1972.

Gornick, Vivian, and Moran, Barbara K., eds., *Woman in Sexist Society,* New York, Basic Books, 1971.

Greer, Germaine, *The Female Eunuch,* New York, Bantam Books, 1972. Paper.

Hall, Radclyffe, *The Well of Loneliness,* New York, Pocket Books, 1966.

Jacobi, Jolande, ed., *Psychological Reflections* (selections from the works of C. G. Jung), New York, Harper & Row, 1961. Paper.

* Where possible, authors have indicated the paperback edition of those titles which are available in paperback.

Bibliography

James, William, *Essays in Pragmatism*, New York, Hafner, 1960.

————, *The Varieties of Religious Experience*, New York, New American Library of World Literature, 1958. Paper.

Jung, C. G., *Answer to Job*, Cleveland/New York, World, 1969. Paper.

————, *Civilization in Transition*, New York, Bollingen Foundation, 1964.

Karlen, Arno, *Sexuality and Homosexuality*, New York, W. W. Norton, 1971.

Laing, R. D., *The Divided Self*, Middlesex, England, Penguin Books, 1971. Paper.

————, *The Politics of Experience*, New York, Ballantine Books, 1971. Paper.

Lifton, Robert J., *Boundaries*, New York Vintage Books, 1970. Paper.

————, *History and Human Survival*, Vintage Books, 1971. Paper.

Marcuse, Herbert, *Eros and Civilization*, New York, Vintage Books, 1962. Paper.

Martin, Del, and Lyon, Phyllis, *Lesbian/Woman*, San Francisco, Glide Publications, 1972.

Millett, Kate, *Sexual Politics*, New York, Doubleday, 1970.

Ortega y Gasset, José, *On Love*, New York, Meridian Books, 1957. Paper.

Rachlin, Howard, *Introduction to Modern Behaviorism*, San Francisco, W. H. Freeman, 1970. Paper.

Reich, Wilhelm, *The Sexual Revolution*, trans. T. P. Wolfe, New York, Farrar, Straus & Giroux, 1971. Paper.

Reik, Theodore, *The Compulsion to Confess*, New York, Farrar, Straus and Cudahy, 1959.

Robinson, Paul A., *The Freudian Left*, New York, Harper & Row, 1969. Paper.

Ruitenbeek, Hendrik M., ed., *The Problem of Homosexuality*, New York, E. P. Dutton, 1963. Paper.

————, *Sexuality and Identity*, New York, Dell Publishing Co., 1971.

Sahakian, William S., *Psychopathology Today*, Itasca, Illinois, F. E. Peacock, 1970. Paper.

Skinner, B. F., *Beyond Freedom and Dignity*, New York, Knopf, 1971.

Smith, Roger W., ed., *Guilt, Man and Society*, New York, Anchor Books. 1971. Paper.

Stearn, Jess, *The Grapevine*, New York, Macfadden-Bartell, 1970. Paper.

Szasz, Thomas, *The Manufacture of Madness*, New York, Harper & Row 1970.

Teal, Donn, *The Gay Militants*, New York, Stein and Day, 1971.

Tiger, Lionel, *Men in Groups*, New York, Random House, 1969.

Toffler, Alvin, *Future Shock*, New York, Random House, 1970.

Weltge, Ralph W., ed., *The Same Sex*, Philadelphia/Boston, Pilgrim Press, 1969.

SUGGESTED READING

A Gay Bibliography: Basic Materials on Homosexuality. Task Force on Gay Liberation, Social Responsibilities Round Table, American Library Association. Lists books, periodicals, pamphlets, and articles. Revised periodically. Free copies on request with stamped reply envelope. Write to: Barbara Gittings, Coordinator, P.O. Box 2383, Philadelphia, Pa. 19103.